Change of View

An Adventurous Love Story!

By Alice Parker

CHANGE OF VIEW

An adventurous love story!

By Alice Parker

EXPLORA BOOKS
700 – 838 West Hastings St. Vancouver, BC V6C 0A6
www.explorabooks.com
Phone: (604) 330 6795

Because of the dynamic nature of the Internet, any web addresses or links contained in this book may have changed since publication and may no longer be valid. The views expressed in this work are solely those of the author and do not necessarily reflect the views of the publisher, and the publisher hereby disclaims any responsibility for them.

ISBN: 978-1-998394-14-2 (Paperback)

Table of Contents

Learning About Life

They say you learn about life,
from living life itself, day by day.
You must live it wholly,
to learn anything from it.

Yet, you need to recognize
what things can teach you.
And, what things you ask?
Ah . . . there is the rub.

For what do you
truly want to learn?
You can learn about love
from a single kiss.

It is much more intimate
and personal than sex.
It may be a song - the lyrics hit a memory,
or the melody brings eternal spring.

It may be glorious nature itself,
for it reflects a beauty open for joy.
To others, life is their pride of people,
family, friends, country - freedom.

Of course, there is faith in spiritual fullness,
of who you are, and what you can do for others.
Life, yes to live it, is to learn
what a precious gem it is that's given.

Whether you take it in measured steps,
or giant gulps to satiate your quest –
Like love, you can only receive more,
when you have given it away freely.

Prologue

This story takes place in the fall of 2010, while the U.S was still in the midst of the housing 'Recession.' While the characters are fiction, the facts are all true.

Modern Croatia was brought to the world's attention when the crumbling Soviet Bloc countries, declared their independence from Yugoslavia. At the time, it was classified as an 'emerging and developing economy' by the International Monetary Fund. Yet, also a member of the United Nations, the Council of Europe, NATO, the World Trade Organization and CEFTA - Central European Free Trade Organization. Most prominently, it was a *candidate* for European Union membership, with a decision expected by 2012.

The two biggest concerns raised by the EU were Croatia's problems with factions of Organized Crime, and their current unemployment. Since their biggest growth-industry was tourism, its expansion made constant news, and focus on those people behind it. Rarely promoted under Yugoslavia, Croatia's newest tourist magnet was its 1200 islands, old walled-cities, mountains and its capital of Zagreb, a modern mecca for the young. Its ferries had vastly connected it to Italy, and its extensive coastline for centuries. And, the recently updated light-rail system, was geared to carry the tourists from one end of the country to the other, quickly. Thus, tourists could travel by ferry one way, and rail the other.

Croatia's ancient history, as an organized group of people - the Liburnians and Illyrians were colonies of the Romans and Greeks in 2 BC. The Croatians established their own cultural independence in the 7th century AD, from the joining of two dukedoms, then finally becoming a kingdom in 925, with King Tomislav. Actually, one of the most powerful, progressive kingdoms in Medieval Europe. For the next 12 centuries, they made unions with other countries, like Hungary in 1102, and were back and forth with the Habsburg's, as well declaring their own independence from Austria-Hungary. Still, their Kingdom of Croatia existed until the end of World War I. Their architecture, during all of these associations, some of the most unique in the world. Battles and wars were fought, including the famous 16th century battle when 2300 Croats held off 100,000 Ottomans for two months - a pivotal-pride point in their proud history.

While the Slavs were a people from northeastern Europe, mainly Catholic or Orthodox. "Bosniaks" were not recognized under the Yugoslavian government - and considered to be Slavic Muslims. Under the harsh Ottoman rule, from the 15th century on, throughout the entire Balkans, people converted in small numbers to Islam, in order to escape the burden of taxation or resulting social discrimination. However, in Bosnia, large-scale conversions to Islam were prevalent, as the central Ottoman control-government there.

In order for them to get the bureaucratic jobs, they gladly converted, while never really a 'religious' belief, as most acknowledged being Muslim in name only. Many also intermarried with Turks to *solidify* their positions of power. Then, many became very defensive of their stance, as the control crumpled centuries later, when the Austro-Hungarian Empire took over again. While the concept of 'nationhood' foreign to the Ottomans, the *Bosniaks* clung onto their name, as an identity of ancestry, since the other Slavic or Balkans had their own.

Croatia was continuously seeking to reestablish their sovereignty, and personal right of independence. Their constant outspokenness, caused many Croats, Serbs, Bosniaks, Roma (gypsies), and all Jews, to be sent to death or labor camps. There were so many various groups turning on each other, for one belief or another, it was sadly estimated, easily three to four hundred thousand people were killed in World War II.

Still much controversy from those killings, as well into the 1990s Civil War. While a Soviet Bloc puppet of Yugoslavia, they all suffered greatly under dictator Marshall Tito, though Croatia had an autonomy beyond other Eastern Bloc-Balkan countries. Their patriotic goals from 1967, morphed into a generic movement for more rights for Croatians, and their decentralization demands of the economy. This movement evolved into what was known as the 1974 "Croatian Spring," with a new Yugoslav federal constitution ratified, which gave more autonomy to the individual republics. Croatia, the wealthiest of the Yugoslavia republics, though it suffered great losses, with the growth in the Civil War.

Interesting side note: In June of 1981, still under the Communist Yugoslavia, six young teenagers in Medjugorje - a small village in the Herzegovina-Bosnia area, southwest of Sarajevo - saw the apparition of St. Mary. It was on the top of an extremely rocky hill, where she spoke to each of them, every day for months.

Then hundreds, thousands, and eventually tens of thousands came to visit, pray and be blessed. The Communist government felt it was a plot by Croatians, since they were considered greatly, devout Catholics, but also yearning for independence. The atheistic-Communists believed there were spies among the foreign religious visitors. No one really knew, or understood how spies, or this apparition could be a benefit for *only* the Croatians. Especially, since St. Mary's most repeated words to the teens regarded, "peace for all."

But, the paranoid Communists, as well as the doubting-Vatican representatives, tested, probed and questioned the young people. Though, they were quite resolute in having seen St. Mary, and identical in reporting what she said to them. Interestingly, *neither* inquisitor group accepted the visions or words of St. Mary. Yet, they could also *not refute* them, or others' belief in them. When heard, the confused/frustrated Communists wanted to arrest the teenagers, but the priest of St. James Church took them into his protection. Mary then began to appear and speak to them, in the rectory.

So, the Communists arrested the priest, and sentenced him to three years in prison for conspiracy. Eventually, the Communists saw they could not quell the throngs, so decided to make money off the religious pilgrims. They allowed the locals to build hotels and inns, taking *60% of the fees* from the tourists, for the government coffers.

Tension among and between the various ethnic groups was always just beneath the surface, and controlled by the Soviet leader, Tito. Yet, riots became almost a norm rising, being quashed and rising again among the different groups of Albanians regarding Kosovo, Serbia and Montenegro. Loyalties were organized, so coups came and went from one leader to the next, grabbing for power and stirring one group against the next. Finally in June of 1991, Croatia declared its independence from socialist-communist Yugoslavia, then the National Army openly attacked Croatia, which meant Civil War *against themselves*. By the end of the year, Slovenia had joined forces with Croatia, so a full-scale conflict, with the new Republic of Serbia.

Simply put, despite religious differences, the Bosnian-Serbs didn't want Croatia to separate, for largely economic reasons. They were more the land-locked farmers, and needed the Croats to move their products from the sea ports. After four years of sporadic, often bitter, brutal fighting, occupying-Serb armies were mostly cleared from Croatian lands. Then, after four cease-fire agreements, the fighting stopped in 1995. Under United Nations' supervision, the last Serb-held enclave in eastern Slavonia returned to Croatia in 1998.

Ethic-cleansing and propaganda, unfortunately common on all sides. It remained a controversy as the International War Crimes Tribunal continued to investigate and prosecute. None of the other countries involved, in the old Yugoslavia group had the extensive history, or establishment of a strong government like Croatia. Much of their success had to do with deep, continuous loyalty to their Croatian roots and ancestry.

The horseshoe-shaped country, of four and a half million people, literally had it all, from mountains in the northwest to its long, incredible coastal-Mediterranean islands heading south. They also have some plains for farming, stretching out from its centralized capital of Zagreb. Croatia's long history revealed in UNESCO rewarding it, as World Heritage Sites for walled-Dubrovnik and Zadar, with its unique Venetian connection.

There were as well, the creative influences of Vienna in many areas. On a more modern note, Parliament approved Jadranka Kosor as Prime Minister in July 2009. Ms. Kosor had been deputy Prime Minister since 2003, and became the first woman premier in the country's history. In respect to her, she is not mentioned in this novel, as said, all characters are fiction.

~ ~ ~ ~ ~ ~ ~

Though Destiny may be guiding and directing our path, it is still our own thoughts and beliefs by our choices, which bring about the actions on our journey. Destiny is usually directly related to our Karma, and those people, situations, events, involved with it, usually need to be healed. Certain couples are sometimes brought together by an amazing circumstance, or sequence of events which defy logic, and may be referred to as 'meant to be' or synchronistic. One might say their love begins through 'Divine' intervention, and many lessons learned. The couple then has an opportunity to create a rare relationship, which has the possibility to positively impact the greater humanity, more than just themselves, or those closely centered on them. Timing, or *Divine Right Order*, as doors open for the opportunity to change lives.

Chapter 1
Moving On

Interesting, in removing the nails from the walls
- It felt as if removing myself from the rooms.
I recognized how my 'things' were a part of me,
they represented who I was in collected memories.

I'd felt for some time 'something BIG'
was coming – Some Really Big Change.
Something to totally change my life and lifestyle,
bring forth who I was meant to be - that kind of Big.

No way, no how would I ever guess, the
'big change' would include physically moving.
'*Moving*' from my dearly, beloved San Francisco.
The city I'd dreamed of living in since 18!

Yes, reality certainly sucks, even more than money.
Though the lack of money helped me accept
my purpose - reasons for moving on - leaving SF.
The perfect apartment, still just a place to live.

Yes, many 'like-minded friends' I'll miss, but
with all our connections, we're still attached,
just as those of my pivotal years in Japan.
And, my reason to live in *this,* most liberal City.

Yet, not just SF changing - more convoluted.
My purposed-destiny needs space, challenges.
Didn't really know, but dissatisfaction stirred. And,
not try to pound square-pegs into round holes.

I knew where I did not want to move to,
but no clue as to *where* I *wanted* to move,
until an unexpected phone call. The surprise,
genuine offer, totally unforeseen. Yes, this is it.

I listened, a calm voice inside me said, …
When it all flows together - it is meant to be.
I knew cleaning closets, cleaned out my mind,
so many buried emotions, I felt so good at last.

Julia would joke later, of how she thought of Sean Connery, when he laughed, regarding his doing the movie, *"Never Say Never"* and agreeing to again be, the quintessential-Bond. The slogan had become her sort of rallying cry, to being open to new things for herself, and others she preached to about being adventuresome.

But right now, she'd stepped down from the foot-stool, trying to find her ringing cell phone before it went to voicemail. Who would be calling on this lovely summer afternoon - another cool, but sunny day in San Francisco? I'm going to miss these days she thought, and wondered why the thought had popped into her head.

When she left the Chicago area, shortly after turning 30, she uttered several times she'd never return there, or even the Midwest to live. More than just 'too hot and humid in the summer and too cold in the winter,' also the stoic-attitude of 'nose to the grindstone, shoulder to the wheel.' Julia had no problem with being a workaholic, now she just wanted more than work - to see more, do more and, of course, be more. She did acknowledge Chicago a good place to be *from*, and she'd kept her strong values of right and wrong.

To the point, even if they didn't always float-well with her various employers, especially the management. So, she succeeded well with several college degrees, lived in six States, Japan seven years, traveling extensively both Stateside and in other countries. Not too shabby for a girl who'd married too young, and kept reinventing herself to be successful in each new career-adventure she jumped into.

Julia had visited San Francisco when only eighteen, and vowed someday she *would* live there. When returning from the seven years as a corporate trainer in Japan, San Francisco best suited her newly free, independent lifestyle. She also had preached to never go backwards, in where she'd lived or what she did - thus regularly adding to her diversified resume. Believing nothing happened by chance or coincidence, when she resigned from her last trainer-human resources manager position, she didn't worry. She then had several good contracts, and enjoyed her free time to write a blog, releasing her stressed-workaholism to reinvent herself once again.

Being a Scorpio, she believed in the whole 'rising from whatever ashes, phoenix-style,' to a better opportunity, challenge and experience. Yet, when the economy crashed, so very heavily and fast in California, she accepted companies could easily get a younger, cheaper-version with most of her assets. Living in the most expensive, little city in the country lost whatever glitter she'd seen. As the money became tight, she decided to downsize, so she could make her somewhat-retirement and small income stretch, till a new job opportunity arose.

Julia's large, sunny one-bedroom in Pacific Heights with great views, might be rent-controlled, but no longer in her budget. So, twelve years of San Francisco, three years prior in Hawaii was probably enough, she acknowledged. Yet, she still didn't want to move back to Chicago, though a job offered through her sweet nephew. Thus, cleaning closets to clear out her mind, questioning where she could be happy moving to. Or, most importantly afford living, when her phone rang that Sunday afternoon. The accumulated frustration of it all peaked, as she curtly answered her friend Cara, calling from the Upper Peninsula of Michigan. Before she could say much, Julia dumped it all out on her - no job in sight once she finished her Census work, and not much of a retirement income left to live on. She'd drained-it out, and charged more on her cards.

Cara was known years back from their old, unincorporated suburban neighborhood. Julia gave her credit in helping to form and make who she was today, especially when it came to men and sex. They'd known each other since high school, and been through a lot of changes together - including their divorces and affairs, so the honesty basic. Julia also considered Cara one of the smartest women she knew, with business success. In those early, freely-divorced years, when they were tearing-up the Western Suburbs, especially Julia over- compensated for being raised so strict and straight.

They even invaded Chicago regularly, so some people called them bawdy, usually when drinking. But only a few small glimpses of Cara's old persona came out these days, and usually just to Julia, or their mutual friend Maura, still in Chicago. Quietly listening, Cara then calmly stated, though late July, 75 degrees and breezy with no humidity. Most importantly, all affordable to Julia's restricted income.

More than a whirlwind, as they talked, and went over the pros with few cons to consider. The moving-seed had been planted, to be mulled over the next few days, yet it amazed Julia how comfortable it felt in her gut. By the time Cara visited the refurbished apartments - fifteen miles from her home - and sent Julia the photos of the renovated, historic building, she was hooked.

The application on its way, as Julia gave notice to her shocked building manager. The clock started ticking, as to packing-up, shipping it all out to Cara's house and truly moving- on once again. Interesting, as Julia began to notice things aggravating her about the city, which had not jumped out before - like the increase of noise and rude-traffic at crosswalks.

Reinventing herself once again, at fifty-plus, most friends were surprised. But her son, Jeremy in Dallas, totally shocked, and worried about the dramatic change. He regularly referred to her as his 'hippie- super liberal' mother, who considered *him* to be conservative. Julia also a source of entertainment for Jeremy's stories to his friends, as 'she's always up to something - never boring her motto,' he often said. "I know Jeremy, this is rather sudden. But trust me, this feels right to my intuition, and I just know it's something I'm supposed to do. It's not just about the money, and I will *not* have my son supporting me, or me living with you."

"Mom, *those people* up there, they are so conservative, and believe so totally different than you do. . . Even your 'wild and crazy' friend has become a died-in-wool conservative. And, what about your movies, you go almost every week, and the symphony, opera, all your museums, the gallery openings with your artist friends . . . and walking everywhere to do things, friends . . . " Julia could hear the earnestness in his voice, and his dire concerns for her mental health.

"I know there will be some challenges, and maybe it's what all of this is about - I've got some new lessons to learn. Please don't worry so much about it, I'm sure I will find some like-minded people. And, I'll survive without my movies or museums. I've adapted before - you know I did it in Japan against all odds, I was quite successful. I think I'm ready to get away from all of the city life, and really get back to nature, for completely releasing my stress. I can do this . . . and if I truly fail, you know I'm the best at coming up with a Plan B."

"I've done it before - remember I survived the business disaster in Hawaii, so I can overcome just about anything." At least he knew better than to say she was too old for another change. He finally surrendered to her, as he knew always a losing battle of the wits. He may be a computer super-geek, but she could out-wit just about anyone with her words.

A few days later, Julia got Jeremy's tacit-acceptance, as he put $1000 into her checking account. This aided greatly to her expense of the continuous - over thirty boxes of her 'life-stuff' she shipped-out daily from her Mail Boxes, etc. two blocks down. After many trips down to the "Out of the Closet" donation store, a trip out to the SCRAP art recycle center, then finally the Salvation Army picked-up what she'd not been able to sell.

Julia finished cleaning the apartment, totally exhausted with the physically-emotionally-busy month. She stretched out on Cara's air mattress, she'd brought to San Francisco, on her first visit years past. It had been fun for Julia, to share *her city* with Cara each trip. Bags for the airport were packed, along with the stuff she was giving to her artist friend Carol, who had also recently moved from the city to the desert. Julia just finished her sandwich, when her phone rang and Cara's name appeared. "Probably making sure I'm all ready for my *Next New Adventure*," she laughed out loud. "Hello My Sweet! Yes, I'm all ready to go."

"Well, is there any way you can put this off? I got a message from the site-manager at the building, and it's going to be at least three or four weeks before they can let anyone move in - contractor delays on some State inspector stuff." Her voice a little pensive, worried about what she'd do with Julia for such a long time

"Cara, where would I go even if I could change the flight?" Julia surprised at her question. "I know it's an inconvenience, but I guess I'll have to stay with you. Can you put up with me for that long?" A mutual concern, since they'd been living far apart for so many years. With only four to five-day visits when together, three weeks together for two independent women, might damage their friendship.

"Well, . . . yeah, . . . sure. It's just I've scheduled to be out of town, and I don't want to leave you by yourself. . . You know, without a car and all."

"Hey, I've been living by myself, and entertaining myself for a very long time. Remember, I'm really adaptable when I have to be. I'll manage to keep busy helping you however I can. I mean if you can put up with me, I can certainly try not to invade your life too much. It *is* a big house and big yard."

Julia could see this would be one of her *first* new challenges. There were hesitations on both ends of the line, realizing what a huge commitment they were both entering into with each other. Neither the same woman, they'd been thirty years before, when their lives had been so daily entwined.

"OK," Cara said cautiously, trying to get a sense of irony into it. "I guess if we don't kill each other, it'll work out." Julia laughed heartily in response, affirming her gut still with her on all of this.

"OK, I'll call you from Minneapolis to let you know I made it so far, and no delays to you." She took a deep breath and drew up some resolve, "I love you and I really am excited about all of this. I'm truly ready for the change. Off to *My Next Big Adventure!*" Now, Cara on the other end giving out a rather loud laugh. What were they doing?

~ ~ ~ ~ ~ ~ ~

With the long wait between flights, after Julia finished her homemade sandwich, she decided to do some deep breathing. She closed her eyes to visualize clearing herself from top to bottom, so she'd keep the positive energy flowing into and through her. For the last couple of years, her positive regiment had really helped to change her around.

She had moved her Metaphysical beliefs into a Spiritual clarity, an understanding of herself. Just believing, better yet knowing she was protected and guided, made staying positive with it all so much easier. Not wanting to come off as another California, or San Francisco airy- fairy space-cadet, she even made fun of, she only shared her feelings and beliefs with others who were open to it all.

She knew and accepted reality, as she had no intentions of being a 'Susie-Sweet-breath' or Pollyanna, but acknowledged everything a choice in one's life. With a positive attitude, it did make a difference in her choices, as well the results. So, Julia promised to herself, no preconceived-expectations, she'd chosen to make this drastic change to her life. She'd then continually remind herself to let it all *unfold*. She took another deep breath, and the relaxed feeling told her once again, the right move to make. She felt more big things coming, stemming from this. She thought, *"There's no asking why or when, let it unfold - be positive."*

Her hopper-flight landed at Rhinelander, Wisconsin's small airport, and she spotted Cara there at the single baggage carousel immediately. She had let her premature, silvering-hair do her frosting, and it looked great with her dark eyes. They were both about the same build, having added a few extra pounds over the years.

With a big hug and kiss, Julia excitedly asked, "So, how soon until I can call myself a "Yooper?" Cara laughed and shook her head, still often amazed at Julia's cheerleader-enthusiasm.

"Once you've lived through one of our winters, and still want to live here, it's that simple. So, we'll see how you do with it. You said it's almost thirty years since you even lived in a full four seasons. ... You look good, all the exercise with packing must have helped. How many bags do you have?"

"I just had to check the one, because of the air mattress occupying it almost totally. A real hoot, too. Trying to tell them at the counter, it wasn't a bomb, without saying the word, since the air pump certainly looks like one." Cara shook her head again, picked up the small tote bag, heading for her white, luxury Jeep - the dichotomy of it totally her. Cara really wondered how this was all going to turn out, as the UP not an easy life she'd chosen for herself to escape Chicago.

Julia had visited the area many times with Cara, in their younger years, as getaways from Chicago, in both the summer and especially the incredible fall. Cara's mother's relatives still lived in Iron County, and it had been Cara's home now for over fifteen years. She'd found a comfortable living, as the owner of a large bar and grill, with a lot of community involvement. Julia's last visit had been three years prior for Johnny's Memorial, Cara's much older second husband.

Settled into the car, Cara turned toward Julia, serious in what she was about to say. "OK, you've heard me bitch and complain about the limited food selection and the people, but I'm telling you, to watch what you say, if you want to be accepted at all." Julia ran her hand through her hair, and rolled her shoulders back stretching to get comfortable. She'd frequently teased Cara, in living as if in Witness Protection, never revealing her wild past life in Chicago, the two had shared after their divorces.

Cara pulled out of the parking lot, and turned easily onto the highway. "Let me tell you about this asshole, who recently moved up here from the Chicago area to open a bar. He then preceded to piss absolutely everyone off, with his mouth and actions." A typical story of some jerk thinking, because they're from the Big City, and had money... Or in his case, actually his father's and fiancée's - they think they're smarter, or better than the local, town people."

Cara had commented in the past about how many people from Chicago, Milwaukee, etc. had moved up there for a stress-free life. Most had managed to fit in, as she did by keeping a low profile, and not bragging about any past success, or in her case, hiding-well past secrets. She then added in the reminder again, how no one knew about any past escapades they'd done together. At this, Cara looked over at her, and Julia slid her thumb and forefinger over her lips, to show they were sealed. As she went on, into detail regarding the asshole, Julia totally agreeing, and regularly responding with the appropriate 'no shit?!' or 'what an ass!' or simply 'OMG!'

"So, you also need to limit how much you talk about yourself - you know Japan and all of your education and stuff - until you get to know someone, or they ask for more details. Just being from California, and especially San Francisco will raise enough eyebrows, and they'll expect some liberal-stuff from you. Now, my friends know who you are, as I've told them you were moving here, and they remember my trips out to see you, along with the food we ate."

She laughed at this comment, as the trips had given her certain bragging-right. "I'm going to miss all the great food. Anyway, I've told you before, everyone is related to everyone, so you need to be aware *not to talk* about somebody, as they'll take offense regarding a relative.

And, that's even if they know the person is a jerk or whatever."

Julia had worked hard on letting go of her sharp, critical tongue, not only against herself, but especially towards others. Though she wouldn't go so far as to say she was compassionate, she had become more patient. She'd definitely given up rescuing people - with two divorces, she learned it didn't work.

"Cara, I've told you before, like in interviews, especially with younger managers, I don't mean to come-off as intimidating or arrogant, but when asked what I've done regarding my resume or past jobs, the reality of it comes out. Having managed a thousand employees is not a throw-away in an interview. I just wanted to say sometimes, 'I don't want your job, I just want a job!' I've thought about it, so I've got my responses why I left SF - too expensive and busy, etc. And, I got too stressed, which is true. I'm not a city person anymore."

She glanced out the window at the typical, open small-town scenery. "And, I've also got my responses, as to them inviting me to things I'm not interested in, so I don't hurt or offend anyone. I know they probably don't understand my whole metaphysical belief-thing. I know you don't really either, but you don't care about how I believe or think anyway, as long as I don't tell you how to. I guess it's how we've continued to get along over the years, as we've changed." Very quiet for a minute or so, then Julia decided to finish it off with one of Cara's favorites come-backs. "All-righty then, I guess we've gotten it all covered." They both laughed, more relieved than satisfied, as to how it was all going to come out for them.

"Since I've come all this way to pick you up, I thought we'd go to Walmart and another cheap discount store, since I don't have one close by. You can get some staples for the apartment. I'll tell you what I've already bought for you, and you can add it to the boxes in the garage." They pulled into the parking lot, and Julia glad to be out of the car to walk around. She was used to so much more movement with her aerobics class, and felt her body getting stiff again.

"You know I really do appreciate all you've done for me with this, … and I sure hope you didn't try to pick-up, or move any of those heavier boxes by yourself. And the last four are coming this week."

Taking the lead, as usual, Cara was striding across the parking lot to the door. She turned as she opened the door, "I had the UPS guy trained to put the boxes in the garage himself for me, and when you mailed the others, the mail-lady put them in front of the garage door, so I only had to kind of shove them inside."

Julia thrilled with the cheap, canned goods and actually excited about going to Walmart, which didn't exist in the San Francisco city area. "You know you really need to get out to do more shopping," Cara laughed at her excitement.

"Yeah," Julia joked, "I'm really going to miss my *Personal Shopper* at Bloomingdales!" She may not always be able to handle Cara's chiding, or especially the sarcastic teasing, but Julia did have quick, humorous-retorts she could unleash. To Cara, they were actually appreciated, and not taken with offense. It might take a bit, but they'd get back into each other's syncopation and the comfortable honesty they'd always had. It wasn't quite a mutual sigh of relief, but it was going to be OK. *"Unfolding,"* Julia said under her breath, "just let it all unfold, and accept it all as it is - *new lessons being learned without any expectations.*"

Back at the house, Cara behind the kitchen counter sipping her glass of white wine, with dinner in the oven and another wine glass waiting. Julia came down the hall from her bedroom with her new bra from Walmart on, since she'd been changing her clothes. Adjusting the straps, tucking her boobs to make sure they were straight and balanced. "Keep those girls straight and looking up," Cara joked.

"Yeah, I really needed a new white bra. So many women don't know how stodgy and old they look with saggy, hanging boobs. It easily takes ten years off, when they are up and perky. I'd show you my new panties, but doubt you're interested." A relaxed laugh,.

Cara slightly shaking her head, and directly asked, "How difficult is all this for you to handle?" A real concern, now Julia there.

"I've told you before how much I loved it here; I'll adapt and adjust to it all."

"No, I don't mean just *here*. I mean difficult not having money, when you've been used to having so much for so long. And, difficult not getting a job or work, when you've got so much experience and education . . . how are you doing with *all that*?"

"Do you have some red wine?" She wasn't ready to answer the heavy questions without a little imbibing. She sat on a bar stool, it becoming her side of the counter.

Cara walked over to the wine rack and pulled out two bottles. "That's all the red I have." Julia read both labels, chose one and put the other back, as Cara pulled out the corkscrew. "It doesn't exactly need to breathe, but it's not bad I understand." Almost like an homage to their years, so long before when first divorced, working in the French restaurant. Julia almost fell off the stool with her laughter, and Cara cracked-up at her own excellent foil.

'Touché' all Julia could get out, while Cara opened the bottle to pour her glass half full. Julia picked-up the glass, clinked the other as she said, "To us, and long may we live and love each other." Cara nodded in agreement.

"Japan taught me a lot about being adaptive, and yes, the money was nice. I loved what it afforded me, so much travel and seeing so much of the world. But, I also had to do without a lot of the things I was used to, when living there. Traveling to Third World countries, you learn really quick to adapt, and the importance of toilet paper." Cara cracked-up, laughing loudly.

"In some other restrictive countries, you learn to be aware, to keep your ass out of jail!" Cara laughed, remembering her story of facing an AK-47, and almost going to prison in some Middle Eastern country, for sitting in the wrong place and letting her knees show.

"But, after I loss so much money in Hawaii, because my asshole business partner had sex with my Japanese partner's wife, really sucking-air for a while, . . . And, afraid how I would survive there, not a cheap place either. But I did, because I had made good connections on my own, and had always treated my clients well. Of course, my one client … well I told you about him …" Julia smiled, as Cara chuckled. Julia took a long sip, thinking of the twists and turns which had contributed to her destination. Usually, she'd compare it to dominoes tipping- over the next and next, as everything so totally interconnected.

"Yeah, I always loved going out to eat, the traveling to the other islands, and doing all of the artsy plays, musicals and buying some decorative things for my home. But, let me tell you, when I had to move out of the condo-rental in Hawaii, . . . To almost a hovel I moved into, and had to practically, kiss-the-ass of one of the most disgusting men I've ever met. Of course, the SRO I had to live in, when I got back to San Francisco, wasn't much better. But as you know, they just don't rent to you, even with money in the bank, without a job."

Cara had taken some cheese and crackers out, as dinner would not be ready for almost an hour. Julia picked-up a piece of cheese. "Yet, I do not look at myself as an older woman who has fallen on hard times. I think of it all as an adjustment - an opportunity to try new things. So, as I said, you adapt. And, when you can afford things you like again, you appreciate them more. I've now learned, how it's a part of the process of the lessons we grow from - stay positive to always appreciate what you have, as well as what you've had." Julia took a swallow and deep breath.

"As with Japan, you do learn what you can live without, and some things you never go back to, even when they are available, or you can afford them. You really learn it is not always just about the money - especially in a job. Besides you taught me, and always said,

'It's only money,' and it is. I think it is the same in choosing and keeping friends, though understanding they may only be passing through your life. There are those like you and Maura, we've been through so much good and bad. So, no matter how long in between the times together, we never have to start over. The real understanding, acceptance and love is still there."

Julia took another sip and adjusted herself on the stool. "You know also, I love adventure, and while I'm not an adrenaline junkie, I do like to have new experiences - *never a boring life.* I think now, I've also learned how long to pound a square-peg into a round hole, or see the writing on the wall - whatever you want to call it. I'm NOT afraid of change, in fact sometimes I seek it out for the challenge, and to make sure I'm not too old to change again." She put her glass down. "So with all that, I'm sure I more than answered your question, I usually do." She laughed again. "I'm going to put my shirt on, as I'm getting chilly. What's on TV tonight?"

Nothing Cara could say, they had always been different. She'd accepted and preferred her repetitive routines, even if they were boring. They were safe, and she didn't have to worry about any extensive challenges or adventures any more. Since her mother and Johnny had both died, Cara basically free, as her son Matt ran her bar. Yet, she'd often not wanted to bother with the driving to Chicago to get direct flights to San Francisco or Florida visiting her other friend Mary. Cara content with volunteering at the animal shelter, her DirecTV and her dogs to keep her company at night. She had her outdoor toys for the summer and winter, but beyond those, little more interested her enough to put the effort into doing it.

~ ~ ~ ~ ~ ~ ~ ~

"It's not easy being me," Julia thought out loud. And, to herself, *"I know, because I've been living with things changing so much, for so long. And, sometimes I don't know who the real me is, or if there really is just one me. I have always been the adaptable person, but now I feel as if I'm shape-shifting, which is a little scary."* More than spunky- independent, with her bent sense of humor. She acknowledged, an older woman who knew herself well, because she'd spent most of the last three years learning to do so, in classes, reading and writing. Giving up her workaholism had not been easy, but truly worthwhile. Most importantly, she'd learned who and what she *did not* want to be, and sometimes *acknowledging it* had been the hardest part.

So, in recreating herself, she'd become the softer, kinder more accepting person, she'd worked on for so long. At this time, in her fifties Julia moved into a rare category for women, she saw no need for any explaining, defending or proving who she was any more, especially career-wise. She'd made her mark, and yes, she may not be working full time now, but her career had pretty much always defined her. No taking away what she had accomplished. So then, what job she did do, going to be her choice, and she wondered what it might be.

Even before the whole job-hunt scenario, Julia had also learned the technique of subtle, sensuous-sexuality - a most wonderful balance of words and behavior. Yes, she'd acknowledged, she'd love to have another romantic involvement. Not sure how far she wanted to go, or ever marriage, but open. Toning-down her lighter blond hair to its current light-honey color, and keeping it a little shorter. She liked her layered, longer shag which easily curled and waved nicely.

She also took the dramatic out of her make-up, with lighter eyebrows, shadows and mascara around her unusual, turquoise eyes. Aware of her full breasts, they were accented casually, without tight or clinging clothes, especially those obviously showing too much of her cleavage. They called it the 'professional-casual' look, San Francisco women were so known for - not looking up-tight or stuffy. She'd learned a long time ago, it wasn't just the looks, but her attitude. The looks would fade and did. Attitude always a state-of-mind over physical matter.

Julia always said, she'd never be the pathetic, older woman trying to look twenty years younger, by her clothing choices or make- up. The slightly fitted tops accentuated she had a waist, but did not require her to hold in her tummy. Likewise, a top may cover up enough of her butt, to not show it off, but reveal had a shapely one. Since she rarely wore skirts, no need for the high heels, and since developing arch problems, she kept all of her shoes between one and a-half to two inches. A good thing, too, Julia had never been a 'clothes-horse,' but mainly about the colors, the material and feeling good wearing whatever. She never wanted ordinary, or what everyone else wore, and laughed at the *fashionistas*.

"Somebody out there will want me, and he doesn't have to have the big bucks, as I've learned to enjoy the simpler life!" Her experience, knowledge and yes, wisdom in the business field was extensive. Even if some management people didn't want to listen, or even pay attention to her training. She'd also learned to tone her opinions down, but she wouldn't play stupid - just wait for them to ask, or question for her opinion.

So much to share, Julia even wrote a book about New Age- style management, which treated employees fairly, and admitted their mistakes openly. Of course, never published, but it felt good to get all of her ideas out, and on the page. In her usual research of any topic, she did find there were some other good thinkers out there, regarding how to do business better and better managers, who were real leaders. So, at least Julia had the satisfaction on her own, of being on the right track with all she knew and believed. *"Clay into pottery, through the heat of the kiln,"* she remembered reading, and it spoke to her.

Perhaps one of the best recent lessons - thus experience - she had working for the Census. The ridiculously long process, tests, evaluations, repeated delays for starting and, the obvious-nepotism involved in hiring, when Julia actually met the Assistant District Manager at a Human Resources meeting. But, at least they eventually hired her, though asked several times why she had declined a supervisor position. "Just want to work as a simply capable body." Julia's experience could be clumped together as to being *comfortable working with people.*

Also, since she basically worked alone, no one to be bothered by her overly-detailed and organized behavior. Maybe why she did so well as an independent contract-trainer. The client had already agreed to what they wanted, so all she had to do was fulfill it, which she did with her own material. Now, only if the economy were better, there might be a niche to fill with her talent, and not have to worry about other people handling or telling her how to do something.

Julia's high energy and presence could sometimes be emitted or slip out - much more than she realized - and intimidate others. If those 'others' were the hiring managers - some mousy human resources person, dead in the water before getting any further in the interview process. One of the more difficult things was having been an HR Trainer-Manager for so many years, especially the seven years in Japan, if they were even cognizant of its connotations. Most HR people she initially interviewed with, were almost half her age, so yes, she'd learned to kill them with her kindness. She might slowly dazzle them with her dialogue, but she rarely got to baffle them with her bullshit, if they didn't have a sense of humor.

There were few who could see through the numerous layers of who Julia was, and what she could do for their company. Many had a fear, others in management might not be so accepting of such a knowledgeable, outspoken person. Sometimes the Boss might recognize the workaholic and see her as the panacea to some of his work load, or be the person to implement all those things he had not put the effort into doing.

One might say, and several of her friends did, she did this to herself in not fitting in - "You are just too much, done too much and know too much! Lighten up, and keep your mouth shut, so you can get a job, for god's sake!" Yes, but, . . . much of the deepening of her Spiritual belief of who she was, she *just could not-not* let her light shine. In a most positive way, Julia exuded confidence and happiness, which for some reason aggravated the shit out of some people. Who could dislike happy people, but in a very down-economy, apparently many did?

The bright side of not having a job, she could reduce-eliminate, all of the stress which had been plaguing her for so many years. And, what better way to break the addiction of being a workaholic, than to be out of work? The biggest down-side, of course, not having the money to live adequately, if not well, in San Francisco. What was the point of it having so much to offer, if she couldn't afford it? So, Julia still had some of her baggage, even after these years of 'working' on herself - forgiveness, patience, acceptance and not trying to control things to make it all 'right.'

Julia could honestly slip into more OCD, than she wanted to. The whole 'rescuing thing,' she'd also gone through classes to release and let go, now sort of working. She understood all about personal responsibility, the other person's, not hers to do whatever. Once she truly accepted the rescuing actually a dis-service to their growth. And, the reality some people would actually later resent, being helped too much, she could then stop doing it. As Richard Bach said: "When you wanted more for the other person, than they want for themselves - you will be frustrated" - and disappointed. Julia had added it to her list of mantras and her affirmations to keep her in the direction of releasing, letting go and getting in the flow, by really living in the 'now.' Though it all sometimes sounded so trite, and way too, New Age for her.

This had all brought Julia back to cleaning closets - letting go, giving away to simplify her life. She could live with less, as even her food shopping had become more limited, since putting most of it on her credit card. She'd never really been into material things, though she did like her collectibles from her years of traveling and living in Japan. Still, with each subsequent move, she had given away a lot of stuff, which she felt she no longer needed in her life, and she'd done it again more easily. Julia had moved on - a new life, in a new place and she'd work to make it turn out better for her. Or, her newest mantra - *"This or something better."* She was open.

Chapter 2
A Serious Man

The doorway is not solid wood, or steel,
it is of glass, tempered safety-glass.
You can not only look through it,
but you may safely break it to escape.

And, what I ask, do I escape from?
Why, those hidden obstacles, so deeply embedded;
those varying shadows of negative feelings, which
need to be revealed, so *you* can be released.

And, if I may ask - what reward do I get,
for doing this deed, I don't think I need?
Oh, you more than need it, alright! And,
it's called freedom, pure unmitigated joy.

. . . But I did not feel, I was not free.
Oh, but the chains which bound you
were not visible to the naked eye –
Since they were created in your mind.

Most of us have them, some of the time.
And others have them, all of the time.
The problem is - you get used to them.
Be strong enough to allow love in your life.

Open up to let your soul guide the way,
for your freedom to grow in boundless areas.
This allows real happiness to bubble-over, as
you live-love in effervescent joy of freedom.

Only one caution: Once you have had it,
you'll never be able to go back to shackles.
Your prior constricted-thoughts will seem silly,
and those limiting mind-boundaries, too absurd.

The JKF Airport Immigration Officer looked through his passport, "Business or pleasure, Sir?" Actually, his ninth visit in three years, though she'd not counted them all.

"Business, thank you," Tomis responded trying to put a smile on his face. He knew, too, to come the week after the American Labor Day holiday, so no loss time in his work. She now glanced at him, and back to his photo on the Croatian passport.

"You have been here many times on business Mr. Kanavelić, you should try a little pleasure. I've heard your country is quite the tourist attraction now, but we have a lot to offer, too." A slow time of the day, so the forty-ish woman in no hurry to let a good looking, older, tall man slip by quickly. From the expensive suit, silk tie and even down to the shiny-shoes, he reflected serious business. You'd never know he'd just gotten off a long, overseas flight.

Feeling he had to say something, Tomis added, "I always ride your ferryboat. They are very good." He managed a bigger smile, but a little forced to please her.

She stared at him. It *was* an enjoyable stare. The English easily understood, with the lyrical-accent distracting her in a good way, but obviously he was all work and no play. "I ride them everyday to work myself, and they're not *that much* fun, but whatever suits you. Enjoy your visit."

Luka had already put his passport down, and she repeated her perfunctory 'business or pleasure' with barely a glance, when noticing only in his early thirties. When he had also repeated 'business,' through a smirk on his face, she added, "I guess you don't have much chance, with him. Enjoy your visit."

Only his second trip over with Tomis, - his boss/client - and he knew there would probably be little free time. And, definitely no partying for him, until he had secured Tomis into his hotel each night. Even back in Croatia, being on his security team often more boring. Though lately, more challenging when the Organized Crime faction came up with some new tactic to give them problems, or try some new way to kill Tomis.

Still, Luka would rather have a client who followed his strong instructions, than one who went off on their own, like *he* knew better than they did. A good gig, and he certainly didn't want anything to happen to Tomis on his watch. He had some good assistance on U.S. soil, but mainly just him doing the protection. When they finally finished Customs, Luka called for the car to meet them at their baggage pick-up point.

As usual it all ran smoothly, with Luka opening the back passenger door for Tomis, while moving to put their luggage in the trunk. And, never more than one bag each, as Tomis very organized, and rarely let his briefcase, with the lap-top out of his hand. The stop at the Consulate brief enough, for Tomis to check any changes in his itinerary, for required dinners with his investors, and pick-up his U.S. business phone. Luka left his suitcase at the Consulate, as he stayed in the staff quarters. He saw which car would be assigned to him, got his New York phone, and also checked in with his supervisor back in Croatia.

Luka then drove to the hotel for Tomis to check-in, shower, and change clothes before they were off to the New Jersey docks. There, the three retired, Staten Island ferries were in the last stages of being refurbished for Tomis' ferry-tourism business. Per usual, once he stepped out of the town-car at the docks, a big smile spread across Tomis' face, as then truly in his element. He looked around, almost missing the time he'd been gone from the humongous facility.

Although late September, still a lot of daylight, and the weather perfect. He reached into his pocket and pulled out a mixed wad of U.S. dollars, giving Luka a twenty for food for them both. Often Luka just took care of it, as he had a generous expense account, especially when they traveled.

Tomis with his long-legged stride, now wearing his khakis, polo-style shirt, windbreaker and sturdy work shoes, met at the door by the security guard, who welcomed him by name. No surprise there, as few people before had purchased three ferries from them for refurbishing at the same time. He led him to the waiting Foreman's office, where Tomis slipped on a hardhat and the day-glow vest for the inspections. The members of the management team would catch-up to them, and do a genuine welcome.

To most, the massive interior noisy, smelly and all of the large equipment rather overwhelming. Though it had been almost twenty years, Tomis missed those days of dock work when and being back around it. As a nine-year old boy, he learned all the jobs to help build the challenging business his father had started. But, making it over and growing it after Croatia's civil war kept his sanity. Not just the extensive destruction hurt, but the deaths of his wife, Celia and daughter, Milos still haunted him from time to time.

The long hours, with continuous physical exertion were the only things to usually help him sleep through the night. The wounds never really healed, they were merely pushed down, as he rarely allowed himself to feel the immense guilt-ridden pain.

Once his father died, more from a broken heart than health, since he'd sent his wife - Tomis' step-mother - and their daughter Talia, to the United States during the war to protect them. Yet, Tomis' own son, Stepan had to raised, as well try to work with his half-brother Ivo, who he'd long ago learned neither a reliable, nor willing dock worker.

Still family, so Tomis' responsibility as promised to his father.

From his own experience in World War II, his father had insisted Tomis learn English. He did two years at Cambridge for business training, after his mechanical engineering degree. Tomis had insisted the same for Stepan, except his degree in computer science. After this last trip to the U.S., Tomis had thought he might visit Stepan in London for the holidays, and travel some, rather than Stepan make the trip home. Yes, a pleasant distraction, and perhaps he wouldn't be so lonely without this project to occupy his mind any more.

The three ferries were due for delivery at his Rijeka dock in October. It did not seem possible it would all be over shortly - no more needed trips to the U.S., or blueprints or all the mechanical specs to be gone over, again and again. Tomis not going to think about it now, but he did need *some-thing* to keep him, thus his mind busy, especially with winter coming. He could escape on his sailboat down the coast in the good weather, though he didn't do it, as often as he *thought* of doing it.

Yes, he thought, it had been three years from him first deciding he needed new ferries, but wanted something more impressive than the ones they had always purchased. With the growing number of tourists streaming into Croatia, particularly the Germans and Americans had more expectations of safety, and wanted more space along with amenities. He had remembered his first trip on the Staten Island ferries, almost twelve years before, after visiting his step-mother and Talia in Chicago. Unlike some businessmen, he still considered American-made to be the best, most importantly when it came to long- lasting ships. He knew he couldn't afford them new, so really excited when he learned the retired ones were available refurbished.

The research alone gave him hours of joy, but it couldn't compare to the time spent crawling over and in the used ferries, until he finally decided on the first two. They had already started the work on them, when he got a call from the company foreman of a 'new- used' ferry. As on its way in, Tomis had dropped everything to make the trip back to the U.S. the next day, and get his bid in on it. Some people thought he acted like a father having a baby, whose delivery had come early. His generosity to the men who had assisted him in his 'find,' became almost legendary in the industry.

Tomis determined to get the three of them done together, as much as a marketing ploy, as the economics of them being done identically. He definitely wanted one for the Italy ferry trips, as they were the year-round 'bread-and-butter' of the business. For the tourists, the growing market for traveling down their beautiful coast, to the various dozen islands or so, of the 1200 scattered along the Adriatic Sea. Then, of course, Croatia's jewel of Dubrovnik. The ancient walled city, a magnet to tourists from all over, and nothing compared to approaching it from a ferryboat. Yes, lucky to have such a great country to grow his business, to occupy his mind and energy.

Some years before this project, the 'light-rail' passenger trains, had connected the capital of Zagreb with the other tourist cities down the coast. Easily, the other cities contributed to the cost, along with government support, as the whole country benefited from the ferries.

But, the 'new' ferries were almost all tourist-oriented. With the help of Tomis' long-time friend Petar, at the Consulate, American investors were jumping on the band-wagon, of the newest growth country in Europe - Croatia. While the other 'civil war' participants still struggled with United Nations occupation, and "War Criminal Trials," Croatia anxious and able to rebuild.

Soon, Tomis also approached by large investors from other European countries. They knew a good thing when they saw it, and he had an excellent record of hard work, with great accomplishments. Still, it took over a year to get the total funds lined-up, before starting work on the ferries. The final element fell into place when his close friendship with Croatia's President, brought the Tourism Board into play to endorse his huge project.

Tomis had then learned to play the game of 'schmoozing' the investors on both sides of the Atlantic. He hosted dinner parties and updates of the project's progress - photographs, charts showing the increasing numbers of various tourists flowing into Croatia each year. It couldn't have been more of a success, but then he worked at it, meticulously organizing the details in every area of the project. Importantly, he *personally* made the trips to the New Jersey dock - though they did give him a satisfaction no one else could have understood.

If it hadn't been for the rise of the Organized Crime faction, trying to prevent Croatia from being accepted into the European Union, he'd have seen the project as flawless. But, they targeted him because of his influential power, and control of so much of the tourism business, along with his strong vocal support of joining the EU. The Crime faction knew eliminating them, almost a requirement to join EU Tomis's close friendship with the President, also made him a target, as him a key spoke-person outside Croatia for the EU. Once several attempts had been made on his life the year before, the President insisted Tomis have 24/7 security, from a combination of State Police and private security. Not easy to get used to, but then he really didn't have much of a private life any way. Of course, a lot of women would've wanted to be his dinner hostess, as well the fact that someone always trying to fix him up, with some friend or relative. Even without his success, an unattached, good looking, older man always a gem of a catch.

Tomis, always polite, accepted the invitations to meet the ladies, or have them join him for dinner, but it rarely lasted for more than one visit. He felt it basic, he wanted a woman who understood business and travel, with the intelligence to talk about them both from her knowledge by experience. He enjoyed visiting other countries, which catered to tourism, and if they had some kind of ferry system, it made it all the more interesting.

But, his point to see unusual cultures, more to *expand* his knowledge of different, perhaps better ways to keep the tourists returning, to enjoy *their* travel experience to Croatia. In other words, he wanted a partner in both businesses, and perhaps personal companionship. He'd learned enough to know, the younger women either wanted children, or had them to raise, which limited being able to travel freely. The experiences of most women were usually cruises, or more of the typical of shopping or trendy 'hot spots.' Rather, he preferred to explore nature, or other developing or 'third world' countries. Not that he didn't enjoy a hot shower and clean bed, but beyond the cultural museums, most large cities weren't much different from one another.

While Tomis had talked to the Tourism Board regarding naming the ferries, in reality he had chosen the names before asking for them to vote on a list he gave. The Italian ferry to be called *Istrian Lady*, after their north-eastern province. It had a majority of Italians, and the home of his half-Italian step-mother. *Dalmatian-Split* would be the island-hopper ferry, as the major city being Split, and the area known as Dalmatia.

Their most historic, the Dubrovnik ferry would be honored by being called *"Adriatic Pearl."* From a quote of Lord Byron, when he'd referred to the city. The ferries were painted red, white and blue, their flag colors, but in different combinations, with their checkered emblem and symbols in predominate locations.

The *Istrian* would have a red hull, the *Split* a blue one, and the *Pearl*, a white one, of course. The same colors of the trim, floors and interiors would vary on each one, to make them more interesting. The President had insisted on giving Tomis three million dollars from the tourism fund, simply so *he* could claim some State sponsorship of the ferries. Though he'd wanted them to be independent, Tomis knew he'd have no problem with interference on his friend's part, but he tried to stay out of politics, if possible. Still, his avid support of joining the EU put him right in the middle of the controversy, and a continued target of the gangsters, who wanted their own rule of things.

Almost dark, by the time Tomis called the napping Luka, to let him know he was ready to return to his hotel. Luka sometimes slept on the plane, as Tomis preferred business class for the quiet comfort, and stretching out his long legs, so also nice for Luka. Yet Tomis never slept, as his restless-mind kept his computer going, or reading an English book to relax. By now, he'd been up at least thirty-six hours. Luka held the door, as Tomis exited and thanked the night guard. Stepping into the back, Luka asked if he wanted to stop to pick-up dinner before returning to New York.

Tomis had to think a moment, as he had been speaking English-only the last four hours. *In Croatian:* "Sure, and please remind me to go back early tomorrow, I have a business dinner at 7pm." Tomis then on the international phone, when Luka pulled through the pick-up, and reached automatically for the food bag, when he handed it back Tomis, he never asked what he'd be eating.

When Tomis exited the car at the hotel, standing from the driver's side, Luka asked what time in the morning, as the doorman had opened the passenger door. Tomis automatically said, "7 am,." Then Luka reminded him to take his bag of untouched food. Tomis chuckled, and said "Thank you, and have a good night." He dug out his card-key, to check the floor, as he had no idea what room. The mundane things just did not stick in his brain, or perhaps he didn't allow them to.

Tomis ate his food, watched some news and read some in his book, before going to bed around 10 pm, with a 6 am wake-up call. He dressed in a clean version of what he had worn the day before, and remembered to put out his suit for the evening dinner. He checked his schedule to see who would be joining him, Petar, his wife Jelena from the Consulate, and probably she'd invited Vesna, her younger sister. Jelena, a smart woman with a good business sense, and a perfect- partner in securing investors, or business supporters of Croatia.

However, her divorced sister Vesna, had no interest in business, unless it entailed the latest sale going on at some high-end store. Jelena had been trying to bring them together for some time, and also knew this would be Tomis' last trip to New York. Her hints had not exactly been subtle, as she kept saying he needed a *real* modern Croatian wife. Yet, he could not imagine Vesna would ever want to live in Croatia, after so many years living in New York. Not that he had any interest *whatsoever* in her. Perhaps the fact, he'd always been polite to her, gave them both ways too much encouragement of more acceptance from him.

By noon at the New Jersey dock, Tomis more than realized not much more for him to do until the final inspections. He totally recognized these were more than competent men, and the few changes he had requested were of his choosing, not of any mistakes. Really no need for him to hang-around watching and looking over everyone's shoulder, he knew how distasteful, or non-trusting it could be. They needed to finish doing their jobs, which were now down to timing, such as each layer of paint had to thoroughly dry before work proceeded. He didn't want anyone rushing, just because of him watching and waiting.

Now Wednesday, the special containers for each shrink- wrapped ferryboat, would not even be loaded on the massive ship until a week from Monday, for sailing out the following Tuesday morning. Final inspection should not even be done until the Friday or Saturday before. Tomis then realized he had over a week of free time - something which rarely occurred in his life. It'd be wasteful to fly back to Croatia and return just for the inspection. He now had to acknowledge it; the project almost finished.

He had to find something new to occupy his time. He did not truly remember being so lost before, except when he accepted his wife and daughter's deaths. Then somehow, he deeply felt it wrong, a job - a project, even a big one he loved so much, like this could be compared to the biggest tragedy in his life.

He looked out the foreman's window at the beautiful fall day. He snickered to himself, as he shook his head remembering the Immigration Officer suggesting he explore New York, other than just his usual ferry ride. Tomis then remembered, he had emailed his half- sister Talia, before leaving Croatia about maybe going to visit her, at her new home in Michigan. He looked at his watch, but she wouldn't be home from work for at least five hours.

Tomis then startled Luka by phoning him to bring the car. He then turned to the foreman, "I think everyone do great job, so I leave you to do it." He reached out to shake the surprised man's hand, as he quickly stood up to walk Tomis out. "Call if any problem, and I return next Friday, … before shipment for final inspection." He waved to several of the workers and repeated 'thank you' to them, as well the security guard, as he walked out the door. Luka just pulling up, and before he could get out, Tomis had opened the car door and climbed in the back seat.

(In Croatian) "Is everything OK? Are you OK?" Though they had been together almost a year now, they were not friends in the true sense, yet Luka had been trained to 'read' people for both the good and bad signs. Something *off* with Tomis, but he couldn't put a read on it. He backed the town car around, and glanced in the rearview mirror.

"Yes, I am OK, everything is OK. They are doing a great job, so I need to leave them alone to do it. Let's go back to New York." A long pause, and Tomis asked, "Where do you think we should go? I mean what tourist attractions do you think would be interesting?" His face could only be described as blank.

Luka stopped the car in the parking lot, put it in park, and turned around to look carefully at his client. Tomis had *never* asked his advice on anything, other than traffic or weather. As it turned out, Luka actually had a list of places *he* had hoped to visit before they left, and some of the men at the Consulate had told him he should see.

Then, Luka *accompanied* Tomis, as they went up the Empire State Building, visited Rockefeller Center, and the 9/11 Memorial Site with the rebuilding, before driving through, and even stopping in Central Park. Tomis also talked to Luka like he'd never before, asking him questions about his life, while they sat on a park bench eating hot dogs. Luka couldn't help but keep looking at

Tomis, as if some *magic* change had come over him, but he could not figure out what.

Tomis then surprised Luka more, as he said, "I'm not sure what I'm going to do, once we get back to Croatia, with this project completed." He paused, "Perhaps, I'll travel, as October is a good time to go to many places." He may have been in the tourism business, but didn't like to travel with a lot of them around. He talked to Luka, as if his best friend, about a few places he wanted to visit, to maybe occupy his time. Luka still hadn't figured out what could be going on with Tomis, but now time to get back to the hotel, for Tomis to get ready for the dinner meeting. He knew Tomis always liked enough time to go over the details of his investors, so he could show a personal interest in them. It always made them feel, he wasn't just interested in their money. Several had become very good acquaintances, and even visited him several times in Croatia.

Since a business dinner, the four men had sat on one end of the table, facing each other, while the four women had sat on the other end. Vesna made a point to sit as close to Tomis as possible, and speaking-up right away to ask how 'his boats were coming along?' His jaw tightened, and he hoped no one actually noticed, but he saw his biggest investor smirked, while bending his head, to take a swallow of his drink.

Tomis answered politely, and returned to the business conversation. Jelena spoke to Vesna *in Croatian,* telling her not to interrupt, but she felt she needed Tomis' attention. Once the entrees were served, the conversations did intermingle and Tomis then noticed how much Vesna kept drinking, as well continually touching his arm.

He did not want to end the dinner or even rush it, as the two men were his largest American investors. He made a point to ask when they might be visiting Croatia again, and it certainly lightened up the talk, and got their wives involved. Tomis then caught Jelena correcting Vesna in Croatian about her drinking so much, and ordered her some coffee with dessert. Going into almost three hours, Tomis relieved when the two wives jointly agreed, they should call it a night. Though Tomis and Petar had insisted on taking the check, *Mr. Big*, the bigger investor just joked, Tomis could pick it up in Croatia. "In New York, at this restaurant, *the boys* would all be very disappointed if I didn't pay, and over-tip them all." The men laughed politely, knowing how true, while the wives all shook their heads. Vesna, however too out of it to get the joke.

Once they all started out, Vesna made a point to ask Tomis to take her home, though she had come with Petar and Jelena. He glanced at them both, and while Petar just shook his head, Jelena gave him almost a begging look. When the group of eight exited, the largest limo waiting, of course, for the two big investors. The only difference between Tomis and Petar's cars, Luka standing outside of his. Tomis had followed the investors to their car, to once again give the ladies the European hug and cheek kisses, and shake hands with the men.

"You shouldn't spoil them like that," the older, wealthier Mr. Big, said. "I can't compete with your looks or charm. It's a good thing I've got so much more money!" He laughed loudly, and Tomis chuckled. A reality he could live with, still smiling as they pulled off.

He walked back and gave Jelena the same hug and kisses, helping her into their car. He saw Vesna gone, so figured she must have had Luka put her in his car. He gave a bigger hug to Petar, who apologized for his sister-in-law, as Tomis told him not to worry about it. "Thank you, as always for all of your support. I'll stop by tomorrow to visit and catch-up on it all."

Once the car had pulled away, he took a deep breath and walked back to Luka standing by the open door. Leaning in and speaking low he asked, "Do you remember where she lives? I may need help getting her home."

Luka then smirked, trying to keep from laughing out loud. "She has insisted, she is going to the hotel with you," he whispered. Tomis' eyes rolled, as his head tilted back, and he shook his head 'no,' getting into the back seat. He thought she'd passed out, but Vesna came alive, flopping her arms around him and trying to kiss him. Tomis just kept saying "No, we are taking you home, … you need to get to bed."

"Yes," Vesna said, "I want to go to bed with you. We can have fun together." Luka sped-off, as he called the Consulate to get her full address and any directions he needed.

Luka pulled in front of the brownstone, and used his flashlight to check the same as the address he had gotten. He then got out to open the back door. "No, Luka, go from the other side, and I'll try to push her out, as you pull her up." Vesna now out cold, and practically dead weight. Though not a large woman, still not easy. Tomis tried to be careful of her dress, but she seemed to be fish-flopping from side to side. Though not as tall, Luka more muscularly built, as a requirement of his job. Finally able to get Vesna balanced, so he could actually throw her over his shoulder, while Tomis carried her purse and cape, going ahead to the door and ringing the bell.

The maid shortly answered, and not stunned at the scene, which quite telling within itself. At the maid's instruction, Luka went ahead and took Vesna up to her bedroom, and deposited her onto the bed. He symbolically wiping his hands - 'finished with her,' as he returned to Tomis at the door, as he had given her stuff to the maid. Closing the door behind him, Tomis began to apologize to

Luka, who now laughing-fully, out loud. He then said, "It's perhaps one of the funniest things I've ever seen . . . And truly, never expected to see in regards to you." Tomis also began to laugh, and realized how good it felt. He did need to laugh more.

Once back in the car, headed to the hotel, Tomis checked his business phone and Talia had left an enthusiastic voicemail from his earlier call. He checked his watch and decided it probably not too late to call, as Talia on Central Time. He'd made three trips to Chicago, once she and his step-mother had gotten settled into both the Italian and Croatian communities. The second for his step-mother's funeral, and the last when Talia had gotten married five years ago. She had proudly earned her nurse's degree before her mother passed, but she'd not lived to see Talia's marriage or birth of beautiful Ericka.

Talia answered quickly, "Tomis, I can't wait for you to spend some time with her also. As I mentioned, the most wonderful season is on now, with our spectacular trees and leaves turning all kinds of glorious colors, like you've never before seen. Besides, with Edward gone these past few months for work on the lower side, I'd really like the company. I'm not sure how much time I'll be able to take off, but I'll see what I can do. How long can you stay, when can you come?"

Happily, confused with some of the English, Tomis replied, "I come on Friday and return to New York on Friday next week, . . . if not too long for you. I check on the flights and see best time."

Talia laughed. "Tomis it is very beautiful and open up here, lots of nature, but very few people, so not a lot of choices or amenities. There is only one flight out and one flight in to Marquette, our only large jet airport. It was a military field. It's best to fly into Chicago, and the American flight leaves there about 6:30 pm, and gets in here an hour later, but Marquette is on Eastern time, so it will say 8:30 pm. I know a little confusing, I will send you an email to make sure you understand. It is a small jet, so you do need to get your reservations, as soon as possible. Trust, me it is worth it, to come here and see it all."

She laughed again and added. "I'm so glad you are coming to visit, I know it will be a great experience for you, and so good to catch-up on your life." Having lived in the States about eighteen years, her relaxed casualness actually made Tomis feel more comfortable himself, and not worry now about his unknown future.

"I look forward to your email ... and make reservation for flights. Tell Ericka her uncle come to visit her. Can I bring her something from New York . . . or you?" He could feel some real anticipation building in having a new 'project' to work on.

"No, no Tomis, just bring yourself, and we'll do the rest here. I'm really excited about this. Love you and take care. Can't wait to see you." With Talia's warmth and enthusiasm, he smiled.

Tomis mumbled a 'love you, too' and thought how long had it been since he'd said those words to anyone. After a moment, he switched back to Croatian for Luka.

"Well, my friend, you will get a short vacation yourself. I'm going to northern or . . . *peninsula* Michigan - not sure what or where it is - to visit with my sister Talia. Very few people, and hard to get to, so I'm sure I'll be safe alone. She is my half-sister, and has been living in the States about eighteen years. I have a niece; her name is Ericka. I must buy her something, but I have no idea what to buy for a child here. Her husband is somewhere in other part of the state working, so she welcomes my company."

Even as telling it, Tomis not sure he understood all of it, but somehow it did not seem important to do so. He had something new to do. She had said lots of nature, so maybe a good experience for him. He wondered a little about why, she'd been so excited about their autumn color, but maybe good to see.

Luka now smiling from ear to ear - time on his own in New York. "You can buy her snow-globe of Empire State Building, all kids like it." Tomis nodded his head, fully smiling.

Chapter 3
A Lovely Accent

A catch in her breath, then a rise of warmth.
She hadn't connected his presence to either.
Flustered. This was not her, not the organized,
detail-oriented her, being slightly confused.

No comprehending his request, words diffused;
her mind played with them, rather than processing.
It was becoming more difficult to breathe,
as the warmth slid-up her chest to her neck.

Her words stumbled, fell out of her mouth,
as he stopped speaking to look at her.
She missed the lovely lilt of his accent,
along with his baritone smoothness.

She blinked her eyes, it cleared her mind,
and she responded coherently to his inquiry.
His eyes locked on hers, a facade of composure,
as warmth touched her cheeks to give a glow.

She knew the gods of fate had kissed her.
She barely concealed her realized emotions.
A naiveté, neither of them knew they had.
The silence, before he walked off she said,

"I love your accent. Where are you from?"
"Croatia. ... I love your eyes, so luminous,
they don't appear real, . . . are they?"
"Yes," she laughed, "what a lovely compliment."

Now they're both faced with the dilemma:
to move forward with their separate lives,
or smile to interact and discover each other.
Love or friendship, just happens sometimes.

Julia had only been at Cara's a few days, but already she'd helped clean out the basement and clear out residuals, from the past few years from the lower-level family room. With the glass patio doors wide open, the woodsy-smell freshen everything. She'd catch herself staring-off across the deep lawn down to the lake, with the sun shimmering off it.

She took another deep breath, so appreciating the glorious nature, as the last bit of stress had been releasing itself from her back and shoulders. She had encouraged Cara to give her any projects she'd put off, and especially the packing-up of the last of some of Johnny's things for his kids back East. They'd also caught-up on details of the past few years, not covered in phone calls.

Living alone, Cara'd expressed now how happy with the company, and glad they had the extra time together before Julia's move to the new apartment. Cara's trip down to Wisconsin cancelled due to an illness, so they could maybe plan some sight-seeing for Julia to get more familiar with places, not gone to before. Considering she no longer enjoyed the driving as much as years before, because of problems with her legs, Julia took it as a really kind gesture.

With Cara's IPod blaring, Julia later on the verandah trying to do as many of her aerobics exercises as she could remember, to the various music beats. She kept thinking how proud her instructor would be of her. She'd managed to work up a bit of sweat, when she noticed Cara staring at her from the open sliding glass door, smiling as she shook her head. When she saw Julia had noticed her, she leaned over and turned off the music, wanting to comment on her arm and elbow movements. "I'm assuming it's some sort of exercise, and you're not trying to fly off the balcony?" Cara always with her sarcasms.

"Very Funny! But I'll have you know, the more you move your arms, especially the elbows, the stronger you make them, and the more muscles you use to firm them. One of the reasons I was able to do so much packing, lifting, etc. for the moving. I'm in better shape than I have been in a long time, and feel really good not having my bones creak at every little move. You should try at least a little stretching to flex your muscles."

Julia grabbed the hand towel to wipe her face and neck, before sitting down at the glass table in the shade of the umbrella. She grabbed up her bottle to chug down some water, as Cara pulled out a chair, and looked at her newly manicured nails, to make sure she'd not scratched them in any way. "I wouldn't like having to limit what I did with my hands, just to protect those nails." More of an observation, still a chide, Cara had heard many times before from Julia

"My hands are one of the things which still look good on me, so I like to keep them up on a weekly basis." No comeback to Julia's exercise or stretching comment, as she had made it clear before, she had no interest in either. They talked a little of some gossip Cara had picked-up, having her nails done, and when she dropped-off the *change-bank* at the bar. "OK, go back to flopping your wings, I've got some bookkeeping to do. I'll see what we can do this afternoon, as we'll be gone all day tomorrow, working at the animal shelter."

She turned the music back on and disappeared off to her office, in the back of the house. Julia took another swallow of water, and returned to her exercises. Much more difficult to do them consistently without the support of her instructor, or the other participants, but she told herself something better than doing nothing.

It had been fun working the front desk with Cara at the animal shelter, and Julia hoped to be able to volunteer with whatever fundraisers they had, or other work they needed done. As frequently as possible, she offered to Cara to take the dogs out, and soon learned many of the routines around the big house and five-acre yard. Her favorite time of year there, so she truly wanted to be outdoors absorbing it all to satiate herself, for all the years she'd missed not living in four-seasons. It'd always been the one big missing piece from San Francisco, no real fall.

Sitting on the wooden bench-swing noting the daily, minuscule color changes in the various leaves, when Cara called down to her from the verandah. "I just got a call from Marge at the shelter, and she's also on the Friends of the Library Board. Since you said you'd be willing to help on any projects, would you like to work the annual book sale, supporting the county libraries this Saturday and Sunday? They're selling all the donated books, so the libraries can buy more new ones. I remember you talking about going to the big, library book sales in San Francisco, so I thought you might like to do it. They'll pay you in used books and donuts - can't beat a deal like that for your diet!" Cara chortled over the temptation.

~ ~ ~ ~ ~ ~ ~ ~ ~

On Sunday morning, Julia came into the kitchen in her sleep shirt, over her underwear to fix her breakfast. Cara just pouring herself a cup of coffee, as she rarely ate breakfast early, but usually grabbed a peanut butter and jelly sandwich going out the door. She stood there, with a smirk on her face watching as Julia prepared her coffee, mixing and stirring just right. She then started her ritual of dressing-up her instant oatmeal packet. "You buy the kind already with stuff in it, isn't it enough? Just like how you always *made-love* to your baked potato, while most of us were half done with our meal!" Without comment, Julia continued her process, then slipped it in the microwave.

"Why have ordinary, when with a little more effort, you can have extraordinary? It's just like I'd tell my clients, referring to customer service, give an extra five seconds to a customer, and it makes you tons of money and goodwill in it, too. And, I don't eat potatoes anymore."

Cara again shook her head, as she started down the hall to her office. "You just always have to be *on*, trying to *convert* everyone to your way of thinking. You wear me out sometimes. Give it all a break, and just let people fuck-up on their own, would you?" Julia burst out laughing, and they were both chuckled at Cara's truism.

"I can't help it. I y'am what I y'am!" At least they could always laugh at each other.

After she finished getting ready, Julia came to have her *appropriateness-check* done again by Cara on her dress, for the conservative attendants of the book sale. She'd passed easily on Saturday, but Sunday may be different. She'd curled her hair a bit, and kept the make-up to a minimum. She looked younger than her years, with a certain something there, not common in the other small-town women. She did not want anyone thinking or saying: "Who does *She* think *She* is?" The subtle-femininity in dressing, but nothing particular someone could point out to being obvious. If she kept a smile on her face, and deferred to others to help her, she knew she'd not offend anyone.

She knew this warmish-weather, could turn cool - much like in San Francisco. Julia wore longer short sleeves and nicer cut-offs, to give-off the casual-yet almost-dressy look. The crisp, fitted cotton shirt could be unbuttoned without directly revealing any cleavage. She thought the whole outfit could work for so many situations. Cara agreed, so they headed out with Julia set to call her when to be picked up. Cara had already scheduled to help her daughter-in-law with another project, since her grandsons had vacated for the university.

Since Sunday the last day of the sale, they expected to be busy. To stretch a little at the check-out table, Julia stood for the big sales to pack the books in boxes, but sat for the smaller ones, which went into plastic bags. They'd been steady most of the morning, but now real lines were forming, as the rooms had gotten more crowded. Being one of those perfect fall days, the old, giant windows of the armory had been opened to the breezes, and the glorious smell of the various leaves painted in autumn colors.

It took her back to when she walked out into Cara's yard with the dogs, she'd examine a leaf here and there. Some actually had what looked like drips, *or spots of paint from the autumn elves, who had been busily switching them from green to vibrant red, ochre, gold or a glowing orange.* It all so delighted Julia, she caught herself sometimes giggling at the thought of how she had gotten there, and how lucky she was. "Synchronicity!" she said out loud, and the curious dogs looked up at her, questioning a word they did not know how to respond to.

Suddenly, she's brought back to the next customer in line, with a question. Embarrassed at her obvious day-dreaming, "I'm sorry, could you repeat that?" She put a smile on her face to make up for it.

"I said, 'You seem to be in-sync with each other handling these crowds, do you work at the library?'" The typical, pleasant, middle- aged, small-town woman.

"No, I'm a volunteer for the book sale, but thank you for your compliment, and for supporting the library. Enjoy your books." The conversation also brought the tall, distinctive looking man into her purview, though she moved easily to the person ahead of him in line.

The customer finished and thanked, he placed his three books of classic American literature down and said, "You have good collection to choose . . . and prices . . . are very good. They are donated by members, yes?"

A catch in her breath, and a slight rise of warmth. Julia had yet to connect his presence to either happening, and she became flustered. Truly not her - the overly-organized, detail-oriented her, being slightly confused. Somehow, she could not comprehend his request, like the words diffused, and her mind played with them, rather than processing their meaning. It became more difficult to breathe, as the warmth slid up her chest to her neck. Her words stumbled, and fell out of her mouth, as he stopped searching through the dollar bills in his wallet to find the right ones, and looked at her.

She had focused on the lilt of his accent, along with the baritone smoothness. When she blinked her eyes, it seemed to clear her mind sufficiently, and she responded coherently to his inquiry.

"Yes, . . . um, so many people are so generous to us." His eyes locked on hers, as she smiled with a facade of composure, just as the warmth touched her cheeks to give them a glow. Julia knew the gods of fate had kissed her lightly with this opportunity of him.

She barely concealed her realized emotions, as the smile broadened across her face, as if in the spotlight. It brought a naiveté neither of them knew they had, and he returned the smile equally, to his own amazement. She had noticed the lack of his use of contractions and articles, so to break the silence before he walked-off she said, "I love your accent. Where are you from?"

"Croatia," he said. "I visit relatives here." He too, then wanted to add more to his short response. "I love your eyes, they are so . . . shiny, . . . luminous, they do not appear real, but they are, . . . are they not?" He felt himself biting his lip a little, as perhaps it had been contrived, and he did not want to appear to be too swooning or something. More than out of practice with these things, and he did not want his uncomfortableness to be apparent to her.

"Yes," she laughed, "they aren't contacts, if that's what you mean. What a lovely compliment." She noted the touches of grey at his temples, almost looked as if they had been individually chosen to release their dark, rich auburn color. His eyes also had a penetrating dark blue, which somehow did not seem real for peering out of in broad daylight, but only in soft silhouettes.

Now, they were both faced with the dilemma: to move forward with their separate lives, or how to interact and discover each other. The growing cacophony of the crowds brought them both back to reality once again. "Well, I'm new to living-up here, but you certainly have chosen the very best time to be visiting. I hope you enjoy the autumn leaf-viewing, as we certainly do have some great nature around here to see."

He smiled again, and thought to ask, "Yes, I look forward to do it. How long are you open? I think I bring my sister . . . and niece to get book and DVD." Clever man, he'd picked up the gauntlet, and took the challenge of what possible opportunity the bemused-fates might be throwing at him, or them. Not a fake line or poor pick-up, as reasonably construed, he felt. There it was: love or friendship just happens, or is on cue in unexpected places.

"We close the doors at 3 pm, but we won't chase anyone out until 3:30, if we're busy. I hope to see you again." Her grinning- response now more natural, as if all as it should be. Julia didn't really care what reason he found for returning, just so she'd have a chance to talk with him again. She'd had her hey-day with men, and still had the vivid memories to keep her warm at night. But, it'd been a long time since putting herself out on a limb, and not nearly as frightened, as she may have expected. *Funny how it goes sometimes,* she thought.

"I come back," he said confidently, as if a meeting he did not want to miss.

Julia watched for a moment, and turned to the next person in line. As she thanked the woman for her support of the library, a wry- grin in return. She leaned in with a raised eyebrow to speak, "Good luck on your meet-up, he looks like a *keeper*." Julia a bit taken aback, on the fact her flirtatious-encounter had been so public.

Then she laughed, thinking how Cara had said people around there, not only all knew each other, but loved to gossip about each other. She chuckled regarding the irony of becoming an item, before she actually became a resident. *"I just love all this small-town stuff, and how they keep themselves entertained,"* she mused to herself. Without the big city stresses in her life anymore, none of it bothered her. She now saw it all, as part of the connectedness they shared, which she'd rarely felt before.

~ ~ ~ ~ ~ ~ ~ ~

It all ran as if choreographed by the best pros: Tomis, from Tomislav - and Julia could not be sure of the correct pronunciation, or even try to spell his last name - had returned with his sister in-tow, and come back through her line just before closing. Chatting with his much younger, half-sister, Talia, Julia accepted the invitation to meet them down the street for coffee when she finished, 'to talk about the 'leaf-viewing,' and sight-seeing opportunities the Upper Peninsula offered.' A good thing she'd done so much reading of the tour books, while at Cara's.

Laughing, Julia told them both, truly not qualified as a tour guide, but happy to share what she knew. She then mentioned Cara going to take her to see Bond Falls, which not too far away, with some really nice trees and falls. Actually, Talia who then asked, "Could Tomis perhaps join you, as his visit had been kind of last minute from his work in New York, and I can't take off work from the hospital - I'm a nurse there. He's only here until next Friday, when he flies back.

I may be able to get some time off another day, before he leaves, but I don't know." Both Tomis and Julia were a little stunned.

Already repeating, "No, too much to ask," as Tomis slightly embarrassed Talia setting him up, or trying to get someone to entertain him, because of her schedule.

Then Julia admitted, "Well, Cara wasn't very interested in driving me, she has a problem with her legs. But if Tomis is *game*, and up for an adventure, I'd be happy to drive him and myself, so we could both enjoy Bond Falls. I have some good maps and tour books. As well, Cara could give me some pointers on not getting lost, and . . . she does have a GPS system in her Jeep, if we do get lost." She laughed at her joke.

When they both looked at her hesitating, Tomis said, "It is . . . in - convenient to ask you to do drive." His hesitating face saying this had all been a mistake.

"No problem, I love to drive and I want the company. We can enjoy it together. I will try to not bore you, or asked too many questions about Croatia." She had plastered a broad smile across her face, "It'll be fun. Talia said you have to leave on Friday, you *need* to do some leaf-viewing before you go!" Her smile still beaming.

49

Tomis took a deep breath, looking from the one woman to the other, accepting his fate. "OK, I pay all expense and promise no problem." Both women laughed lightly, as it had actually been them who had hood-winked him into the trip.

Julia turned to Talia, "If you'll write down your address, or if there is some other place you want me to pick up Tomis, and give me some contact numbers, I only need a time." She then gave her new cell number, and Cara's numbers, so if any changes or problems, they would all know how to contact each other. She wanted to reassure both of them, she wasn't really as flighty, as she may have seemed.

"I'm actually quite the intrepid-traveler, as I've been to thirty- six countries and even forty of the fifty States, driving in most of them. I even drove in Australia, which is right-hand driving, not easy for us left-hand drivers. I worked in Japan for over seven years, but I never brave enough to drive there." Now, the two of them looked at her, as if amazed at their find. Tomis looked a little confused by it all, but Talia was delighted.

"Wow, that is impressive, and you will have a lot to talk about with Tomis, as he's had to travel so much with his company these past years. I only traveled to Italy before coming to America, when I was teenager. My mother was half-Italian and Croatian, of course, our father was full Croatian. He had insisted we leave when Tomis' wife and daughter were killed. We first lived in Chicago with some friends and relatives, then mother died after I finished nursing school. I moved up here when I got married - my husband has relatives here. He's working out of town because there is no work here now."

A more familiar lilt in her light accent, which Julia had noticed slightly different from Tomis', and now she recognized it as the Italian. Shocked at the cool revelation

50

regarding his wife and daughter. But before commenting on her Chicago connection, to not dwell on it, Tomis spoke first. "May I ask question; my English is not … so good some-time?" Having tried to learn some basic Japanese, Julia knew she'd been able to understand more than she could speak, which usually grammatically wrong.

"Never apologize for your English. Like most Americans, I don't speak a second language fluently. I'm sure, like most Europeans, you also speak other languages fluently. A business teacher-trainer in Japan, this takes me right back into the mode of English, and yours is very good. I do sometimes speak too fast, especially when I'm excited." Julia trying to give him an understanding smile.

He paused to look at her almost intently. "What was word you said before 'traveler'? I do not know it?" She had piqued his curiosity, and sense of being quite different from most other American women he'd met.

Talia shrugged her shoulders, but added, "He speaks Italian fluently and conversational French." As quite proud of her brother.

Julia had to think for a moment. "Oh, the word, 'intrepid' traveler. I often say it, because it means 'fearless, or adventuresome' or not afraid to try something new."

Tomis nodded his head. "Thank you, good word to know. So, you go to 3 - 6, thirty-six countries and 4 - 0, forty States in America?"

Julia now nodded. "Talia is correct, it is impressive. And, you teach business in English in Japan?" Again, Julia nodded and smiled broadly. "I am happy we take drive together - interesting. I can learn much from you, … and I am happy to talk about Croatia for you." All were now smiling.

"We have even more connections," she laughed. "I'm originally from Chicago, and my friend Cara's parents were both Croatian, with her mother being born and raised right here in the Upper Peninsula." Tomis fully laughing, disbelieving how much they had to talk about together. His niece Ericka began to fidget, and Talia knew time to get her home. Since neither Julia nor Tomis were any longer uncomfortable alone, and she felt Julia could handle his English, she figured she could leave.

"I let Ericka choose the ingredients for our take-and-bake pizza, so she is anxious to get home and cook it. Tomis take your time with Julia, and call me when you are ready to return and I'll come later to pick you up. Julia, I'll be happy to take you home also, if you want." Tomis had risen to kiss her on the cheeks and give her the usual European hug.

"No, thank you Talia. I called Cara before, to let her know of meeting up with you two, and told her I'd call later to be picked up." She rose also, but reached out to shake her hand, as the cheek kisses and hug seemed too personal.

"Both of you, please take your time and have some dinner, this is a nice restaurant you can enjoy." She took Ericka's hand, and Tomis walked part way to the parking lot with them.

Just then Julia's phone rang showing Cara's number. She listened as her usual cautiousness expressed, and Julia's usual adventurousness blew it off. "I'm staying for dinner because he's interesting and I want to do this. It's a public place for God's sake, what can happen? I'll call you later, Bye." She hung up before any more warnings could be issued. Tomis sitting back down, as she slipped the phone into her purse.

"Is everything OK? Do you need to leave?" It *was* a disappointed concern.

"No, not at all. Cara called and I told her we're going to have dinner. . . "She then realized he had not even asked her, as Talia who mentioned it. Julia laughed, "I'm sorry, I'm assuming since Talia left. You did want to have dinner, didn't you?"

"Oh, yes. Dinner is nice idea. I did not have lunch. Do you want to go inside?" They had been sitting in the outside area, which had a few tables. Julia nodded agreement considering how cool it could get, and Tomis waved the waiter over. "We want to eat dinner inside." He got up and helped her with her chair, as she had a few books she'd chosen from the book sale. They had taken theirs back to the car before she arrived.

Julia happy Tomis didn't hesitate to ask about any unfamiliar words on the menu, as they ordered and ate dinner. She felt his English, especially regarding business, good enough to not slow down her talking-speed noticeably, but she did get more selective in her idioms and figures of speech. They talked continuously about various international food and foreign travel experiences, since entering any new friendship-relationship stuff new territory to them both.

Yet, Julia began to realize he looked at her as more of a tutor, or business companion sharing information. Perhaps it best, as he'd only be there till Friday and most likely she'd only see him for the trip on Monday to Bond Falls. Even, she'd suggested it as a matter of convenience to tour together - *"Don't make this more than it is,"* she told herself.

When Tomis noticed a man wearing a tie in the casual surroundings, he laughed lightly saying, "I bet you do not know tie or 'cravat' invented in Croatia, in 17th century?" Julia a little stunned, yet happy to know even with the language variance, he had a sense of humor. When she chuckled in return, commenting on his use of English, he then informed her more than fifty percent of their population spoke some, and it increased to seventy percent for those under thirty! The laughter, and subject of age, became a great leveler in making them relax. He looked at her intently for a moment and said, "I like how you laugh . . . is so full and natural . . . you do not hold back. It is very real, … hearty, I think is word . . . I am not sure how to say what I want to say."

Very nice, and telling, to know how vulnerable in his emotions, not just because of his language. She'd have usually avoided such a good-looking man, as she'd often found them to expect the compliments, rather than to give any. More than an ego thing to most of them, kind of an entitlement, but he'd shown no tendency for it.

"Well, thank you again for such a generous compliment. I don't laugh at jokes I don't think are funny, or give compliments which aren't true. I'm rather straight-forward and a bit out-spoken, so I don't play games, if you understand what I'm saying. Yet, some people say I'm complicated, or what I call layered, or deep . . ." She used her hand to show the layers. "So, I can't quite say 'what you see is what you get,' because I'm much more than meets the eye."

She suddenly laughed, with no idea why she'd said all of it, and knew she'd confused him with the way he stared at her. Then she felt it might be better to move on to easier subjects. "Never mind . . . So, your turn, please tell me more about your business, and what you are doing in New York."

"I am in tourism industry - much growth last five years. My father starts ferry business down coast, and our islands and across to Italy. His father starts as fisherman, many boats. I add 'light-rail' trains for passengers - most tourists to visit places of sight-seeing and Dubrovnik, which is old-walled city . . . over one thousand years. It is opposite - far from capital - modern city Zagreb.   I want to get new, big ferries - very expensive. I learn New York Staten Island Ferry sell used   cheap, and can be refurbished. I go to New York to find best old ferries. Over three years now, I get investors and government support." His face lit up, as a smile broadly crossed it. "Many trips and investors, and job finish this week in New Jersey dockyard. I am tired and happy." True pride, without any ego, as if he knew he had only been the facilitator to get it completed.

Julia not really surprised, but impressed at how almost perfect his long speech. He must have memorized it from having to give it to some American investors many times. This truly clarified many of his mannered actions and how sometimes his English could be so good. "Wow! That's truly amazing, and I can't wait to pick your brain about your wonderful country. I'd not been able to go when in Japan and doing so much travel. I've heard about it being so popular with the tourists, and even read a blog from some friends visiting there this past summer. So, I do look forward to visiting it one day. I've traveled through Italy, and around Austria and Czech Republic just north, so I'm really looking forward to you telling me more about it." They were both smiling at each other having found another mutual topic to share with each other.

He told her of all the extensive beautiful National Parks and nature areas in Croatia, which were proudly restored after the war. No doubt of his love of his country, without any dwelling on the destruction or blaming of anyone. A subject she'd avoided asking him about, as she knew no one in his small country had escaped being affected by it. "I've been to several places devastated by war, but of course, I can't imagine the horrors you and your family experienced."

Tomis then told of getting Talia and others out of the country to America, had been a benefit for them, but a sacrifice for others in the families. As he started to become somewhat quiet, Julia quietly interrupted, "You don't need

55

to go into the details, they are safe and happy now. Tell me more about some of the tourist sites to see." She hoped she projected a compassionate smile, and she'd not unintentionally released any sad memories for him.

Slowly smiling, Tomis nodded. "We are more Mediterranean climate on coast, so do not get much Autumn like here. So, I look forward to see your nature and leaf-watching with you tomorrow." He had looked at his watch and could see it was almost seven. "I am sorry, but I need to make calls to Croatia tonight - it is soon Monday morning there." Finally, an evening he honestly wanted to continue. Though what could come out of their meeting, he had not even thought of or considered. "We talk more tomorrow."

This escape visits to Talia's, had been meant to clear his head of those business problems back in Croatia. Yet, his only immediate concern to not have any more ferry problems, and get back to the dock in New Jersey by Friday. But, right now Julia's happy, positive talk a surprise-salve on his worn emotions and body.

As starting to get dark, Julia agreed and said she'd call Cara before she settled in for the evening. They had walked outside and were both on their phones at the same time. Tomis then pulled a small notebook from his jacket pocket and wrote down his temporary business phone number, as he used his international phone only for keeping in touch with Croatia. She said she would call once Cara had agreed to loan her the Jeep, and she got directions for their excursion.

Waiting, they both lingered to comment on the wonderful weather, and hoped it would be another beautiful day tomorrow for their trip. As she thanked him again for dinner, he said very genuinely, the pleasure all his, and what a wonderful evening she'd given him. Julia walked with him to the curb where she figured Talia would drive up for him. She went to shake hands and while he took her hand, he also put his other arm lightly around her shoulders and kissed both cheeks, European style again. Julia determined not to read more of anything into it.

His lovely accent lingered in her ears, as Talia arrived before Cara. When he offered to wait with her until she got there, Julia insisted it would only be a moment or two longer. Talia stepped out of the car to call a 'thank you' over to Julia, and quickly returned to the driver's seat. Once Tomis got in the car, he turned to wave to her, as Talia drove him away. Julia felt her mind take the bulk of the day and rewind it to replay - stopping at the key moments to thoroughly enjoy them once again. All had been almost too special, avoiding the word 'magical.' She'd almost completed reviewing dinner, when the quick horn beep brought her out and back to see Cara waving at her.

"So," Cara asked, "what is this all about? You can't control yourself from picking up the first man who compliments you?" She jokingly laughed, but also somewhat serious about Julia's unexpected behavior. In their past, she'd been the one more comfortable speaking to strangers than Cara, which had gotten them both in trouble.

Julia took a deep breath and released a big sigh. "I have no clue at all, what all did or will happen, or why or anything. He's only here through Thursday, he flies back Friday morning to New York or New Jersey, . . . whatever." She sighed curiously again. "He's refurbishing three ferries to be shipped back to Croatia - he's in the tourism business with the ferries, and also light-rail passenger trains for tourists, mostly." She took another long sigh, thinking about it all.

"I may not even see him after Monday's trip or Tuesday, as his younger half-sister is a nurse at the hospital. His visit kind of last minute, so she's had to ask for some time off, and she won't know for a day or so." Julia stopped, realizing herself rattling, and to think what else to say. Obviously, her feelings were really stirred up. She sounded much like a squirrelly-teenage girl, and she did not want to admit those feelings.

Cara glanced over at her, and when she got no additional information, she chortled, "What the *fuck*?!" Julia looked back over, rolled her eyes and shrugged her shoulders, which Cara could barely see in the fading light. "You spend almost four hours with a man - a man who had come back a second time to see you with his sister in tow, and that's all you've got to say - 'he's in the tourism industry and refurbishing ferryboats in New York or maybe Jersey?" Now they were both laughing wildly at the absurdity of it all. They had been separated for so long, but their actions had not changed.

"We talked mostly about Croatia, and he asked me a lot of questions about working in Japan, and other places I've lived. It was either about tourism or business - interesting to us, but probably boring to you. His sister left before dinner to take her daughter home and bake the pizza they had picked up." Again, she shrugged her shoulders. "I told you I have no clue. I think it will be a fun distraction and I'll get out of your hair for a day or two."

To be funny and play with her frustration, Cara asked "What kind of pizza?"

"You are such a smart-ass sometimes!" Julia took another deep breath and added, "He's the most interesting, polite man I've met in years. I think he's available, though I felt some sadness when he mentioned about rebuilding after the war . . . "

"Duh?!?! What do you think? A long, ugly war, they're still doing those War Criminal trials, or whatever they call them. He's probably married with six kids at home and the wifey-pooh doing laundry everyday." She chuckled at the visual she made.

"I doubt it greatly! I think he's rather a successful businessman, though I don't know what all it entails in his country. He is obviously educated, and his English, especially related to business, is very good. But I think my extensive travel and being around foreigners, especially working with men in Japan, makes him more comfortable with me. He's also around my age, so he can't have any young children, I'd think. Something about him seems vulnerable, like he's not used to being around women and a little uncomfortable. He seemed to feel like Talia trying to fix him up. I mean his wife and daughter died in the war. His son is at college in Cambridge."

"Vulnerable, what does that even mean? How is a man vulnerable, other than an erection? She's probably trying to get him occupied, so she wouldn't have to worry about him wandering around." She snickered at the thought of a man actually being capable of being vulnerable. "You kill me sometimes, with your Dr. Phil psychology and BS."

"I will ask more questions when it seems more appropriate." Julia frustrated from Cara making such a joke out of it all. "I don't know   What does it matter, he leaves on Friday, and I'll go back to

getting my new life together here. End of discussion." No, it wouldn't be for some time to come. They pulled into Cara's long driveway, and Julia remembered she had not actually asked if she could borrow the Jeep for the trip.

Cara said yes, as glad to not have to be driving, and before she could bring up about the gas, Julia said he'd mentioned he'd pay for everything. Cara went over the tour book and map with Julia, then took her out to show her how to use the GPS. She then reminded her how to get back to the town center, where Julia was to pick Tomis up in the morning. "And, if you do get lost, just call me - if you can get cell-service out there." She laughed again, as the whole expedition more of a joke, than the adventure Julia referred to it as. What was she getting herself into Now?

Chapter 4
Colorful Leaves

Colorful leaves dance by me in bristling wind,
like they know me, or remember we met before.
I still want to Live the life I dreamed of having.
Never too late to change my life, to do as I choose.

I've learned Life is nothing but my choices,
every day, or moment, or hour. My Choice, truly.
Dealing with what comes - obstacles or gifts.
Handling by choosing love and truth over fear.

My words, actions, emotions, attitude,
let them point to love around - within me.
I'm in control, I think, I feel - I own it.
I let anger go - it's not worth keeping.

If I am more positive in all I am and do,
I am Surrounded by more positive people.
As I change my thoughts, I change my life,
Thinking positively, creates a different reality.

I want a partner who leads during a dance,
through the leaves, the rain and the snow.
Even with age, Sexy is a state of mind.
I embrace who I am, Loving fun and to laugh.

The next day, Julia picked-up Tomis near the business area where they had met, as a close drop-off for Talia on her way to work. They were both again casually, but nicely dressed. She had the tour guide and maps to take him to the amazingly, beautiful Bond Falls. With her basic directions from Cara, an easy, almost hour's drive. Even along the way, they both 'oohed and awed' to each other regarding the turning trees, on the rolling hills to get there. In a more open area, Tomis chose his words, "You travel many places, may I ask if you have favorite city . . . or country?"

Julia glanced over with her bright smile, "Oh, yes. My favorite city is Prague, since not bombed during World War II, and I really love old buildings. If you've been there, you know not just the famous buildings, but even the homes and apartments in the old sections are like works of art. The windows, doors, roofs - everything decorated with metal, wood, stone - just beautiful."

She glanced again and saw his smile. "Oh, I should have known you've been there. OK, Mr. Tourism, have you walked the Charles Bridge - in the full moonlight? In fact, a Blue Moon when I was there! How about that?" She saw his brain running the translation. "OK, got you on *Blue Moon*. It's the second full moon in a month, rare, only one or two a year."

"Interesting," he said as he took out his little notebook from his inside pocket and wrote it down. "No," he smiled, "I have not walked Charles Bridge in full moon or Blue Moon." He liked how she talked to him, though difficult to understand all of it sometimes.

"And, my favorite country is Malaysia, not just its beauty and Colonial British buildings, but for the fact so many different kinds of people live together, not just peacefully because the government is strict, but most of them do seem to get along." She glanced over again to make sure he had understood her. "I think it is really important. We all, not only need to get along, but to accept each other in every way."

She could see him processing it all, so decided to continue. "I must admit though, my favorite country for *quirkiness* - you know 'unusual behavior' is Australia. They are very funny in what they say, and how they do things. Also, I'm really fascinated by their Aboriginal people, and *their* amazing history. I did a three-day cultural study on them. Unfortunately, the whites there were as bad as us Americans in killing them off, like we did to our Native Americans, before they accepted they could learn something from the Aboriginal people. You know, the ones who actually had owned the land, and protected it before they got there. But, I won't go on my soap-box about all of it. I'm sure you've been there, haven't you?"

"Yes, I have, . . . to both countries." He then paused to choose his words. "You have good opinions on many things. That is interesting." Julia laughed, then giggled more to herself, as so much more true in his statement, than the words had said. Tomis looked at her closely, as he realized more to her laugh.

Tomis then decided to change, and asked her more about her work in Japan. They dialogued for some time with her details, his questions and her funny stories, until she felt she had talked enough. Then Julia asked more about the different tourist spots, especially the old walled-city of Dubrovnik, she'd read about. She enjoyed it all, as she carefully listened to his wonderfully, accented English.

After they parked, they were both impressed by the lovely boardwalk up to the main viewing of the falls. While it kept them off the ground, there had been a minimal removal of trees, of which they both stopped to

touch and even finger the variegated leaves. She had the guidebook folded in her tote bag, so when he asked if she knew what kind of trees they were, she swung it off her shoulder, took the book out and read him the information. He smiled as he thanked her, realizing not only how organized, but she also wanted to know, too. It did help him relax, and to be more into enjoying the surroundings, knowing Julia very happy to be there. She also pulled out her visor cap, for the sunny open areas. She looked around, surprised there were a couple dozen other people visiting, but the area quite large, so the viewing open. When Tomis saw the "Sunshine Coast - Queensland," on the front of her bright-pink cap, he asked if it was Australia. Surprised, Julia answered congratulating him, "Right on! My friend Barb, who lives there, gave it to me on one of my trips, after I lost my sun-hat." A moment of acknowledgment for
them both.

He led off, and took her hand to guide her around the rocks at one end, open to the public, then continued to hold it for awhile, as the nature lovers traipsed around. He had brought his business phone, which had a camera in it, and told her he had sent photos of the ferries before and after to his office to share with his investors. Now, he wanted to take photos of them together, and just of Julia with the glorious falls as the backdrop. He also photographed the walkways, later the gift shop and other areas for reference to be used in Croatia for their tourists. Like Julia, he continued to stop to examine the amazing colorful assortment of leaves within reach. She then showed him two with the 'drips' of color on them, smiling. "I believe *'leaf-elves and fairies'* come every night to paint the leaves, and sometimes these little drops are mistakes the inexperienced ones make."

He had listened very carefully to what she said, and was translating in his head, when he saw the smirk on her face. They both started laughing loudly, and several people around them stared, like wanting to know their joke.

"You are very funny. *Elves and fairies* not easy to translate. I read fairy story to Ericka last night, so I learn word." Proud of himself, he said, "I am best student in class."

"That's Great," Julia said, "Touché - a new word you probably won't use in business." They were both laughing again.

"No, probably not in business. But please explain how you mean, touché?" She laughed and explained it to him, as they walked to the other end of the boardwalk.

She began to note how good he was at picking up her phrases and repeating them. "Also, I have a very *bent* sense of humor. Using 'bent' in it being odd, or strange, or unusual or different. So, I like to say silly things, like the elves. Do understand?"

He again looked at her processing it all. "Why do you like to say silly things?"

She laughed, "Because I have a *bent* sense of humor. It makes things more fun. When I gave up being a workaholic, I also gave up being so serious." She watched him.

He then laughed and said, "Touché - is correct use?" She now laughed so hard, she could hardly get the 'yes' out, and lightly jabbed him with her knuckles in the gut. It startled him at first, and he laughed more. "You punish best student?" They both laughed more, as she grabbed his arm and kissed him on the cheek, then walked off laughing. He stared at her retreat, not knowing what it had all meant, but she didn't react at all.

They had walked around for over an hour. Julia glad Tomis not one of *those* people who take one look and are ready to go.

"Do you want any more photos here, because I thought we'd stop at the gift shop and see what all they have?"

He looked around before answering, to make sure they had covered both ends of the walkway, and there were no more paths to explore. "No, I am ready."

They both walked slowly back, touching the hanging branches and leaves. Julia then took out a re-useable plastic sandwich bag from her tote, to put her collected leaves into. He watched her and said, "Very smart." He slipped his chosen few into his shirt pocket. She then scooted ahead to a tree, at the end of the walkway. She turned back to look at him, as she threw her arms around it, as much as she could to give it a hug. He laughed and took out his phone to take a picture of her again. When she turned to smile at him, he took another and said, "You are perfect 'tree-hugger,' . . . is word correct?"

She let go of the tree, as he walked up to her. "Wow! I'm impressed. You must have some environmental magazines in Croatia, or you have heard about Eco-tourists, who want the trees protected." He smiled broadly and nodded. "Touché, again!" she said. In the gift shop they both wandered around looking at the displays, and reading the information on the trees. Again pleased, his interest genuine, as he wanted to learn.

When they'd gone off in different directions, he came to find her to ask her to explain what some of the gifts and souvenirs were. She added "tacky," "chintzy" and "fake-faux" to his vocabulary, laughing at her explanations. "I think all souvenirs *should* be made by local artists, or at least made in the country you're visiting." He looked at her closely, and finally nodded in understanding and appreciating the information. "I believe your tourists will buy *more* authentic items, representing your history and culture." Tomis then smiled at the useful compliment.

She then moved on, to look at some really lovely carved wooden loons and bears, picking them up and checking their prices, as well as where they were made. He had been watching her for several minutes before he came up behind her, "I want to buy you a *sou- venir*, . . . you know thing to remember trip. Is correct word?"

A little taken aback, not only by his closeness, but he'd obviously been watching her. Nice, but unexpected. "Oh, no, it's not necessary." She turned to walk away, and he touched her arm. He had a soft, almost pleading look on his face.

"Please, I want to buy for you. What one do you want?" She looked at him, and saw the genuine emotion of wanting to show his gratitude for her time.

"OK, but you tell me? Which one do you like best? I really like wood, and birds, and I love dragonflies, but I didn't see any." She saw the questioning look on his face, as his brain must have been scanning his vocabulary, and she knew it was 'dragonfly.'

"Let's go ask at the counter first, to see if they have any dragonflies, because I don't know how to explain it. It's a lovely, flying insect, my favorite, and actually the second oldest insect in existence, but nobody likes cock-roaches." She'd now lost him totally. When she reached the front counter, with Tomis following behind, the older man seemed anxious to please her determination. "Excuse me, do have anything at all with a dragonfly on it, or in it?"

"Well, yes, a few things." He took them over to a corner she had not seen, and showed her several things. As soon as the clerk picked it up, Tomis recognized it, and nodded OK. "We also have a necklace, a charm, and a stained-glass piece."

"Do you have anything with wood, or on wood?" The man shook his head. "OK," Julia said somewhat excited, "Can I see the stained-glass?" Tomis had become fascinated by the whole process, and watched closely. They walked to another corner and he took down a rather large, but gorgeous stained-glass dragonfly on a water scene. "Oh," she said, now rather disappointed. "It's very beautiful, but kind of large. Do you have anything smaller?" The man looked around, and held up his forefinger, saying let me check in back, as he walked out of sight. She turned to Tomis, "He's looking in the back for a smaller version. I really shouldn't be getting anything new. I told you; I got my unpacked boxes in Cara's garage for my new apartment."

The man came back out smiling with an 8 x 10 flat box, and carefully opened it up, as he spoke. "We just got these smaller ones in last week, but haven't had the time to unpack and hang them up." Slipping it out of the tissue, he held up the most perfectly-designed dragonfly on a branch, with colorful leaves over water.

Julia breathed excitedly, "Oh, Tomis! It's perfect with the autumn leaves, I love it." Before she could ask how much, he'd taken out his wallet and given the man his credit card. He really smiled now, as he knew he'd made her happy. "Oh, thank you Tomis!" Before she realized it, she had kissed him on the cheek again. They were both momentarily embarrassed, then she blew it off, so he wouldn't misconstrue its meaning. She then began profusely thanking the clerk for his effort.

He listened to her thank the clerk, and recouped well, figuring it must be her habit to kiss cheeks and responded when she turned back to him. "You are welcome, my thank you gift to you." Once she'd gotten the box into her tote bag, he asked, "May I ask favor to help me choose some souvenir to take to Croatia?"

"Oh, sure, who are they for?" Julia delighted to help him shop. He had an embarrassed laugh again, when he realized souvenirs were usually bought as gifts.

"I want to show to tourist board . . . suggestion to sell to tourist. Do I need to buy for people also? . . . Friends in Croatia ask me to buy things, so I buy . . . what they ask me only. Is that mistake?" He had a concerned look, not wanting to make a mistake.

Julia pulled in her lips, trying to not laugh out loud. "Some people *expect* souvenirs, in Japan *omiage* - souvenirs were almost required of overseas tourists. And, other people may consider them just to be *trinkets - tchotchkes,* you may know the word or dust- collectors. They have some very nice things here, and you may want to get something for Ericka.

She is young and would probably like something from you. Though I don't know if Talia will be taking you other places, which would have some souvenirs." She paused to make sure he had understood what all she had meant. "Show me what you were thinking of, and I'll help you choose what may be good and easy to convert or copy for your National Parks."

Julia helped him choose about a dozen items for the Tourist Board, making sure none had been made in China. She also suggested some distinctive post cards, as he had commented on their unusual beauty. Then, she couldn't help but notice, he'd taken out a very different credit card to pay for them, and the other one again for Ericka's stuffed animal.

She figured careful to use one for business, and another for personal. When they headed back to the car, Julia asked if he was getting hungry, but when he didn't respond right away she added, "Cara told me about a little general store, not too far away, which has sandwiches and ice cream - homemade. How does that sound to you?" She had opened the back hatch for him to put his bags in, and headed for the driver's door. He almost rushed over to it.

"I do it for you." He'd surprised her, so smiling up at him, and got in the opened the door, as he smiled in return, then added, "Yes, I am hungry. Sandwich and ice cream sound good to me." He closed her door, walked back to close the hatch, and continued around to the passenger side to let himself in.

She wound them through the other parking lot, and back out to the other entrance for what she figured the general store. Considering there were only a few buildings or businesses out there, easy to spot. It also had several cars, as it was after one o'clock. They decided to split a sandwich, when they saw the size of the ice cream cones, as they both definitely wanted one. The crowd had cleared by the time they got their cups of ice cream and moved outside to sit.

Eating the homemade ice cream, brought more giggles to their mature bodies, adding a youthfulness neither of them expected. Sitting on the wrap-around porch enjoying her chocolate, Julia gave him one of her big smiles, "It's always the simple pleasures, which really make me happy, especially when surrounded by so much nature." She watched as Tomis nodded, and broadly grinned in return. He totally filed away her comments and actions, as most of the day had been spent taking in the abundance around them.

For Julia, this had been a fascinating way to get to know a man, so much better than a dinner - movie date. She'd seen him in this non-threatening, platonic situation where he had relaxed, which she doubted he'd done in a long time. She could tell he wasn't used to being around a woman like her in this capacity - not a client, investor or employee or even a date.

She did not want to do 'twenty questions' on him, though her curiosity had not been slaked at Sunday's dinner, and about to get the best of her in this calm. Did he just 'want her company to share and view nature,' as he said? Could it all be so simple? No, she wasn't going to slip into Cara's conspiracy-theory stuff, as if he had some ulterior motive. Tomis had been quite open about so many things, and had politely asked her regarding particular questions about her training work in Japan. Then, for her explaining more about her experience in Human Resources.

He did not hesitate to compliment her on her business knowledge, and openly surprised she was not working full time. He'd been nothing but a considerate gentleman, and though some of her quirky comments had thrown his English sometimes, he didn't hesitate to ask for a clarification. That alone, in her book had moved him into the 'secure man' category.

"I cannot remember the last time I sit outside to enjoy ice cream. This is good!" He seemed amazed at the small notch of land, which had been cut out of the woods, at this intersection to the highway. "It does not seem real . . . so many trees and few people, but good roads and things to see." Tomis' personal relaxed feelings surprised him. He didn't have to 'be' anyone around Julia.

"We do take pride for our large nature areas in Croatia, but I never see so many trees on drive here." After surveying the colorful trees again, he turned to look directly at her. "You call them rolling hills, and I see why . . .they remind me glide sailboat on Adriatic Sea, down pass all our islands." He looked out, almost dreaming, smiling at the memory.

"I would like that, kind of riding-off into the sunset. But, I can't be out in the sun and water too much, as I burn like a crispy- critter. But I love sunsets, especially on boats."

"What is 'crispy-critter?' I do not understand?" He stared intently again.

She began laughing and chuckling. "My bent sense of humor. Let's see if I can explain it. When you cook something on a open fire - do you guys bar-b-que?" His head tilted questioning the words again. "Never mind. When you leave something cooking too long and you burn it, it turns into a 'crispy-critter,' because it no longer looks the way it is supposed to look." She looked at him. "I'm rather allergic to the sun and get sun-burned easily, especially around water. But I love the water. I love to snorkel - you know with a mask and breathing tube? Did you ever do it or Scuba dive?"

Now openly laughing at her, as she had been gesturing so many different ways, to describe all of the actions. "OK, Bub!" She leaned over to jab him in the stomach again. "Stop laughing at the circus clown!" This made him laugh more, as if real entertainment.

She had the giggles also, and they both finally calmed down, and he returned again to look at her. "I feel so relaxed here . . . and with you." Without realizing it, Tomis now surveying Julia, with a realization of how true what he said was. The look went deep past her eyes and touched her soul, as it lightly *tingled* other parts.

Her knees might have buckled, had she been standing. She felt she needed to move, to break his mesmerizing hold. A look which can tell you more, than a hundred words in perfect English. She understood clearly what his look saying - 'there is more here than meets the eye.' At the same time, she had a creeping-fear of falling for him, yet still elated to know he cared, on more than a business-tutor level only.

For the first time since their meeting, Julia felt the slight rise of warmth come up between her breasts, starting to flush her neck and tighten her throat. "Well . . . thank you. I'm just . . . playing a rather inept, tour guide here . . . just sharing with you what I've read and Cara has shown me." As much as she loved the spell he'd put on her, she did not want to get swept away by this man. "You've been a really good sport about it all . . . and I'm glad you're so relaxed, so am I." Or at least she was until he made *her* a part of his whole enjoyment.

"Without being too intrusive, could I ask you what your plans are, now your ferryboats are finished?" She knew her subconscious had spouted it to break the spell, and it certainly did. "I mean, I don't want to get too personal, just curious. You seem to be a workaholic like I recently was, and it's not easy to not have a project." Now, she wished she had allowed the moment to continue, at least a few minutes longer.

Not quite startled, but a little taken aback, by the abrupt change of subject, and he ran the words through his mind to make sure he thoroughly understood what she had said. Tomis then noticed the pink in Julia's neck and cheeks, realizing maybe he'd gotten too personal with her. "I am not sure," he lied, not really knowing why he had said it, rather than talk about him just traveling somewhere. "Do you think I am stuffy, old business man - engineer, like Talia say? I do enjoy nature at home, but do not usually have time." Somehow he felt a little defensive and wasn't sure why.

Slightly embarrassed, Julia could hear Cara in her head chastising her about her flippant mouth. "I'm sorry, I really didn't mean to get too personal. I mean things pop into my head sometimes, and I say them. Just wondering if you had other projects you'd be moving on to." She put a lot of effort into a big smile.

"I told you I'm quirky, . . . and sometimes, when I feel relaxed with someone. . . I apologize. And, no, I don't think you are a stuffy, old business man. Also, my second husband a mechanical engineer, and so were most of the Japanese men I trained. I'm used to technical talk, I actually, find it interesting." She silently watched, as Tomis sorted through what she said, while staring at her, he burst out laughing, not sure why.

"You are very surprising . . . uh amazing! I never meet woman like you before." He chuckled, "I mean, I always think American woman outspoken, and I like it, . . . and I can see Talia change in five years, I last see her. And my niece, she also become very independent *American* woman, I think is good." He looked at her very intently. "But you are more, . . . very business knowledge and much travel experience . . . you surprise me many ways." Before she could respond, he added, "And, I am fifty my birthday next May. I like to stay active . . . *what difference is age?*" He couldn't imagine anyone doing as much as she'd done, so she had to be at least fifty, or so.

Now Julia stunned. What could she say to all that? The age thing would put it all back into a relationship, or even friendship perspective. She certainly didn't want him to think she classified them together in any way. She took a deep breath. "OK, . . . got the point clarified, so I'm just going to go for it . . . " She wasn't sure if she should refer to his late wife as 'died' or 'killed,' as she certainly didn't want to bring up any downer-thing regarding the war.

"I'm divorced twice, the whole 'been there, done that' and no interest to do it again. But, I guess just curious, as to why you didn't remarry . . . or if you did, or I would think you would at least have a lady-friend back in Croatia, or why you wouldn't bring her with you to visit the States?"

He had stood to drop his empty paper cup and spoon in the trash. "I mean, you are a rather good looking, successful man, and I would think you would have a lovely, young woman by your side for all your business and political functions . . . ." Her voice trailed off, as it almost rambling, and sounding like 'celebrity reporting' or something.

Tomis sat back down, as Julia continued to sit a space away on the bench, holding her empty cup like a life-preserver. Her mind racing between wanting to retract all she'd said, yet the 'inquiring minds wanted to know' popped in, to put a pinched smile on her face.

"Well, what is you say, 'quite a mouth-full?'" He slightly chuckled, realizing some feelings between them, and though he couldn't remember the last time he had dealt with this kind of conversation, it might be good for him to address it as well.

"It was four - five years between war end and recovery, . . . work help me not remember so much . . . loss of wife Celia and daughter Milos. I concentrate on son Stepan to grow up." Tomis took a breath, as Julia did, too. "I think last five or eight years maybe call normal, and much better than under Communism." He looked directly into her pale-turquoise eyes, which had distracted him so, the first time he saw her.

Self-consciously, Julia ran her hand through her hair, her usual habit to help her focus. A rarity - a man who talked openly about himself. With her non-native English experiences, she couldn't help but recognize it, when he used phrases he'd obviously picked-up from reading or perhaps English television. Kind of a time-warp for her, to those years of speaking English to so many foreigners, it intrigued her. "Yes, I am work-ahol," he stumbled a little on the word usage.

"But I date ... some younger . . . pretty women when business start, ... for events ... to become successful. But they did not understand what we know of war, . . . My son and Talia have little memory of war . . . and it is good thing. I hope they never know war,... except in movies or television." He glanced away, forming his words, then back to her.

"We watch much American television, same most of world. I do not feel . . . I need young, pretty woman by my side . . . or in my bed to make me feel good or feel success." He smiled, knowing this a good thing for him to acknowledge to himself. "I like woman who has business experience and understand work-ahol. She never needs me to explain or entertain her. We do things together and talk about much. Age or beauty are not part of equation - not to sound too much like engineer I am." With a wide grin he finally added, "In three days I fly to New Jersey. . . I hope you spend more days with me." He glanced around again at the surrounding nature. ". . . maybe we enjoy more trees together."

Momentarily they sat looking at each other, his backstory had basically been filled in now, so up to her to drop in more bits and pieces about herself, as he had asked few personal questions of her. "Well, thank you," Julia sounded almost sarcastic instead of perky, so quickly toned it down.

"Really, few American men would share so much, so openly. And, to change the subject again, if you think this is a lot of trees, and if Talia is still tied up working tomorrow, *and* you are up for it, we can go to Michigan's largest area of *undeveloped* wilderness. It is so open and empty; you can drive if you want. You told me you drive on the right in Croatia, so I think it will be safe, and I can navigate. I haven't been there before, but it looks easy on the map." Again, a lot to drop on him, but she'd see how he processed it all. She had no plans to comment on any of the things he had so personally shared.

She'd gotten up as speaking, to finally drop her paper cup in the trash, "By the way, is your son still at the university? Mine graduated a few years ago, but he was late, from fooling around and being distracted with girls." They both laughed, and it obviously felt good for them, in clearing any residuals. When she turned back, he was standing right in front of her. He gave her a big hug and kiss on the cheek, as if to say it's all we need right now. He didn't want her to get skittish again, so let go of her stepping back.

"He finishes at university computer science degree, and now study English and business at Cambridge, to decide work he want. You say your son do computer, too. It is young people career. I can do it, but not easy to do it." Julia laughed in agreement, as they walked to the car, with Tomis opening the driver's door for her as before. As they headed back, he asked about the music on the radio, if what she liked to listen to.

"Cara has the satellite radio, and I would never change the station. It's mostly R & B, you know, rhythm and blues, with some jazz and old rock. I like most of it, and most of the older songs and singers. There are a few of the newer singers, who do ballads and jazz I like. How about you?" Glad to get onto a common topic.

"I think American music is how we learn English. And, I like same music. Do you have favorite song or singer?" A comfortable way to know her personal side.

"Oh, that would be very difficult for me. I guess I could say, most of the Beatles, but some classics of groups like the Eagles, or Earth, Wind & Fire, even Santana and some Sinatra. I don't often listen, just for the music. It's usually background to something else I'm doing, or like driving in the car. I loved going to the symphony, we had a really great one in San Francisco, the Opera and I loved seeing Broadway musicals, as quite a dancer in my day." She laughed like it had been ancient history. "So, tell me your favorite songs or singers." Again, he agreed with her choices, and began to mention specific songs he liked, and what they sometimes reminded him of doing at that time in his life. Julia heartily agreed, as they continued to throw songs back and forth to each other, not always remembering who had sung them. The time flew by quickly.

He had insisted on filling Cara's gas tank, as they got back into town. "Please thank Cara to use her car. I do appreciate it." He had gotten directions for her, so pulling into the driveway of his sister's small house, Tomis leaned over to kiss her again on the cheek. "I talk to Talia to use her car, you trust me and direct my drive, so we do not get lost." He leaned back into the car after getting out, "It was perfect day. I call later to confirm details." He gave her another look, as if wanting to remember something about her, and smiled before closing the car door.

Julia watched as he walked up the sidewalk, turned and waved before knocking on the door. As she pulled away she could see Talia hugging him and his niece waving out to her. As strange as their arrangement might seem, it felt natural in its unfolding. They had both agreed they needed, and also wanted to spend time with their respective loved ones in the evening.

Though Julia doubted Talia would be quite as questioning as Cara could be, she did wonder what Talia thought of them being together. Perhaps his idea of getting them joined for dinner, would quell any concerns either of them might have. Julia trying to tell herself what it was - just one of those 'out of the blue friendships' which happens on vacations or business trips. She shook her head, *"Wrong-o Kiddo!"* She heard it inside, and said out loud. It's going to be more than a vacation friendship. It would not be convincing to Cara either, but she would try saying it.

~ ~ ~ ~ ~ ~ ~ ~ ~

The dogs had probably been announcing her arrival, from the moment she entered the long driveway, so no sneaking in, even if she had wanted to do so. As soon as Julia had parked the Jeep in the garage, Cara had let the dogs out, so before running into the yard, they had greeted Julia. "Do I need to check for any scratches or dents?" Cara half-seriously joked.

"No, just a lot of killed-insects on the windshield, I tried to clean off, while Tomis filled the tank." She got the rest of her stuff from the back seat. "I think it is all intact, and we both thank you very much. I didn't really have any problems at all. I didn't even have to use the GPS, and I found the little General Store easily, too." Cara had looked back at the car, as she had walked out part way into the driveway to watch the dogs pee, or if she needed to scoop up any poop. "I've got to pee, so I'm going in, OK?"

Julia went up the stairs and on in, heading back to her room to dump all of her stuff. She peed, went back to get her dragonfly gift to show Cara, then poured herself a glass of red wine and sat down on her bar stool at the kitchen counter. The dogs came in happy, greeted her again, followed by Cara, and they dispersed. She picked up her glass of white wine, took a swallow and stared at Julia a moment. She began to take the framed glass out of the box and unwrap it to show her. "Isn't this gorgeous?" In her usual subdued way, "That is nice. Where'd you get it? How much was it?"

"It's from the gift shop at Bond Falls and Tomis bought for me, I have no idea how much it cost. He is a very considerate man." Cara kind of hummed, neither agreeing nor directly any disagreeing. Julia chose to ignore it by making no comment. "We had a great time, perfect weather, talked a lot and he's going to call later . . . to let me know if we're going to Porcupine Mountains tomorrow - we'll take Talia's car, so you won't be stranded at home." She added it to quickly counter any reaction to the next trip.

"Why? . . . You know it's over two hours to get there? Are you going to drive her car then?" This now getting bizarre to her. "Hand me the dog's water dish and bowl, I may as well make their dinner, since we'll be eating soon." She took another swallow of her wine and shook her head.

Julia got up to get the dishes, and passed them over to Cara. "You know I've been reading all those tour books, and I know you really don't want to make trips you've already made, or just long drives. So, I suggested it to him, if Talia hadn't gotten the time off to be with him, and if he's interested. And, 'no' I'm not going to drive, he knows how to drive on the left, and the roads are so empty, I figured he could do it." They talked about the details, as Cara prepared the dogs' dinner. Julia went to get her tour map to show Cara the trip she planned. "We will leave a little earlier, and probably get back a little later, but I think we can do it, or know we don't want to spend any more time together, after being so confined. Either way, I still basically get to see some of it." Julia decided to reveal bits and pieces of their conversations to Cara, as she reacted.

After situating the dogs in their eating spots, Cara refilled her glass and headed for the Lazy Boy chairs in the living room. "We've got about a half hour till dinner."

Julia followed her in, and plopped down in her designated chair. Cara had automatically turned on her big screen. "Also, Tomis wants to take you and Talia to dinner Wednesday evening. It is kind of a thank you. We talked about where would be a good place to eat, and convenient to you both, so I suggested Brule Ski Resort. You had said how much you and Johnny had enjoyed it, when you were first coming up here. I want to see it, and we should get some nice sight-seeing from the ski lifts, since they're open limited hours for all the 'leaf- peepers' pouring in. There were quite a few people up at Bond Falls." Trying to be casual about it all, but knew Cara would resist it.

"You know I don't like to get dressed-up to go out." She studied the line-up on her DirectTV, planning their evening's viewing.

"He really wants to do this for both of you - whatever you want to eat or drink, how can you pass it up? You don't have to cook for us, and you know you don't really have to dress up to go there. Come on, it'll be fun, or at least entertaining to meet his sister, younger half-sister, anyway." Cara conceded, and they talked more generalities until the timer went off for dinner.

Once they had settled into their chairs with their dinners, Cara paused the TV. "You know I gotta ask, so what happened to his wife, why doesn't he have another one or a girlfriend? You'd think he'd brought someone here for the visit or even New York?"

Julia had to laugh, as she told Cara how she'd asked almost all of the same questions, and gave her his answers. "But there's got to be more to it, than all that, I'm sure." She thought for a moment before going on. "It's like he has an old, buried pain, . . . a guilty burden connected to the deaths of his wife and daughter. A loss which does take a hole out of you - I don't have to tell you after losing your son Jimmy almost twenty years ago. I think Tomis always a hard worker with his father, but became a real workaholic after they died. And, when his father passed, I think he felt it necessary to carry-on the legacy. I'm not going to pry any more than I have. We're having a good time, he's interesting, and I'm seeing the sites without any strings attached, or emotions invested."

Julia went back to eating her dinner, but the last comment made Cara stop eating hers, and look over at her. "You sure about that? If you start denying something you say isn't there, then there's something there." A slightly-raised determined voice she used, and the dogs looked up at her, noting something wrong.

Julia sighed, swallowed her food and took a sip of wine. "Cara, he flies out to New Jersey *early* Friday morning, he reminded me, when we talked today. Nothing will change those business plans. This is a really big project he's been working on for a couple of years. And, a few days later, he flies back to Croatia. I stopped doing one-night stands a long time ago, . . . and it is *not* what this has been about."

She paused to get the analogy she wanted. "We're just two tourists combining resources to site-see, . . . that's all . . . really." She tried to go back to casually eating her dinner, but *even* she didn't believe what she had just said, though she wasn't totally sure why.

"Really?!? *REALLY!* Can I hold you to that when you get all mopey? I *will* say, 'I told you so.' And, you know I'll have the *right* to do so." She laughed rather sarcastically. Something to be said for all their years of knowing each other, and how they'd lived their lives.

"Whatever! I don't want to talk about it anymore. What's on tonight?" An hour later Tomis called to say Talia happy to let him use the car. He'd be back to the house by eight-fifteen, if he didn't get lost returning from her work. When Julia told Cara, she cackled loudly.

"Yeah, right! *Just* two tourists, *just* sight-seeing together! We'll see about it." She shook her head and laughed again. She paused for a minute before adding. "OK, yes, I'll come to dinner. Let me know what time tomorrow… I've got nothing better to do."

Chapter 5
Trees and Big Water

Is it the fog, or do my thoughts rise
Because they have no weight?
I have never thought of them as fluff.

Why is it, some people think they need
to explain me to their friends?
Do I look as alien as I feel?

I believe I can speak for myself,
but then there are some people who
are not worth the full explanation.

Do I need wine in my blood to sing?
Or is it just having an audience,
who knows how to listen to life's music?

A once remembered fantastic lover . . .
Where do those energies all go,
when they dissolve over the years?

Passion could be called episodic,
for it lacks a notoriety of long use.
Where is the replay button when needed?

Even a long distance runner crosses a finish line.
Mileage is the experience which youth
will never understand, until they have it.

So, Tuesday had Cara dropping Julia off early at Talia's house, and Tomis at the car closing the trunk. He had obviously, successfully driven back from the hospital, where she worked. He walked over to the driver's side, as Cara lowered the window.

"I am glad you join us for dinner tomorrow at ski resort. Julia has plan to get there at 4:30, we can call you or come at 5pm. Talia feel better for her Ericka to stay with baby-sitter, she does not sit well for long time." He waited to see if Cara would respond right away and added, "I drive today, but Julia navigates map. I hope we do not get lost, too much." He could feel the strong vibe from Cara, and felt it probably better to let her go. His smile now a bit forced, as he stepped back.

The window moving back-up, as Cara finally responded, "I'll be there before 5, have a good time, and drive carefully *on the left side please*!" She had attempted to smile, but she didn't feel good about this situation at all. They had not exactly argued last night, but she just could not understand why Julia had wanted to spend time with this stranger. As she slowly drove away, she watched Julia put her arm around his back, as he swung around to kiss her cheek to hug her fully.

Or, even more so, Cara questioned, why he wanted to spend time with her? Though Julia looked really good for her age - he was younger, very good looking and probably even wealthy, considering the tourist business and his expansion.

Three more refurbished ferryboats, still they couldn't be cheap. What did he really want with her? It wasn't a Green Card thing, as he wasn't at all enamored, or wanted to live in the U.S.. Julia really no longer had money; yes, very pretty and smart, but could it be just easy sex? She shook her head, hoping she'd find out more at tomorrow's dinner. And, see how his sister - much younger half-sister at that - thought about it all. If she had no concern, then definitely *something* was wrong.

Julia put her tote bag with the sandwiches, snacks, water bottles, wine and wine opener with plastic glasses in the back seat. She had the map and tour magazine in hand, as she climbed into the passenger seat. "So, as I told you last night, it is about a two-hour drive there, spend three or so hours there, and two hours back. If, and it may be a big 'if,' we can still laugh *and* enjoy each other *and* want to site-see more together, it will be a huge accomplishment for *any* two people who choose to spend time together."

She looked at Tomis, waiting for him to finish examining the dashboard and driving panel. She had no idea, and he had no intentions of telling her, he had not driven himself in a car for almost a year. He had certainly not wanted her to know about his security and life-threats, since really no need to tell her any of it.

He turned to look at her, "I am proud, I did not make mistake . . . drive back alone. I do not think we run out things to talk about, but I bring music, . . . too." Smiling, he handed the CDs to her. "Pick one you like." He'd also thought about the long time the two of them would be in the car alone - almost the whole day. It would be like a test of how *compatible* they were. He wasn't worried either way, but curious.

Julia cracked-up laughing, understanding he had put some thought into their long day alone in the car. "OK then, go back out to the main road and head for Hwy. 2, going back West. We are going one way straight to Porcupine Mountains Wilderness State Park, where it cuts off from Silver City and Lake Superior . . . "

"Do you mean real Lake Superior or is town name?" He looked at her in total amazement. This was going to be fun; he had no clue at all of the wonder she was about to show him. Almost like taking someone to Disneyland the first time.

"Yes, My Dear, we are going to be driving along-side the *real* Lake Superior, which may remind you of the Adriatic Sea, as you cannot see across it. We'll explore the Park, and above in Lake of the Clouds is where we'll have our picnic. And, it's where we can see Superior from above, very unique experience, I understand. After, we'll explore some more, and onto the Ontonagon area. We will then head back a different way, and if all works out as planned, I should still have you back to Talia by 4 pm." Now smiling from ear to ear, like a boy on his first road trip, who couldn't wait for all of the wonderment and excitement of it.

"I have no idea such big trip in one day. Lake of Clouds and Onton sound wonderful. I know you have much information to tell me. You *are* good tour guide!" At the flashing red light, he looked at her, "I know we have fun. And, this is new to you?"

"Yes, so please don't shoot the messenger, I will navigate to the best of my map-reading abilities, but they are all highways. Most of the names come from the Native Americans, so my pronunciations may not always be correct either. This is really going to be an adventure for both of us, but we have food, water and fuel, so off we go." She looked through the CDs and picked out the Beatles album, which Talia had in her collection, then put it in the player. She listened for a moment, nodded her head, "Yeah, this is going to be a good trip." He smiled in agreement.

She began to read to him about Lake of the Clouds being situated in a valley between two ridges in the Porcupine Mountains, surrounded by *virgin* wilderness - she stopped to explain what the 'virgin' meant, and he could not believe her. There were still trees which had never been cut. "Yes, it says: 'This one is a true wilderness, with nearly 59,000 *acres* of sprawling mountain rivers, lakes and dark stands of virgin hemlock, pines and hardwoods. They are the largest virgin hardwood-hemlock forest in the United States. Some of these forests' monarchs are 200 years or more old. It is 92 square miles, with scenic waterfalls, rugged Lake Superior shore line, remote rustic cabins, 87 miles of hiking trails with few roads.'" She glanced at him and could tell he was listening intently.

"We will only be walking in about a mile to the overlook area for our picnic, and some other trails. There is a full Visitor Center and it says, 'stunning vistas of the lake, which is 1000 feet down, is a popular destination for hikers, campers, and fishermen.' Wow! That is impressive. It's too bad we can't spend the night, because they have 'a nighttime sky watch, where *while lying down* you can watch for shooting stars and orbiting satellites, as a Park Guide points out the constellations and stars.' It is also said, 'the howling of a wolf can be heard during this nighttime sky watch.' How about that, for backwoods-wilderness experience?"

"When I was young boy, before mother die . . . I was ten, my father takes me up our high mountain Dinara in Alps, and Mt. Biokovo on weekend - you say camp-trip? We fish. But she got sick . . . we never go again . . . He marries my step-mother and no time. . . Ivo, half- brother came and Talia . . . I not think about fish trip . . . for very long time. I think this trip bring good memories for me."

"Oh, I don't remember you mentioning a half-brother before. What does Ivo do in Croatia?" Not wanting to ask too many questions. "He works with me, help with ferries and tourist-trains or what

we need. He calls to tell me problems with unions and things. He is not work-ahol like me, so he need much supervision   Tell me more what we see. And tell me to turn." She learned, like herself, he changed a subject when he didn't want to talk about something.

"Just so you know, the correct pronunciation is "*workaholic*" - just add the "ic" and it's good. And, may I remind you, I was one - a workaholic - for over twenty years also. But have finally let go of it. OK, don't worry we have a long way to go. You don't have to turn until we get to Highway 45 at Watersmeet. And, 'The Park is Michigan's largest area of undeveloped wilderness, established in 1945, and later designated a Wilderness Area made for multiple use management. Which means, . . . designed to accommodate the camper, RV-camper and day use visitor. It also has a complete winter skiing complex and snowmobile trail system.' Have you ever snowmobiled, or do you ski?"

"I ski few times years ago . . . I was at university, but never . . .

snow-mobile - it means ride on machine, right?"

"Yes, I'm just the opposite, I've snowmobiled, but never snow skied. I water skied, when young, but nothing in years. Oh, it says here: 'There's a new wooden boardwalk which leads from the parking lot on M-107 to an overlook at Lake of the Clouds and one for Mirror Lake.' Oh, this is interesting: Ontonagon County named by the Indians after the bowl-like shape of the mouth of its River at Lake Superior, since a center of transportation and traffic. The name originally discovered written on a Jesuit map in 1672.' I love history, where little things tell you so much about an area."

Tomis glanced at her and smiled. This, exactly the kind of time he enjoyed having with someone, and he couldn't remember when he had last been able to do so. "Yes, I know what you mean. I try to explain to tourist bureau people, to say more things our wonderful history and heritage. But they think no need."

"Oh no, they're wrong! As much as I've traveled, *historical and cultural* places have always been my main interest. I've always looked for the info, which has the most colorful background stories, or interesting notes about a place or the people. Here listen to this: 'Copper was discovered in the late 1700's, which included the Ontonagon Boulder, a short distance up the river - then an Indian shrine, a place of worship. It contained over a ton of the pure metal.' WOW! One, Single Boulder! Wow! Isn't that interesting?"

He glanced at her again and remarked, "I love how *'enthusium'* you get." He smiled, turning back to the road, shaking his head learning to enjoy her quirky behavior.

Julia so enthralled, she hadn't bothered to correct him. ". . . and listen to this, it 'was eventually brought to the Smithsonian Institution'- it's the National Museum in Washington DC - 'where it can be viewed today. This brought a surge of settlers to the area, to start mining in 1772, and culminating by the late 1800's. Afterwards, lumbering flourished in the area, until the turn of the century. Today, paper-manufacturing and tourism remain the county's primary economic resources. With over 24 waterfalls, dozens of rivers and inland lakes, not to mention the Lake Superior coastline, fishing and hiking top the list of recreational attractions. The Porcupine Mountains State Park, featuring Presque Isle Falls,' not sure if I'm saying it right, 'and Lake of the Clouds, is the number one place to visit, and definitely make coming here a worth-while experience!' I'll say.

"I'm so glad we're doing this. I know Cara would not have wanted to make the drive with me. I know she went up here with her late-husband, Johnny many years ago, and snowmobiled in winter, too." She looked around at the surrounding trees. "This is great!" Tomis looked over at her again, and their eyes met. "Yes, it is and I thank you to ask me to go." Julia had seen he also had something else on his mind, but now knew to give him a little time and space to formulate up his questions. She glanced back out the windows and pointed out some unusual colors from time to time.

Finally, he asked. "You say Johnny, Cara husband, … I think you say he die, was why last time you here, yes?" He kept his eyes on the road this time.

Julia wasn't sure where this was going, but it didn't really matter. "Yes, Johnny died from a stroke over three years ago. I came for the memorial she had, over the 4th of July, and I did his eulogy - you know the talk about him. I had known them both going back over twenty years, when we were in our twenties. But Johnny, twenty-one years older than Cara, and she had always known he'd die before her. Did you have some questions about them or him?" Glad they had decided to have Cara and Talia meet over dinner on Wednesday, since they may get delayed today with the long drive. Also, Julia wanted to make sure they both had time to make whatever needed arrangements, so they could both come.

"I am not sure I can say correct." He took a breath and dove in. "I try to talk to her at driveway . . . and she is not happy . . . is me, or us or dinner tomorrow. I want you to know. … I feel very strong feeling from her." They then both saw the sign for Watersmeet.

"OK, we're coming up on Watersmeet - it's another Native American name, just so you know. You'll turn right on Highway 45, which goes north, then another straight drive to Bruce Crossing, and turn left on Route 28, which takes us West. I'll let you know."

Rather point blank, being honest also, "No, Cara doesn't trust you, or most men . . . and can't understand why you want to spend time with me. But I don't care, as it is your choice and my choice, which is all that matters, right? I'm not going to let her get to me, and I don't want you to either. Does Talia have any concerns about me?"

Julia glanced over at Tomis, as she had really put the whole 'big question' right out there. What were they really doing together, or did it matter, or did it even have to be answered at this time? She had felt the whole dinner thing like them going to 'meet the parents' or some strange thing, to get *approval* of their spending time together. Seriously, it's only a couple of days together . . . supposedly. She wasn't working or had any obligations, and Tomis on vacation, so what if they spent time together? He was much more fun, and really interesting to talk to about all kinds of things.

Tomis chuckled a little. "No, Talia not say she concern, . . . but does not understand what you see in me. She thinks I am only *workaholic*, boring engineer. You know, only think about business and how to keep tourist happy, to come to Croatia. I think I never talk to her about women in my life. I mean, she knows I am not monk, or not like women."

Julia now laughing hysterically, as the last thing she would have thought about him. "She and husband are . . . separate he has to travel to find work, he laid-off last year. Maybe he gets good job here again, it works out. I only know him at the wedding, seven years ago and not come here before."

"I'm sorry to hear about her marriage. I know it is very difficult to raise a young child alone. I did it for nine years with my son. I hope they can work it out. But I must admit, it is really very funny, Talia and Cara neither understand why we would bother spending time together. You're on vacation, and I'm not working now, so why not?" The irony of it all almost too much for her to keep to herself, but she knew she must. Talia thought Tomis almost asexual, and Cara thought he only wanted her for easy-sex. "You are a much better substitution. I'd probably be reading, doing some long put-off project for Cara, or playing with the dogs in the yard."

"Right, I read or watch television, or call Croatia to check everything OK, with me not there I plan to be New York tourist, but I call Talia and she alone, so I come here to spend time, when she at home from work." At the stop sign, he turned to look again at her, and with his pause she looked up from the map to him. "But now I know, I *meant* to meet you . . . and we spend time together." At that moment, the Beatles began to sing "*Something in the Way She Moves,*" and Tomis leaned over to turn it up. "I like song very much." He looked at her with a very wide smile.

"Wow! I DO TOO! Thank you for bringing the music." While they quietly listened to the song, her mind going a-mile-a-minute. He had said he knew, "*meant* to meet you." Now the whole ballgame changed. There were many things she had pondered when, where or even if, she should share about herself. But now he had somewhat - maybe not in his opinion, as it could be just an English expression he'd learned to use.

Yet to her, it opened-up the whole area of her beliefs, and certainly the idea of *destiny* in relationships. She knew he was Catholic, as what she had learned from Google, as almost ninety percent of Croatia. Religion had been at the crux of the war, though basic-central Croatia had been ethnic and religiously mixed since before World War I. But in the border towns, once they declared their independence, much of the brutal - 'ethnic cleansing' - mainly against the Islamic Serbs or 'Bosniacs' took place. Of course, behind the religious zealots were those hungry for power, who knew how to turn one group against another.

Julia had studied many religions, and knew enough not to argue with some people about theirs. It had led her into Metaphysics years before, with her study of Zen Buddhism and Spirituality, as in being open and accepting of All being One. Much of her personal writing, of her own learning experiences, and believing her angels had guided her to make the move to the Upper Peninsula of Michigan.

Yet respectful of others' beliefs, as long as they did not try to get her to join them. So, her quandary was to find out just how expanded his belief of the more *unexplainable*, or as Cara said of herself 'a lapsed-Catholic.' With his background more technical, science-engineering, which usually less of a die-hard belief of the organized- religion and their dogmas.

Pointing to the CD, Julia commented. "I think the best words are the honesty of saying: 'You're asking me will my love grow, *I don't know, I don't know.'*" She smiled from ear to ear. "I believe we have to let all things unfold, . . . and trust it *will* work-out, as it is supposed to for the best. It's why I am also a believer in *synchronicity*, as there's no such thing as accidents, or coincidence, etc. I kind of felt, it all really fell into place with me *just happening* to volunteer, you standing in my line, and of course, me even being there. If my apartment had been ready on time, I would have been tied-up with moving in and all." He still sat at the stop sign looking at her, so she decided to spout it out to see his reaction. "I've been a longtime student of Metaphysics-over twenty years. A good thing so little traffic.

He turned the CD back down a little, and a sort of crooked- smile crossed Tomis' face, she didn't think she'd seen before. "Yes, 'Wow' you said. I did not expect you to say." He'd crossed the other small road, and glanced over to her, seeing her watching him. "What was word you said - syncor?"

Surprise an OK response to her espousal. "Oh, *synchronicity* - the unexpected coming together, or several things-people being brought together, unexpectedly. Have you heard it before, I mean in English?" She certainly didn't want him to think of her as too, *New Agey* or an airy-fairy - space-cadet. Which, of course, she did not consider herself to be.

"I do not think we have word in Croatian. I check dictionary later, so must be English, but I cannot remember how or why I hear it." Tomis reached in his coat pocket for his small notebook. "Please write down word." Now quiet, and Julia waited for him to respond further, or simply change the subject. "Yes, I think good description how we come together to meet . . . at time and place."

She waited feeling he had more to say. "Talia ask me go to Walmart-place again. We go there on Saturday, and I see no need. I saw in newspaper book sale, and classic English book difficult to find and expensive. I enjoy read when time." He paused again momentarily. "So, you study Metaphysics. I have read about it, . . . can you teach me? I think it is interesting."

Julia had to contain herself from jumping over and kissing him. Again, grinning from ear to ear, "I would be most happy to do so, though I am no expert, but there are many sources, if you have questions I can't answer, which I'm sure with your brilliant, technical mind there will be." She sat there beaming, so happy with all that had happened in the last few days, and kept saying *"Thank you"* to God for believing in herself.

He looked over at her again, and could also feel the warm energy coming from her. "I make you very happy to say 'teach me,' I am glad." Throughout the day, especially with the water viewing, the picnic and in the long stretches of driving, Julia would mention something more of Metaphysics. While he concentrated on the road, she could see him nod, and occasionally glance over to question, or ask her to repeat or explain something a little more. They were very good questions, which impressed her. She swung into her trainer- teacher mode, praising him, as he delighted her as a great student.

The Visitor Center excellent with animal displays, dioramas, and even a twelve-minute visually-stunning video. Tomis studied it all, for future use in Croatia's tourism, noting as nodding his approval. He commented at how impressive for the other people, who obviously enjoyed it, as much as they did. Both thoroughly educated on the surroundings, back to the car and onto the "Jewel" of the park.

As much as Julia had traveled, even though her love of nature always affected her directly, a site rarely took her breath away. Getting closer, she had an excitement building from what she'd already seen. The boardwalk slightly inclined, with a jog right, then left offering look-out points and seats to thoroughly enjoy the unlimited vistas.

Once they got to the first full escarpment view point of the Lake of the Clouds, they were both momentarily speechless. Then, when her breath returned, she simply said, "Oh . . . My . . . God! This is so incredible." Tomis likewise stunned, could only keep repeating 'how beautiful.' As many photos and descriptions, Julia had seen and read, they did not begin to depict the depth of its grandeur.

It truly had to be seen to be believed, as the park itself simply too overwhelming. They followed the jockeying-wooden walkway around and up to stop, as more and more of it all came into their view. Finally, they had reached the rock cliff, and Tomis started up, shifting the tote bag to his other shoulder. He then turned to take her hand, as they both climbed the last twenty-feet up the rocky mound, with the almost 360 horizon view.

The river from the lake could be seen going off into more forest, which continued rolling, as far as the eye could see. Julia said, "This Lake had to be from a glacier formation." She paused for more encapsulation of the view. "This is like a gigantic, super-plush, multi- colored carpet rolled out in front of us, with the cerulean-lake and its river being spilled-ink in the middle of it." How much he understood, she hadn't stopped to think, as she continued staring.

When they walked to the far end, Tomis asked if it *was* water at the horizon. Julia told him, yes,' the maps had said Lake Superior

1.6 miles from the Lake of the Clouds. Since they'd pulled over to look at the surprisingly sandy, but rather narrow beaches of the Lake before coming into the park, he could now see it from an altitude of its full-breath. They then picked a spot where several of the boulders gave them a place to put out their picnic, to eat and drink. As they ate their lunch, they just kept pointing and talking about how amazing their surroundings.

They walked back down by the winding-path through the virgin-woods, while Julia reminded him these trees had never been cut. They could see old fallen giants, which were almost disintegrated, and the smell very musky, with new trees stretching to reach for sunlight in the tightly-gathered forest. Back at the car, they drove to the falls, while impressive it could not compare to the breathtaking awe of the glacier Lake, or of course, Superior.

While Tomis had truly been mesmerized from the escarpment, at its majestic beauty and the endless trees, especially the utter magnificence of Lake Superior, which he could not totally comprehend. She had her print-out sheet of its most impressive facts, yet as he later stared out at it, now at ground level, he kept asking her if sure they were correct. They had walked silently along the shore for some time, until she had said they really must go on into the small town, as getting late for them to leave.

They were almost on schedule, as they headed out of Ontonagon, and back towards home. "OK, you take Highway 45 back down South to Bruce Crossing - this is the section we did not drive before. Then when you get there, you will again take Route 28 left, but this time we are going East to Covington, and finally South on Highway 141 South." She looked up from her map. "I think we're going to make it almost on time, which is truly a miracle considering we could have stayed so much longer in each place. I hope I didn't rush you too much, with it all." She really could have stayed days with him and never noticed the time spent.

"I see why you so successful in Japan, you explain things. . . easy, good for me to very understand. I like to stay long in some places, but I am glad we see all of best places. I take many photos today to show people . . . not believe my wonderful tour guide take me in one day. They also not believe I drive on left side of road." He laughed, very full and hearty. It would be a trip to remember, in more ways than just sight-seeing.

Julia laughed too, at his compliment of being a good tour guide. Ecstatic in being in her teacher-element once again, and feeling quite appreciated for her talents. "A good trainer knows it has to be a process, an unfolding in natural steps. It should be logical, and easily understood with lots of analogies or examples, and even practiced exercises the students can relate to in their life."

She glanced over at him, and he nodded again, as he turned to smile at her. "It's why they say you need to know your audience, so you can reach them. I always did my assessments to learn as much as I could, about whomever I taught. Or, if a difficult subject - like sexual harassment or discrimination - if going to be accepted or reacted to by them."

Tom is then quiet for a minute, formulating what he wanted to say, "I need more English words to ask question, and to say about business and many other things. May I ask why you left Japan, and why you not work now? You know so many things, and I think you are good for company business."

"Wow. I didn't see that one coming, . . . My Japan experiences many years ago - my past glory. I haven't been out of the country in several years, and it a vacation in the Bahamas." She chuckled.

He realized how uncomfortable she was. "I apologize for direct question. You do not need to answer it. I am sorry." He didn't know what he had said to upset her.

"No, no it's OK. You aren't the first, and probably won't be the last to ask why I'm here in this beautiful, but rather desolate place for business. And, especially when I do have so much education and experience, but I don't have a job. As Cara says, it's my 'damn principles and my big mouth." She looked over at him to see if she had lost him or not, and not really sure.

"Do you understand what I mean with both of those things? I have very strong beliefs - principles about right and wrong, and how things should be done, and how people are treated. I cannot accept discrimination of any kind, or bullying or *harassment* either … sexual or religious otherwise. I actually had special training for Domestic Violence - you may know, like within the family or extended family. I am also very honest and cannot cheat, especially on forms, though I get rather creative in my choice of words when I'm speaking, so as to not say certain things." She looked over at him again, and he glanced at her. He seemed to mostly be with her.

"So, first of all Japan. I loved the people, but hated the society, culture and government, all which controlled them, manipulated and lied to them constantly. *Stoicism*, a heavy word. Do you understand it?" He thought for a moment and shook his head no. "I will write it down for you. OK, this is probably more me than Webster's definition. It is basically to be without passion or emotion. Which could not be more opposite to me. It also refers to people who believe we must suffer to show our endurance or worth."

She took a deep breath to continue, "Wrongo! Again, I don't buy into the belief. So, when you've got a society built on sacrifice, it leaves it wide open for the government, and other groups to take advantage of them. This droves me nuts, as I'm a huge believer in choice, freedom, independence and not doing things just to please others. The biggest overall problem, it limits, or controls creativity, which is what change is made up of. *So being stoic, means you are not carefree and happy, or into change*, which is growth." She looked over at him, probably mulling much of it over. "Did I lose you? I really kind of rattled on."

"I want to read more to understand *stoicism*-word fully. Please write down all different way to say word." She took the notebook from the cupholder, and wrote the variations. She unknowingly hit a key.

"You really do blow my mind, at how you want to expand your mind. Engineers have a tendency to be stoic, you are not so much. I'm glad." He smiled at her sharing her thought, though not sure how true.

"To continue, why I left Japan. I felt I was losing my individuality, being *too* adaptive to get along with the Japanese. I'll tell you a comparative story of Australia, the exact opposite of Japan - but another time, I digress." She laughed, as if he knew the word.

"I also didn't like the easy money getting to be addictive. I didn't want to be like other foreigners who felt they were *entitled* to special treatment, because of the money or simply because of being *white*. It's a weird dichotomy, some unworthy-people develop when being in a very privileged minority. The stories I could tell you!" She laughed more to herself than to him. "Also, I knew of several people who had left after being there a long time, and they couldn't adjust to their homeland. I didn't want it to happen to me. I mean just be an ex- patriot in Japan - for life. I wanted choices and being an individual."

She glanced at him again, and he seemed to be intently listening. "So, my last two, full time corporate jobs fell into similar categories - upper management didn't like me doing my job *so diligently*. I chastised or criticized other supervisors or managers for violating the cardinal rules of Human Resources - discrimination and sexual harassment."

"So, if someone tells me how to do my training, I protest, or they try to get me to lie, I warn them. Then I resign when they don't believe me. But, I am proud of Japan and my other jobs. I did make positive changes for people, and I had a thousand employees. And, I know because they told me again and again. At least I made a difference in what I did do, and I'm proud of it." She watched him again, as still processing.

"Now, we have a really big recession, and lots of people out of work. It's easy to hire someone who will do the job the *management* way, which usually means them *Not* following the law on sexual harassment. They may not have all of my varied experience, and are usually much younger and cheaper. So, I'd rather work for less money, than compromise my principles. Thus, why I'm here, and happy to be free." It felt good to get it all off her chest, even if he may not have understood it all. "I know, very long and convoluted or confusing. But, I'm willing to answer questions to give you more clarification." She genuinely smiled, watching him. She then felt the energy in the car change, and not sure of his reaction.

It took a minute for him to form the words right in his mind, since he didn't want to frighten her, or give her the impression his country barbaric. "Discrimination and sexual harassment, you talk about . . . are big problem still in Croatia. Young people accept tourists are different, . . . they come from all over world and must be nice to them. But, some bad influence by older family members . . . they cannot forget or forgive loss in war."

He glanced over to her, and she could see the deep sadness in his eyes. "I sure your training knowledge in work, you call Human Resources - is good term - be helpful in Croatia." The subject still uncomfortable for him to talk about. He paused again, and even took a deep breath.

"Difficult to say correct to you. Many young women hear talk of rape, it happens so much in war . . . power and control. Most people do not understand . . . rape also destroy men, who care for women it happen to. . . . Then, many women want death after . . . and not want to live with rape-shame. You know, people talk about what happen."

This now getting way too personal, and painful, though Julia had never experienced it. She had been trained and certified, regarding rape and domestic violence victims, though thankfully, had not had to use it too much. But, she also knew Tomis needed to speak about it.

"I think subject, you say 'need to be addressed' so young people can understand. Good training for my employees to have . . . to handle many tourists - foreigners. It influences country." When he turned to look at her, hope growing in his eyes and across his face. She could almost see the many wheels of his brilliant brain, racing around with something churning through it.

The sign came up for Bruce Crossing, and a perfect way to change the subject. "Can we stop for coffee or ice cream? I think long drive now make me tired."

Julia a bit surprised, but had no hesitation. "Of course, we can stop. I always like to stretch my legs and chocolate ice cream always works for me. And, I can finish the drive back, I am actually familiar from Covington." He surprised her by taking her hand, as she exited the car, and they walked into the small restaurant together.

Another hug and cheek kisses, as Julia left Tomis at Talia's house, only about twenty minutes later than planned. Since she'd called Cara from Covington, and waiting when they had pulled up. They were both exhausted from the drive, and some of the heavy talk, which Julia felt Tomis cut off, when they stopped at Bruce Crossing. Again, her jaw and cheeks were almost sore from so much laughing and probably talking.

So, Monday had turned into Tuesday, of which they had both obviously passed the test of not just surviving each other, but looking forward to Wednesday's itinerary. And, even possibly a Thursday for them. She had never thought they'd have more than one day - he'd be busy or not want to be bothered with her. Now, like they had acceptable, adult play-dates. She began to wallow in every minute they had together, sharing their talk more personally, deeply and intimately, with the sight-seeing being a beautiful backdrop.

~ ~ ~ ~ ~ ~ ~ ~ ~

As she drove off, Cara let Julia settle in before she started her twenty- questions. "So, enlighten me, how was the long haul? I still can't believe you did the whole trip in one day - was it worth it? I saw you were the one driving home, did his driving scare you?"

Julia did not hesitate to elucidate on the abundance of beauty in what all they had seen, and how much they had both enjoyed it, wishing they had more time. She mentioned his driving being fine, him bringing some of Talia's CDs, and how fun sharing the music. They were almost home when she had wrapped up most of the details.

"Well, did you learn any more about his personal life, or has he turned out to be gay?" Cara laughing, as Julia chided her.

"I wouldn't mind it, if he was gay! You know I don't want to get married again. I just want a romantic adventure. Well, hysterically enough, Talia agrees with you! *But,* she can't understand why *I want to* spend time with him, as he is such a workaholic and possible monk, with no real interest in women. What can I say, we're an anomaly, we just enjoy spending time together." She paused waiting for a response from Cara, but only got a short laugh. "He is interested in learning more about Metaphysics, so I have a convert-over to my way of thinking. Interesting, how he talked about going fishing in the mountains with his father, before his mother died." She paused to look out the window.

"Of course, he's never seen so many trees in his life, and couldn't get over all the facts I read to him about Lake Superior. What you gave me, thanks." She concluded as Cara pulled into the garage, and went up the stairs to let the dogs out. Inside, Julia put the few leftovers away and emptied the wine into a glass for herself. She thought about it, and no need to bring up to Cara his topic of women being raped during the war, and it still being an aftermath there today. Not like it new-news, and even Julia not quite able to understand his concerns. She'd moved over to her bar stool on the other side of the counter, as Cara took her position on her side with her wine glass back in her hand.

"We're just going to have left-overs tonight, so I'll let you know what all we have. You can either eat as a salad, or heat up in the microwave. So, where to tomorrow before going to the Resort?" Apparently, Cara going to leave it all alone for now, figuring she'd ask some of her own questions at the dinner on Wednesday. "That's really funny what his sister thinks about him. A monk, huh? Glad to hear it."

"Going to ask you, besides the resort if something you can suggest for us to check out. Any particular things to see around town, his sister might not have taken him to?"

With their dinner of left-overs, their talk varied, and Cara mentioned some general gossip she'd learned from the Bar. She said she'd have to think of other places to visit, then updated Julia with other tidbits of people she also knew. Tomis called to say he'd be driving again, and ask what time Cara would drop her off. He shared how he had been telling Ericka and Talia about their wonderful day, and she had to promise Ericka they would go visit when her father returned.

He began his usual looking forward to seeing her tomorrow, and added he had some calls to make to both New York and Croatia, *so would see her tomorrow*. He then repeated himself again, in saying how much he was looking forward to it. After she hung-up, Julia knew he had been distracted, so something else going on in his mind. She curiously wondered what he would spring on her. Julia felt another new, but different vibe in him. She held onto the phone, as if looking for it to give her some hint, as to what decision he'd made.

LAKE SUPERIOR FACTS

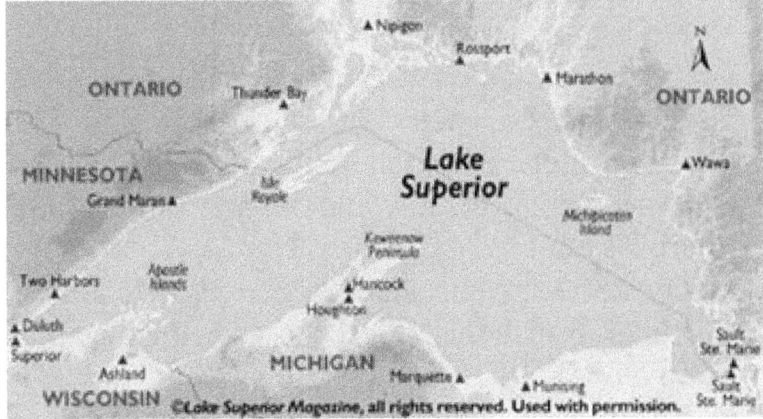

- Lake Superior contains ten percent of all the fresh water on our planet Earth.
- It covers 82,000 square kilometers or 31,700 square miles.
- The average depth is 147 meters or 483 feet.
- There have been about 350 shipwrecks recorded in Lake Superior.
- Lake Superior is, by surface area, the largest lake in the world.
- A Jesuit priest in 1668 named it Lac Tracy, but that name never officially adopted.
- It contains as much water as the other Great Lakes combined, plus 3 extra Lake Eries.
- There is a small outflow from the lake at St. Mary's River (Sault St. Marie) into Lake Huron, but it takes almost two centuries for the water to be completely replaced.
- There is enough water in Lake Superior to cover all of North and South America with water a foot deep.
- Lake Superior formed during the last glacial retreat, making it one of the Earth's youngest major features, at only about 10,000 years old.
- The deepest point in the lake is 405 meters or

1,333 feet.
- There are 78 different species of fish who call the big lake home.
- The maximum wave ever recorded on Lake Superior, 9.45 meters or 31 feet high.
- If you stretched the shoreline of Lake Superior out to a straight line, it would be long enough to reach from Duluth to the Bahamas.
- Over 300 streams and rivers empty into Lake Superior with the largest source being the Nipigon River.
- The average underwater visibility of Lake Superior is about 8 meters or 27 feet, making it the cleanest and clearest of the Great Lakes.
- Underwater visibility in some spots reaches 30 meters.
- In the summer, the sun sets more than 35 minutes later on the western shore of Lake Superior than at its southeastern edge.
- Some of the world's oldest rocks, formed about 2.7 billion years ago, can be found on the Ontario shore of Lake Superior.
- It very rarely freezes over completely, and usually just for a few hours. Complete freezing occurred in 1962, 1979, 2003 and 2009.

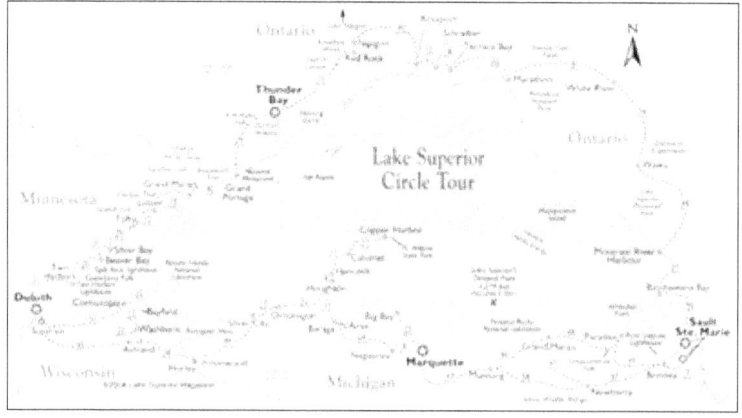

Chapter 6
Getting to Know You

Our hearts are the memory keepers,
recording the imprints of our life.
We may not want to discard
the past to move forward.

Though we are also burdened by
the painful details of our story.
We do have the power to heal,
release and let go of them.

As well, we can create new imprints,
and experiences through our new life.
Erasing those hurt memories is
sometimes easier said than done.

Setting our own lives in order,
should not put it off kilter so.
Though we may have been brought
into a deeper state of awareness.

Are we striving for self-mastery,
or ownership over our own lives?
We are meant to live in the moment.
Now is all we really are given.

Love is always the solution, and
Loving ourselves is always the cure.

This morning, though starting later, ending at dinner with their two 'guardians.' Tomis waiting by the car, again dressed in his khakis and a nice golf-style shirt, while Julia in her nicer linen-style cut-offs, with a slightly dressier top and a nicer necklace added. She'd not been to the resort before, so she did want to look nice for dinner. It should be quite *interesting* to have them all interact, if nothing else.

A little after nine when Cara had dropped her off, she drove off before any encounter with Tomis might happen. He walked over to hug Julia, and Cara again saw them in the rearview mirror, driving away. She could not help but still wonder what could it be all about.

They talked for a moment, before Julia put the tote bag with the food and drink goodies in the back seat. He held the door, as she took the map and tour magazine out of her bag, to climb into the passenger seat.

"So, shorter trips today and starting with Canyon Falls, which is where we'll have our picnic and onto the Horserace Rapids - what a great name? And, we finish at Brule Ski Resort - I made reservations for 5 pm, but I think we'll have extra time, if you see anything else you might want to do before. Otherwise, we can sit in the bar until Cara and Talia get there. I'm sure Cara will be early."

She turned to look at Tomis, as he pulled out of the driveway. Something kind of unsettled, or some agenda or decision to make, she could feel around him. Vibes came back to her from the phone call the night before. Not quite negative, just something with some very strong energy. She had shared very little personal information about Cara, when he had asked about Johnny. Perhaps, he felt her holding back, or being secretive, yet she'd not asked many personal questions about those around him either.

Or, maybe a little miffed Cara did not say anything to him, though she'd waved from inside the car. Julia had told Tomis Cara a private person, not into personal touching, and usually didn't open up to people, until she knew them rather well. She decided to see if she could figure out what was going on inside him. "You know you don't need to pay for everything, in fact Cara may insist on paying for drinks before, or after dinner."

"Which way Navigator?" He looked directly at her, and gave his often-beguiling smile. She wondered if he knew she'd read his energy, and trying to figure him out.

"Same way out, and we go straight until we come to Highway 141, then turn going back toward Covington." She'd wait for him to respond, as he always did.

As he slipped onto the main drag, he took a breath. "I think we have good idea of dinner together, and my appreciation for your time, and Cara and Talia cars. I plan to pay for dinner, . . . but if Cara must insist to pay for drinks, it is OK. I do not like to argue." He turned and smiled at her again. "I am sure Talia does not care, but I think she like to get to know you more. I will not worry, as you say, about Cara and how she feel about me. OK?" Though Julia nodded, she did continue to look at him, she felt more he wanted to say.

"After I finish calls to Croatia last night, I read on computer about Metaphysics and want to ask more question, OK?"

Julia smiled, slightly relieved. "Sure, fire away. I'll see if I can explain enough for you."

He nodded and kept looking forward, "Talk to me about Karma. I know we have same thing in Croatia, but I want to hear you tell me in English. Is it like Bible say, 'Eye for eye or what you sow, you reap?'" He glanced toward her, and back to the road.

"Wow! OK, start with a big one and yes, . . . and no, not quite the same as in the Bible." She went on in detail for several minutes, then realized at a stop sign and needed some directions.

"Oh, you turn East - left here and take 41, up to just before the little town of Alberta. I'm sure there will be a sign which says Canyon Falls. It's supposed to be a really, cool canyon with a nice boardwalk up to the falls." She continued to talk some more about Karma, until they saw the sign, and pulled into the roadside park area. "We can come back for our food and get a table under one of the trees over there."

The map showed just one trail, a quarter of a mile to the Sturgeon River, and a full mile to the end. The boardwalk in parts over creeks and low patches above the ground foliage, while granite slate worked as steps in the gravel. Once they saw the first of the river water rushing, there were huge outcroppings of rock with a path to go down to look out over the water. Tomis took her hand, in a perfunctory way, then released it as they stood looking at the water. "Wow, it's so crystal clear and clean," Julia said.

"Yet, like a watered-down coffee- color from all of the iron in it. It looks so cool."

She glanced over to him, but he seemed lost in his gaze, as if never having seen something like it before. As the river turned, every twenty feet or so, another outcropping for them to walk out on. By the third one, Tomis had become much more attentive to watching her walk down, and holding her hand longer. A small thing, but Julia noticed it without comment to him.

All much longer than Julia had expected, and more numerous pines framed it, as the various trees decorated in between in their blazing colors. Tomis took more photos at each stop, and said he did not get tired of looking at the water, or the trees. "I know now why Talia happy for me to see trees. They are … *unique* … in beauty." She agreed with him, and so happy he not only enjoyed it all, but comfortable saying how much he liked it. By the last few turns of the river, the higher canyon walls had narrowed the flow, so really rushing water, as it descended further into the rock barriers, with a sharp curve finally taking it out of site.

With the 'End of Trail' marker, and an opening in the wooden- rock protective fence, they carefully walked down to the final granite- outcropping. Tomis had taken both of her hands to steady her, and had put his arm around her shoulders and slightly squeezed her to him. She took it, as if to say, *how glad to be sharing it all with her*. They quietly stood watching the water from both directions, with the giant rock wall hiding them from seeing very much around the bend. Julia thought, how interesting, *all quite telling of life, etc.*

On the way back, as they had before, they each picked a few choice leaves. Sitting down on one of the look-out benches, Julia shared, "I've been collecting them in a air-tight, plastic bag. I know they'll eventually turn brown, but for now they're holding their color - reminding me of these wonderful trips." As he had done before, he nodded, smiled, looked deep into her eyes, and kissed her - this time on the chin. Different she thought, *and wondered why, then why not.* He had been exuding more and more positive energy, and also it seemed emotional feelings toward her. Now, quite curious, as to where this would all lead.

At the picnic table, they had finished their little lunch, and the general talk about the view. She then read him more about the park and the area, wrapping it all up like a good tour guide would. Tomis reached across the table, and stunned Julia a little when he took both of her hands. "I want to talk for minute about thought last night - your work in Japan, Hawaii . . . and California. I do not know what job ... or work plan Cara have for you here in Up-per Peninsula, but I want you to think about work overseas again . . . In Croatia, training for my company . . . and others."

He watched her face intently, and saw how her eyes widened, then her head moved back a bit. "Do not make decision now, but please make before I leave Friday. You can ... if you want, come for visit - vacation - I pay for you . . . everything, of course." He looked closely at her face, almost blank in such shock. Not often Julia at a loss for words, and he appreciated it.

"Tomis, I told you before, my experience and knowledge is from years past, some . . . out of date . . . I mean…" As shocked and excited as she could be, she did not want him to misconstrue what she knew, from how much she'd talked about it all.

Tomis took a breath. "You know more ... we can ever learn - especially your travel experience about tourist business . . . handle people and what you call 'knowing first class customer service.' This is all very important to business growth."

He studied her for a moment. "I know ... you do not know me

… well, and job can be separate from friendship we have. I not say a lot of things to try to convince you, … but I want you to think ... we talk more tomorrow." He'd taken another breath. "Thursday   I do not know how . . . complicated, or how soon I can get my investor or Tourist Board approval. I have some investor … not like until they meet you. I talk last night about you … and there is interest. This is from me, … and may be another reason why we meet. Can you just think about?   Please do not mention to Talia or Cara tonight. I need to find out how to move forward … before you give me a decision, or we tell them." The smile, which had once been rare, now again spread across his face.

Tomis raised up her hands, as he leaned forward to kiss them long and softly. He squeezed them gently, before releasing them. He then rose from the picnic table, as if his words had not been as life- changing to him, as they were to her. He stood at the end of the picnic table, and calmly-reached his hand out to her. The still-stunned Julia, glanced back at him, like she had no clue why his hand there. "Is Horse ... Race Falls next on list?" He asked, smiling like he enjoyed the fact *he had now thrown her off track.*

Julia looked at the map, but could not get her eyes to focus. To say all of it came totally out of left field, and once again a whole new ball game, to put it mildly. He had just crossed-over to intertwined her emotions with her career. It didn't get much more personal for her. She stood up, swinging her leg from under the picnic table, took his hand working on controlling the zillion questions she wanted to ask.

"I have to look at which direction we go, once we get out of here." She glanced at the map, as they walked back to the car. "Well, it looks like we retrace back where we came from, down Highway 2 and 141, and continue South, then East until we see the Horserace Rapids Road sign for the Falls."

Julia looked back up at him, trying to keep her composure, as her mind raced, and smiled. "So, some of this is going to become well- worn and traveled to us - the usual coming and going to get somewhere else." He stopped, as if processing what she'd said, and laughed heartily again. When she also processed it, she saw the irony and joined him. "Yah, I guess it's called *life.*"

When Tomis shelved something for discussion, until after facts were gathered, he meant it. Julia tried a couple of different ways to bring-up, what she had considered a tentative job-offer. And, each time he politely put her off, until after he made more phone calls, in the evening back to Croatia. He made a point to ask her to put another CD in the player, and after he reached to turn the sound slightly up. He'd make his point another way, so she'd stop with questions.

Finally, so she'd appear to be handling it, she asked. "Oh, I did mean to ask, if everything is going along as timed for the ferries?" Since she'd asked before, he turned down the CD a little and gave her the latest positive update. But he also made a point, when she didn't request any more details, to turn the CD up again. Clever, engineer.

The rest of the trip to, and viewing of the rapids, more of a distraction. They were a different, but not dramatic spot. While they did talk, they were both somewhat holding back. To break some of the spell, Julia suggested they take the county roads over to Brule, as they may be more interesting. The signs were all clearly marked, as the only real resort in the area. He took her hand as he helped her out of the car, and guided her in the direction of the ski-lift.

Tomis must have felt the slight riff, so decided to break into another subject, to distract Julia from trying to figure more ways to talk about the possible job. "Oh, I want ask you to explain about past lives, or I think word is re-incarnate? . . . It is very interesting to me." He smiled again, as he looked at her, not really hiding his reasoning behind it, though the subject had intrigued him.

He had certainly taken her aback again, but in a good way this time. And, while she could easily see through his ploy, more than willing to play along, since it one of her most favorite topics.

"Well, you know how to ask the right questions for a good continuous discussion. And, the word is *reincarnation*, though most people talk about it more in the plural of 'past lives,' . . . unless they are referring to a certain past life, which they may have become familiar with through *regression,* flashbacks or dreams. Let me start by explaining 'regression' . . . "

As they rode the ski-lift, the trees looked again like a multi- colored carpet, unfurled below them in the valley for the magnificent view. The outcroppings, of the giant granite rock, starkly reminded them of where they were, as the Brule River came into view in the distance. They were both almost silent, just absorbing the bird's eye- vista floating above the glorious trees. Once an occasional tall pine, looked lonely among its brightly leaf-colored companions, getting their day to show their palette.

"I'm sure you've skied more impressive mountains, but this is appreciated for the area, and lots of family fun."

"Not at all," Tomis smiled as he looked at her. "This is like some I ski - but more trees." Interesting, when they switched lifts to ride back up, the ascending view felt like the trees were covering over them. Since Julia had rarely ridden a ski lift, a surreal-feeling of being carried off, feet hanging above ground, so far below. For several moments, she drifted away, and when she came back to look over at him, he'd been watching her with a smile on his face. More telling of his feelings than she realized, but gave her a warm closeness to him.

Back on the ground, they both looked back. "So much more than I expected. Really wonderful." Tomis nodded and beamed at her. Not sure why he acted so happy, but glad it had certainly brought them back to each other. Then off and running with her spiel again on reincarnation, even as they walked around the property.

"Now, where was I . . ." She'd also segue between reading him info on the resort, or commenting on the scenery, or where they should head next from the resort map. It became a joke between them, eliminating any separation she felt, from him not revealing *all* to her about the potential job. She could be rather obsessive, wanting to know things concerning her, which not unusual for *some* people.

"OK, 'The Homestead Lodge is actually a restored 1880's homestead,' and it says it is 'accessible via Homestead Trail and North Forty Trail.' So, we may want to drive over there, as it looks like quite a walk back and forth, as it is not where we're going to eat." They drove over and checked out the authentic pot belly stove, looked around at the antique photographs and farm implements, once used to work the land the lodge sat on.

"Oh, look, it's an authentic Homestead Act for the lodge, signed by President McKinley, on the wall. Do you understand, 'homestead,' it meant free land, if you lived and worked it?" From his blank response, she went on to explain the great value of it all in developing the land, and bringing many people there.

They decided to have a snack and some of the famous hot chocolate out on the deck for the view, before driving back to the Hillside Dining at the Brule Lodge. Julia decided to tell Tomis about her past life experience at the pyramids outside Mexico City, to keep herself from thinking about the job. It worked well for her, and fascinated him. Since they'd planned to wait for Cara and Talia at the Saloon, though still early upon their arrival, they relaxed at the bar. Julia then ordered a glass of Pinot Noir.

Tomis asked what kind of wine it was. "A soft, red wine, similar to Cabernet, but nicer I think." He then ordered it also, and they toasted each other, only regarding their sight-seeing ventures. She finished talking about her Metaphysics for the time being, and asked about resorts in the mountains of Croatia.

She loved to hear about it all, and knew he loved to talk about it. They had both learned, how to easily change a subject into what they each liked to talk about. An understanding many couples, or even friends never learned, no matter how long together.

Though it had not been as exhilarating as the day before, it had held some interesting twists and turns, especially in their relationship. While Tomis in the restroom, Julia thought about some of the signals, and questions or comments he'd made, when she'd referred to different things she'd done with prior jobs. He had seemed a little more intense today she thought, but maybe because of Cara, or the job offer or, as she recalled also his attentiveness, maybe because he'd be leaving soon. They only had one more day together . . .

Julia felt his hand on her far shoulder, and she turned to look at him, smiling as usual. Then he kissed her on the cheek, and his hand slid across her back, down to her elbow where it lightly remained. "This is another great day of sight-seeing and leaf-viewing." He chuckled a little, knowing it had been so much more. "I thinking these days - memories help me ... to easy do my work in New Jersey, . . . but I know I miss you and all the beautiful trees."

He kissed her cheek again, as he sat on the corner of the barstool, then held both her hands in his. It could not have been a more perfect moment, as they both looked at each other smiling, until Julia saw Cara coming into the Saloon. When she pulled back, he followed her gaze to also see her.

Unconsciously, he looked at his watch, seeing it just past four- thirty. But he rose, and went to greet her with a hug. Julia caught herself from giggling. Though Cara had not rebuffed the cheek kisses, she had been a bit stiff, which not out of character for her. Tomis pulled out his stool for her, picked up his glass and moved to the other side of Julia. He spoke, "We talk about beautiful resort, and I tell Julia about resort in Croatian mountain." He noticed she did not do any kind of friendly greeting to Julia, so maybe cool trul her style.

Directly to Julia, Cara said, "I see you started without me." And, before Tomis could offer her a drink, she ordered a high-end brand gin gimlet, specifically adding to put in extra Rose's Lime. Julia took a small breath, knowing the alcohol would add ammunition to her stockpile of clever-quips, and comments she'd probably planned to use. Though she also probably knew, few would Tomis understand.

Tomis again on the corner of his barstool, with his leg on Julia's stool, as she could slightly feel his knee against it. He also had put his hand on the back of her chair, as if to stay connected to her. Knowing he had no knowledge of how Cara could be, yet Julia wanted to support him in some way. Without much thought, she leaned forward slightly to put her hand back, and lightly touched the inside of his knee. Since she'd never touched other than his hand or arm before, except when hugging, he almost flinched at the personal connection. If either of them had been looking at him, they'd have seen his eyes blink, and widen in response.

Julia had wanted to position herself physically between them, yet not blocking their view of each other. It turned out to be an uncomfortable position, so she turned on her stool, removing her hand and leaned lightly on the bar. This way, she could look easily at them both. She smiled easily at Tomis, and nodded to make sure he was OK.

He smiled back more comfortable, having her hand gone from his knee. She had no idea, how her touch had sent such a quick physically-surprising, sexual-sensual reaction through his body. After the moment realized, for him it began to fully change their relationship from 'just friends' to more.

During the whole shifting around scenario, Cara had been watching her drink being made, and tasting it to make sure of no mistake. She looked up at the bartender and said, "Perfect, you can come work for me any time," as she rattled off her bar name to him, then turned towards them. "So, what tom-foolery have you two been up to today? Still playing tourist - tour-guide?" She took a sip, enjoying her inquisitor-position.

Julia giggled, having felt the tingle when she touched Tomis' knee. She thought how one of the best things of the day had just happened under Cara's own eyes, and she had - thank God - missed it. "Oh, just as I told you this morning going over. An easier day than yesterday, with all of the driving, but still nice and colorful. The Canyon Falls were more impressive than I expected. And, the resort is really nice, I told Tomis you and Johnny stayed here several summers before you moved up here."

Cara then looked directly at Tomis, "So, you haven't gotten tired of her sandwiches and *what-evers* in her picnic bag? She always brings wine back, so I guess she doesn't get you drunk or anything?"

It took him a moment to understand all she'd said, as Cara expected it would, and she took another swallow of her drink. Julia had decided not to intervene and rescue him, as it would only cause Cara to make more remarks.

"I like her sandwiches . . . and a little wine is good. She is very good to tell directions . . . and all *informations* on many things. I learn much from her." Julia smiled at him, and tilted her head back to Cara, as if to say - 'the ball is again in your court,' he volleyed just fine. She then felt his hidden hand come up her lower back lightly, connecting them again, knowing they were in this together.

Without quite saying touché, Cara released some of her angst, and decided to see if his version of what he did was the same, as what Julia had been reporting the past few days. "Well Julia has told me some of what you are doing in New Jersey, but maybe you can give me a few more details or background on your refurbished-ferries." Julia beamed, as Cara had no idea how intelligently this man could talk about what he loved, and obviously did very well. Interestingly, Julia also caught how many words and phrases Tomis had picked up in their few days together.

Tomis had just taken a sip of wine, and smiled at Julia first. "Wine is very nice Julia; I forget to tell you." He then looked directly at Cara, "I hope Julia not mind hearing all again. Do you know Staten Island Ferry in New York?"

"I've never been there or ridden it, but I did ride the ferry in San Francisco with Julia." A part of her beginning to regret having asked him to explain.

Tomis nodded, "Well, when they retire, they go to company in New Jersey and depend on condition, they are rebuilt or refurbished or sold to other country for scrap. We - my company and my investors - decide more three years ago we want to expand more ferries to Italy and down Croatia coast to Dubrovnic, our old history city. We have many islands and many tourists come last few years, and they are very good for my business . . . " He went on for over five minutes talking with very few mistakes and more details than Cara had ever expected, though she had nodded with a few agreements.

Still talking when Julia noticed Talia coming in the door, and nodded to Tomis of her arrival. He excused himself to Cara, got up immediately and walked over to give her a hug and the usual cheek- kisses. Cara had caught Julia's eye, and rolled her own regarding his talk. Julia merely responded by mouthing out to her, *"You asked."*

She then got up to greet Talia in the same fashion Tomis had, with Talia rather delighted by it. They brought her over to Cara, she did not rise, but extended her hand, knowing Talia had lived in the States for almost twenty years.

While Tomis ordered her a drink, Cara said, "I understand you're a registered nurse, so is my daughter-in-law - actually she's a surgical nurse, so works with all of those surgeons, and blood, etc." Tomis handed Talia her drink and this time, Julia who offered her barstool and moved her drink down, as Tomis moved his.

They'd all just settled in, when the restaurant manager came over checking to make sure he had the right party. He welcomed them to Hillside Dining at the Brule Lodge, and indicated their table ready. Tomis asked who needed another drink, and only Cara said to the bartender, "I do in about five minutes, and please make it exactly the same way, it was great."

Julia happy Cara had made no move to pay for hers, or anyone else's drink. This told her, perhaps she'd not play any more games.

The ladies followed the manager into the dining room, while Tomis paid the check, and the bartender said he'd bring the drink over in a few minutes. Since only one other couple in the bar, it shouldn't be a problem. Tomis thanked him, and tipped him ten dollars - his time in New York had taught him well.

Amazingly, the talk rolled along, as Cara liked Talia, and since Tomis only spoke English to her, she asked "Do you still speak Croatian?" Tomis reminded Talia, Cara the one Julia had mentioned, whose parents were both of Croatian decent, and her mother had lived in Upper Peninsula. A wise move on his part to show he had remembered, and liked the association.

"No, not really, just a few basic words and phrases. I can understand more than I can speak, which I understand from Julia, is usually the way it is. I left in late '92, just before I turned seventeen. And, we lived in Italy for almost a year with some of Momma's relatives. I don't know if you are aware, but Istria, the far North- Western area of Croatia - closest to Italy - is mostly Italian people. It's where Momma and Poppa had met, and Italian is commonly spoken."

Talia took a deep breath to continue, "We were both passing as Italians, as I was illegal, so she didn't want me to speak Croatian out in public. Momma never fluent, love brought them together, not the language. We could both speak some English, and she wanted me to learn it for coming here. I actually came over on an Italian cousin's passport, Momma still had hers." She took a sip of her drink, and continued.

"Before we left, Momma actually went back to Istria a few times to spend time with Poppa, but he insisted we stay in Italy. Poppa very afraid for both of us, especially after Celia and Milos died. I know all the family sacrificed a lot, and did so much to protect me."

She looked at Tomis, who had become somber and pulled back somewhat from the table. "We finally found some Croatian and Italian relatives in Chicago, who were willing to sponsor us. So, we got here in late 1993. I remember Julia, you and Cara were born and raised in Chicago. I was able to finish my school there. My older brother, Ivo came to visit in 2000, and very upset I spoke so little Croatian then, . . . and he still doesn't speak much English, so we don't talk very much."

"I send him to English school for the tourists, so English is better," Tomis added.

"You have always protected and taken care of Ivo, Tomis. But he is lazy, not stupid, and he will never be half the man you are, because he has no ambition. Momma spoiled him so. He dropped out of university before even the first semester ended, and has bad habits of drinking and gambling, and you rescue him from having to pay." She'd been looking back and forth between Cara and Tomis, knowing he was not happy with what she was saying.

"He is good worker for me, and I do not want you to talk bad about him, please."

Talia shook her head, indicating Tomis a bit hopeless in how he felt about Ivo, so she dropped it. Still, quite a telling-thing about Tomis, and his relationship to his younger sister and brother. "I met Edward when I was in nursing school - he's Polish and Hungarian with relatives up here. Momma had died right after I graduated, and when Tomis came to Chicago."

She smiled now, "Then we got married, and we moved up here just after Ericka was born, so it's been a little over five years here. I was really thrilled when Tomis said he was coming, because it had been a long time since I'd seen him. I really wanted him to see how beautiful Ericka is." She took a sip of her drink, and looked directly at Julia and Tomis.

"Julia you have made Tomis very happy this week, he has always been such a workaholic with the ferries, and after Poppa passed, he started planning for the trains. And now, the tourists take up so much of his time." Talia leaned in to Julia, "Really, with me having to work, it meant so much to me to see Tomis so happy and talking so much, about all the places you took him."

She then took Tomis' hand and brought it to her lips to kiss. "I don't want to bring any kind of downer to this happy dinner," she looked directly at Tomis. "But I don't think I've ever really thanked you - *hvala mnogo*" she said in Croatian, "for all you did for me and Momma, especially since you lost so much in the war. Edward will be coming back this weekend from working out of town for so long, and I'm very, very happy. I doubt I would have all this in my life, if it had not been for you and Poppa protecting me, by making us leave. I love you for the real sacrifice, I just wished Poppa had lived long enough after the war, for us to see him again. Thank you for my life." Talia crying now, and Tomis had tears in his eyes, as he then took her hand to kiss it.

"I didn't mean to go on so, … about all of our ancient history, or upset Tomis. I'm sorry for getting so weepy, . . . please, I really am very, very happy." Her smile crossed her face, as the tears slipped down her cheeks. She used her napkin to dab them away.

Julia and Cara both did an embarrassed chuckle. "Hey, . . . we understand, and we are happy for you being so happy now," Julia rattled and Cara chimed in a 'yeah.' The timing perfect, as the bartender had brought Cara's other gimlet, and she took a quick sip.

Julia rubbing Tomis' back without even realizing it. "And, I'm glad I made you happy this week, and you certainly have made me happy, also." He then leaned over and kissed her on the cheek. "Thank you, Sweetie." The first time she'd used such a term of endearment, so directly to him. "So, now," she turned to Cara, "all we have to do is make Cara happy, like the rest of us!"

Cara picked up her drink and took another big sip, "I'm happy now, and I'll be even more happy when we order." She caught the waiter's eye and asked for the menus. Never one to wallow in emotional things in public, she looked at Julia and rolled her eyes again. The energy changed back to positive, as they all laughed and received the menus to peruse the goodies.

With no more dissertations on rebuilding ferries, or escaping from being raped, the meal went swimmingly-well, with everyone talking and enjoying their food. Cara asked Tomis about some Croatian food she was familiar with, and if Talia planned on visiting it again, since it now had become such a tourist mecca.

"I think I'd like to take Ericka to both Italy and Croatia, when she is about ten or so, and can understand the wonderful *good* histories of the countries. I'm sure Tomis will welcome us, and give us a ride on his new ferryboats. It all sounds like so much fun I never knew of, and certainly don't remember doing such things. Well, I'm stuffed, but I'd be willing to share a dessert with someone."

Julia smiled at Tomis, "Well, Tomis and Cara both know I'm a chocoholic, and this week I've usually gotten Tomis to share something with me. Maybe you can twist Cara's arm or have just a bit of ours - whatever. I'm sure they must have something on the menu with chocolate."

The plates were being cleared, as they looked over the dessert menu. Cara then surprised them by saying, "There looks like a few things which could entice me, but I'd also be happy with an after-dinner drink. What do you like Talia?"

~ ~ ~ ~ ~ ~ ~ ~ ~

Cara sipped on her after dinner drink, having only shared a few bites of Talia's dessert. "So, Tomis, you've talked about the ferryboats and tourism, what problems does Croatia still have? I know the War Crimes trials are still going on." Julia sighed, saying Cara's name, and gave her a look, like trying to cause problems again. Cara responded back with a head tilt, and what she called her 'inquiring-mind' in pursuit-look.

Caught a little off-guard, but Tomis had prepared, from Julia's warnings of Cara's 'conspiracy-theories,' disbeliefs of government and politics. "No, Julia, not a problem, as you say. Croatia is *developing* country, almost two thousand years old, and still have problems." He took a sip of his wine, gathering his words. "We apply to EU - European Union - and hope accept next year. We must have our fiscal

... and internal structural reforms completed. This mean ... any political corruption, or organized crime must be gone."

Julia tried to cover the surprised look on her face, as Cara echoed his words of corruption and organized crime. "It may not make

... your news last year, national newspaper editor ... killed by organized crime car bomb. It ... not the War Crime they report. We find them, trial ... and punish to prison this year. Now, they are . . . " He tried to find the word. "Get into?" He looked at Julia.

She quickly said, "interfering with?"

"Yes, sorry my English is sometime loss. They *interfering* with unions, ... and make me problems. I have several phone calls from Croatia and much concern - my ferries and trains are union, ... of course. They know I am strong for union, ... and have many tourists, so I am '*big target*,' I think what you say. I have good support ... and we succeed on this, I sure. I need to call many people tonight again. I know we win; I fight them. Before they do only gambling, drugs ... illegal things for money. Now, ... do more violence to keep Croatia to not be member of EU, so they can keep to do these things. ... Julia calls these people 'bullies' and true, ... but more. Most are unemployed or ex-military from war, *not Croatian* ... and do not want to work regular job. They want easy-money or hurt people." He took another sip of wine, as it felt good to release it.

Suddenly Julia very frightened for him, yet couldn't believe these mobsters would actually harm Tomis or his business. "I'm sure you and your investors will get it all taken care of soon." She reached over for his watch hand. "Well, it's after seven, so maybe we should call it an evening. I know you have called this evening." She squeezed the top of his hand lightly. "Thank you so much Sweetie, for this wonderful dinner, *and* the opportunity to get to know each other so much better."

Julia pulled her hand back and looked directly at Talia. "It's been a joy to get to know you, and please give my best to Ericka. I hope to see her again, and even spend some time with her." Talia and Cara started talking and thanking Tomis, as he kept nodding and repeating 'of course' and 'no problem' and 'you are welcome.' He had waved to the waiter, and gave him his credit card for the bill.

In the parking lot, Cara talked more with Talia by her car, as Julia talked with Tomis by Talia's car. Tomis holded her hand close to his side. "Yes, I have many calls tonight, so not sure if I can call you . . ."

"That's OK," Julia interrupted. "I'll pick you up a little after nine, as I come from dropping Cara off at the shelter for her volunteering there. We can visit the places I mentioned or not, so we can decide and talk then. I have to pick her up at 3 pm, so it will be a little shorter day - our last one though it is"

Tomis swung his arms around her, and kissed her on the lips, with a surge of passion for a few moments. He then held her back from him, as if he needed to limit his involvement. He momentarily looked at her, then kissed her cheeks as usual. His look surveyed her, and how the day-evening had gone. He drew a conclusion of satisfaction, in all which had transpired for them, in their shared talk. He had not expected Talia to reveal so much but, of course, good she had. Those were things he'd never have mentioned.

"Yes, I look forward to it. We have many things to talk about," he said almost calmly. Silent Julia still stunned from the kiss, as he took her arm and began to walk her over to Cara's car. She almost stumbled, in such a daze from her emotional stirrings. He opened the passenger door, almost perfunctorily, and called to Talia.

"I am sorry to interrupt, but I am late to make business calls." He looked back at Julia getting into the car and smiled, "I see you tomorrow," and closed her door carefully.

He walked over to give Cara another small hug with the cheeks kissed, and at least this time she laughed. Julia watched as he escorted Talia over to the driver's side, to help her in. He waved again at Julia, and got into the passenger side of Talia's car.

Cara talked, as buckling up, while Julia stared after them pulling out and driving off. *What just happened, she kept asking herself?* A very broad smile came across her face, and she whispered to herself, *"I think I'm falling in love and so is he!"*

For many women, it is always about *the 'kiss,'* and the importance of the *first big one*. The kiss speaks of romance, passion and intimacy,. Whereas, a man can have sex with any woman, and not even look into her face or eyes. And, very simply, if the *kiss doesn't* take your breath away the first time, it may never really do so. While she'd thought she wanted the kiss, she didn't expect it - which is sometimes the best kind. For a man who hadn't been involved with a woman for a long time, he certainly knew how to kiss. The whole process of him pulling her to him, replayed before her eyes, in her mind on a continuous-loop.

"I said, 'Are you going to buckle up?' I'm the one, as usual who drank more than anyone. What's wrong with you, … you're mumbling?" Cara backed the Jeep around to pull out. "I didn't even realize, who brought Talia over here, her babysitter?" She concentrated on the road blanketed in twilight, with all her alcohol. Obviously, she'd *not* seen the kiss Tomis gave Julia

Julia turned to look at Cara, still smiling and thinking of his 'kiss.' She automatically began to buckle up, as she answered. "Yes, her babysitter drove her over, since she'd picked-up Ericka at school, before she went to the hospital to pick Talia up.

She really is nice, and I certainly didn't expect her emotional out-pouring. Tomis said, she had been expecting to hear from her husband, about his return, so maybe what stirred it up." Julia took a deep breath, happy also it all finally over, and didn't go too badly. "Well, you seemed to have a pretty good time, and I'm glad you got along so well with them."

"Yeah, I did have a better time than I expected, and his English is pretty good, though I had to listen a little more closely sometimes. I guess you're used to beaten-up English, after all your years in Japan and traveling. I must admit, it took me a while to get used to the accent and speech pattern up here, after only being in Chicago."

Quiet for a moment, Cara checked traffic at the stop sign. "I don't like the idea of them having organized crime, and their using car bombs. I guess I'm just used to it being so quiet and peaceful up here, away from all of it. But, I know other places like LA, and now the drug lords in Phoenix are really dangerous. I'm glad we're not there, aren't you?"

"Yeah, I guess so." Julia really didn't want to think about the violence Tomis might be facing upon his return. She also didn't want to admit, how much she had become enamored by Croatia, from what he'd told her, and she'd read about it. Then, she remembered their secret of him asking her to work for him. What would she say, now knowing the job may entail some dangerous people or conditions?

Talia also telling Tomis what a good time she had, and how much she really liked Julia, though Cara *just* interesting, her nicest description. "In many ways, you and Julia are so much alike, with similar experiences. I'm sure you are going to miss her, aren't you?"

Tomis stared out the darkening window with the sun now gone. "Yes, I think I am." He had no idea what kind of woman he'd be getting himself involved with. He vaguely remembered, her describing herself as *layered and complicated*. In the past few days, he'd seen it very true, likemultiple people, depending on need or circumstance.

Perhaps a good thing, he thought, as adaptable. Still, a good match in she'd been a workaholic, which he respected, though admitted she had *worked* to let it go the last few years. He'd definitely seen tonight, much more to her than her fountain of information, or fascination with nature and history.

Tomis seriously wondered how he'd not noticed before, how sexy ... or another word, *sensual* maybe, he'd have to check out its meaning. But a basic key in their match, he appreciated her brain and experience, *without knowledge* of her sexiness.

For most men, Julia perhaps too much *woman,* with her out- spoken independence, intelligence *and* sexual presence. The more he thought of all her layers, he began to question, if she would be too much woman *for him, too?*

Chapter 7
Approval

I'm thrilled to press an ear against my love's chest.
I listen to our heart's song, know we sing in harmony.
An infusion of light, fills hope into our moments.
A glimpse of kismet-dreams are born to come true.

No need to speak of time, for love is timeless,
as everyone knows who's felt its powerful flow.
To speak of one's love experience is different,
as everyone's love, is uniquely experienced.

Few hearts have no scars to talk of, or reveal.
More than once, most have played the fool.
Love's fire burns both ways, of glory and pain.
A game that can burn, and consumes you fully.

Call it desire, or lust. It beckons us into dust.
More than being weak, it's being unable to resist.
More have forsaken all, for a chance love exists.
Easier still, walking on hot coals, or a high-wire fall.

In healing, the soul yearns to be a moth again.
New fires lit, hopes - dreams created of hearts -
perhaps beating as one to our song's sung.
It's life, living and giving of love again.

Julia proud of herself, she'd kept their secret about the job offer, though with all the alcohol, Cara probably would not have remembered. She certainly hoped Tomis would have the details, and approval from his investors for her to work for them. And, their personal relationship certainly moving forward, it could be a bonus to it all, as far as her concern.

Then, her human resources-hat popped in, and loudly said, *"Nepotism!"* Oops, she didn't want to come off as, *'don't do as I do, do as I say.'* But, since there hadn't been any sex before the job offer

… Perhaps splitting hairs, then laughed at herself. *"And, they happen to be pubic hairs!"*

Tomis sat on the steps talking on his business phone, as Julia drove-up a few minutes after nine, Thursday morning. She jumped out of the car to rush over to him, but when he'd not gotten-up, she realized he'd be speaking in Croatian. She stepped back, as if to not intrude, and leaned against the car to wait for him to finish. He kept looking at her, then raising his eyebrows and his hand, to indicate trying to end the conversation. It seemed not easy, so the person must be very important.

"I am very sorry to keep you waiting, he is my big investor." He rose to come down to meet her, as she walked over, and he gave her the usual hug with cheek kisses. The shining sun, told of another beautiful day. Tomis motioned for her to sit on the steps.

"No, not at all, I thought you were waiting for me, until I saw you were on the phone." They both sat back down.

"I came out to see weather and phone rang inside, so I came out again to talk in sunshine and wait for you." He hesitated, then said.

"We talk about you and other business things. Do you want to talk about job - do you decide answer?" He could really be direct, and Julia felt, *not just* his sometimes, limited-English language-decorum.

"Well, yes, we can do it now, if you want to here." It came out kind of wrong, but he had thrown her once again.

"Oh, I am sorry. Do you want to come in to drink coffee or something?"

"No, no, I'm sorry, you just threw me . . . " when she saw the lost look on his face, she added, "Never mind, just confused. Sure, let's talk. I think I'm going to say 'yes,' but I would be remiss, if I didn't ask for more details."

She saw him a little lost again, so changed it again. "Go ahead and tell me about the job, and I will give you a definite answer." She kind of sighed, at suddenly having so many glitches in their English, for an easy conversation. They were both clearly nervous about it.

Tomis sighed also, then began to give her more details on what they had discussed. He saw the many different ways she'd be able to help his business, and others who dealt with tourists.

"I think best title for you is 'Consultant and Trainer,' but would not be English teacher - we have many of those. I know I need to better my English with you." He chuckled a little, and relaxed some.

"It is about doing best business in more professional manner. We want you to come and meet many tourists worker, and talk about things we need to learn. We pay you to come for a few weeks - you can see Croatia like tourist, and see what we can do better, and what kind of training need for them."

He paused to finish his talk. "We pay for meeting and talking to business people you can help, and if they want to join contract with you. We pay all expenses - first class, of course. We want you to see everything, tell us mistake - so maybe three weeks better you visit, take business vacation." Satisfied with his practiced speech he presented ito her, now smiling waiting for her answer.

Julia, again overwhelmed, of course, putting it mildly. Here the opportunity at the dream job, in what seemed like a delightfully old - new country. And, also rather importantly, being offered to her by a man, who also seemed like a dream come true, too.

The romantic adventure she'd wanted for some time. Did she need someone to pinch her? Could it all be too good to be true? She then remembered one of the basics of her Metaphysics - *"Be careful what you ask for, as it may well come true!"* It usually came with lessons, but did not seem so, at this time.

Yes, she'd asked the Universe many times, these last couple of years to be *wanted and appreciated* for her business experience, and well accumulated knowledge. Since *definitely not* ready to be retired at her age. And recently, she'd greatly missed the international travel, which had been a side benefit of working in Japan. And, she truly did want to make the world a better place.

So, what better place to start, than with a country which had recently suffered so much, yet trying so hard to make it better for its people. She then realized Tomis holding her hand between his two. She focused on his eyes staring so deeply into hers. She took a deep breath, feeling her intuition speak for her. "Yes," she had to joke. "As long as it's first class, and not Motel 6. I would love to take you up on your offer, . . . - how soon do you want me to come to Croatia?"

Tomis quickly grabbed her by the shoulders, pulled her up as he stood, wrapping his arms around her. He kissed her deeply on the lips, without hesitation or any pull back. "I am so happy you want do this!" And, he kissed her on the lips again, though not quite as passionately. When he released her, he asked, "What is Motel 6?"

Julia laughed and explained, but Tomis not sure, but she laughed, so he did, too. He then pulled out his phone to immediately start to call. "I will see how soon we can get a Visa for you, and we can see about your flight."

Julia again stunned, not only at what she had said, but of the multitude of reactions she'd gotten from him, including the two kisses. He intertwined her strong feelings for him, and a job she'd love to have. Several levels of emotions on his face. He stopped speaking Croatian, "Do you want to go with me to Croatia or later?"

"I …guess if I *could* go with you, I would prefer it . . . " She couldn't imagine how he could pull it off, unless he knew people in really high places. It'd all be quite amazing, and maybe even perfect, since she still had several weeks yet, before her apartment would be ready.

"I do not know to spell your full name? I apologize." Suddenly so embarrassing to him, he could not spell her name. She'd only mentioned it once, when they met for the first coffee, then used it for the reservation last night.

To most people, she'd have said, just as it sounds, or the usual way. But Julia knew he'd be aware of different pronunciations and spellings of names. She knew her full name, as on her passport needed. She remembered, an envelope from the management, still in her purse and handed it to him.

Tomis slowly began to spell each letter into the phone, pronouncing them carefully. To make sure when he finished, he had it spelled back to him. Another few more sentences of Croatian, and he hung up.

"OK, they call me when the Consulate has Visa ready." Then, rather than giving the envelope back to Julia, he folded it carefully and put it in his pocket. "In case I need it again." He smiled broadly at his accomplishment. "This is wonderful, you can go to Croatia with me. I am leaving Tuesday evening, after the ferries are shipped-out in early morning."

He sat back down on the steps and looked at his planner book. Julia sat next to him, fascinated by his similar looking Day-Planner, but with the strange writing and European-style written numbers. She'd not seen his handwriting other than his signature, and rather revealing. He turned to look at her with a very open face. "Do you want to visit New York a day or two before flight?"

"Well, yes, it would be wonderful, it's been a long time since I've been there. Do you have time to site-see with me?" She really didn't want to wander around the city alone, but it would be fun to have him play tour-guide to her, as he'd been there several times over the past few years.

"Yes, all is finish Saturday night, and last inspection is Sunday morning. You take same flight I take tomorrow, and get there Sunday afternoon, so we have two days. Is it good for you?" A growing hesitation in his voice, and in his actions, she didn't quite understand.

"So, I would leave Sunday morning from Marquette to fly to Chicago, then to New Jersey? And, we go to New York for two days, and ffly to Croatia on Tuesday evening, is that correct?" A little complicated, but she'd made more convoluted trips in the past, without any problems.

Tomis thought back over what she said, nodding his head, "Yes, it is correct! Is it OK with you?" Still a hesitation lingering in his voice.

"Well, OK, I'll have to ask Cara to drive me to Marquette, but one way or the other, I will get there. I will have to write down all of the details, or you can email the ticket info to me, once they have been made. WOW! This is really getting exciting, all happening so fast."

Now came the hesitation again. "I have nice hotel . . . and I sure they have nice room for you . . . or . . . "

Suddenly, she got it! "I can stay with you, . . . if you want me to, … and I would like that." She saw his face starting to blush. *He did have the same similar feelings she did*, so they may as well get them out there. Julia definitely the more direct one, when it came to arranging personal time to be together. Almost like, having an arrangement to make love, or more basically, finally experience sex.

Neither of them wanted to be made a fool of, or have so many insecurities showing. The tenuous, thinking-hoping the other person *as interested* in you, as you were in them. Yet, wanting to make sure, so no one got hurt or embarrassed. Having been out of the playing-field for so long, both more than just rusty.

"Are you sure? This is not for job or trip. I want to have time with you, . . . if you want." He now felt very confused, hoping it would not all mix everything up too much. "Maybe this is not good, it complicates too much … many things, and how you feel about job."

Julia knew not to laugh, as Tomis very vulnerable right then. "It's OK, we are both adults, … who have feelings for each other, and also want to be working together. *I can* do this, and I think *we can* do this, and not complicate things too much. Are you afraid some of your investors will think I slept with you to get the job, … is that it?"

"I am not sure. I want them to respect you and your experience like I do." He seemed very torn over how their relationship might affect her work for him and others. She really liked the idea, him being so protective of her and her reputation. She knew a world-wide, 'Hollywood' projection of American women, being so open about sex, which true in her case. She'd certainly become more open over the years.

"OK, don't worry about it. I know how to deal with people like that. Most of the men in Japan I had trained, had never had a woman teach them before. I will dazzle them with my education and knowledge. I *can* do this, trust me!" Now she laughed, though had not mentioned the word, 'nepotism.' And, yes, she knew there'd be at least one wife of an investor, who'd say it.

"OK, I call and get reservation for all." He leaned over to kiss her on the nose, and she moved her lips-up to kiss him. A little response, then he pulled back to take another call. He spoke Croatian, and took the envelope out of his pocket to spell her name again for whomever handling all of his stuff. "OK, she email to me and I email it to you." Now, totally confident, he stood up, pulled her up to his side, and started down the steps. "Where do we go sight-see?"

Julia laughed again at the quick transition, and him being comfortable with her. She had just agreed to have sex with him, but he'd 'compartmentalized it, to move onto sight-seeing! "Well, I thought we'd go see our only Nationally-Designated Historical Buildings, the Iron County Court House in Crystal Falls, and the Harbour House Museum. We may even be able to go up in the clock tower, as the view is supposed to be spectacular down to the river valley."

She paused to see if any question or response from him, when neither she continued. "Then, after all that, we'll take a long lunch, since you told me not to bother with a picnic just to remind you, in Iron County you are never more than five miles, or eight kilometers from water - a lake or a river. So, maybe after we'll go to the Boardwalk, along the Paint River." She smiled.

Then she remembered, "Oh, we'll drive past the dam, but I don't think you can go inside, and don't be disappointed, it's not really big. And, there's also ice cream in the deli, at the bottom of the hill, just so you have some more memories, if you want. I'll bring you back to

Talia's after your tasty treat. I'm sure you have packing to do, but if you see something, or I think of another stop, we have time to do it . . . and talk more also."

Tomis looked at her carefully. "You only live here short time, but you have much pride in area." She thought about *his* organized mind, and how she loved *it* also.

"Yes, but remember I came here several times over the past twenty years or so. I may have been living as a city-girl, but I do love nature. I recognized its extensive beauty here a long time ago." She now looked at him carefully.

Perhaps by compartmentalizing decisions between those made, and those which didn't need immediate action, his way of handling the more emotional subjects like their future making love together.

Julia had to giggle when she thought of their secret, future event together. For them, it would definitely be a day of moving slowly to unfold, lingering over little things, and lightly kissing each other regularly. As they were finishing, Tomis turned to look at her. "Again, I know why Talia so excited for me to see her autumn here. You with me leaf-watching more ...unique, not just beautiful. I will tell Talia 'Thank you,' again. And, your memories." He kissed her.

Julia determined not to cry when dropping him off, so she had insisted to not get out of the car. Tomis did not quite understand, but followed what she asked, as he stopped to kiss her again at the driver's door. "Yes, I know I see you again, soon. Not sad good-bye for us. I think again of your word syn-chron-icity, and how wonderful it works for us to be together." Not easy, Julia pulled her lips in tightly, waited until he closed the door, turned and waved good-bye.

~ ~ ~ ~ ~ ~ ~ ~ ~

When she got to the animal shelter, she simply rattled-on about their experiences, especially going-up to the clock tower and the spectacular view. She wanted to wait until they got home, before she told Cara she needed to talk to her, as something had come-up. The catch in Julia's voice told her, more than their sight-seeing.

"What you're pregnant?" She laughed, grabbed a wine glass, "I have a feeling I'm going to need this." Julia plunked down on her usual bar stool, and waited for her to take her first large swallow. Cara started freaking from the other side of the counter, as she calmly informed her about joining Tomis, the following Sunday at the Newark Airport for his return to Croatia.

"As you know, he has an early flight in the morning for his ferries in New Jersey - they've finished the changes he wanted. It's a three-week vacation, he's gotten me a round trip . . . "

"You didn't have sex with him . . . did you?" Her voice raised to such an extent; Julia knew what would be next. She reached for her wine glass to fill it also, ready to duel it out.

"It's not like I'm 25 or even 35, when more about the sex than the person! You think we'd go to some motel, or the inn in town to be gossiped about?" Julia gathered her emotions, "It's much more than just sex, we have a connection, neither of us wants to let go of it. It's only three-weeks, I'll make more decisions over there. I wish you'd quit worrying, and being so paranoid."

"Are you sure he's not one of those war criminals? They still haven't finished those War Crime Trials . . . " Her voice rose higher, and Julia could see how upset she had become. Yet, not going to let Cara's fears invade her feelings.

"You met him and his sister, how could you even say that?!? They got his sister out of the country to save her. He could never hurt anyone like that!"

"Yeah, they said it about Ted Bundy!" She used her warped sense of humor to contain her visibly-affected feelings. "It's your *life*! You know it's not like you're just going to *Cleveland*. You're going to a country with a war history, brutal atrocities ... especially to women." "The war has been over for years. Thousands of tourists are going there, it's safe or they wouldn't be. He has only kissed me twice passionately, and he's the one to pull back." She looked at Cara, as her shoulders slumped and released, so her face relaxed a little.

Julia breathed deep, understanding more about herself with her revealed-realizations about Tomis. Not to get into the whole war scenario, she added, "Besides, you know I like to take risks, and while *some* times it gets me into trouble, or . . . "

"Like what got you here to begin with?!?" Cara interrupted.

"I don't deny it, but he's paying for everything . . . and risking also got me to Japan, where I *was* very successful." Julia sighed, accepting how very different they both were. "You know I believe in synchronicity - the apartment not being ready, my meeting him the way I did . . . I haven't traveled abroad for so long, and he's in a position to make it all happen, . . . and maybe it'll turn into more. I'll email or call you on a regular basis."

Cara paused to find more ammunition. "What about your new apartment? Are you just going to let it go? Have you even talked to Jeremy about him, or this trip?" Julia's son would be the final card up Cara's sleeve, she could play.

"If I don't come back in time, another apartment is always available. I learned from both Hawaii and San Francisco. And you know, I don't tell Jeremy who to sleep with or live with, . . . I will talk to him this weekend. If you get worried, you can have me tracked by the State Department, since my new passport has one of those chips in it." Julia sighed again, and took another deep breath.

"It's three weeks . . . and if I decide to stay, you can send me my boxes - my life stuff, as you say. If not, I'll let you know when and where, to pick me up." She got up, then added, "Oh, he even gave me a hundred dollars for airport incidentals - food, etc.   Please be supportive of me on this   I feel I have a chance I may not get again

. . . especially at my age."

"Does he know you're older than him?" Julia wouldn't take it as a low blow, just a reality check from a concerned friend.

"He didn't ask, and even said age doesn't matter, so I didn't tell him. It's only a few years. Are we done here; I have to decide what all I need to pack. I may need to get into my boxes for some clothes for New York and my passport." She hadn't meant to let it out just yet. "What do you mean New York? I thought you were flying into Newark - New Jersey, where his ferries are being refurbished?" Her pitch had gone slightly up again, as if finding out secrets being kept from her.

"Yes, I fly into New Jersey, it's closer. We're going to have two days in New York, then fly out on Tuesday evening from JFK. You didn't give me a chance to give you all the details. He wanted us to have some personal time together before we left, since he expects to be really busy once we get to Croatia. It may be a vacation of sorts for me, but he wanted me to understand he wouldn't have the time like we've had here to spend together. I think he's being very considerate about it, . . . and I'm looking forward to sharing his bed."

Julia rose from the stool and glanced at Cara, who beamed from ear to ear. "Did you really think I'd go half-way around the world with a man I hadn't slept with? I haven't changed that much!" She laughed, and giggled, as she walked down the hall to her room, with Cara's chortled laugh echoing behind her.

"That's the good, ole Julia I remember!" She laughed louder.

Julia emptied, then sorted through her suitcase, laying out the items she'd take for her trips - sorting the New York stuff from what she thought she wanted and needed for Croatia. Though sort of a vacation, she knew she'd have business meetings and some functions, in which she'd need to dress both professional, and for entertaining.

Once she had it all organized in her mind, she'd go into the garage with her box list, and dig out the other things she felt she needed to take. Determined to make it with just the one suitcase and tote bag, as her usual way in traveling, to not be weighed-down by frivolous items. Mild weather in both places, she could easily wash or reuse the clothes for actual sight-seeing, it did simplify things for her

Shoes and jewelry were basic, figuring only a few showy pieces necessary for functions, and one pair of dressy, stacked-heels needed, she felt. A smile crossed her face, as glad she'd gotten some new underwear at the Walmart, remembering time with Tomis would now be on a more romantic involvement level. A shot of nerves went up her spine, and she shivered at the prospect of what she would be doing. She immediately went into her well-used mantra of the past years. "I can do this. *I* can Do this! I CAN Do This!" She sat on the bed deep breathing, feeling better after a few minutes.

"Now, ask yourself Julia, WHY are you doing this?" She took another deep breath to clear her emotions, and answered herself out loud. *"Because you not only care about Tomis, but you also like the idea you may be able to*

help him, his business and maybe even his country. Boy, that sounds egotistical,*"* she sighed. *"No really, no expectations, even if it only turns out to be just a vacation, it is excitement enough to go."* She thought again, *"Where is your trust - do you feel any concern for your safety?"*

She felt some mixed feelings, which kind of surprised her, and she got a definite response to be *'aware.'* She had always practiced keeping her awareness up, when traveling on her own to *any* third- world, or developing country, and . . . *keeping the Golden Light around her constantly.*

A bit of a surprise, her intuition reported the feeling, but it had been quite a while since she'd been overseas. Always some laxness in safety, when she had been secure for so very long. With another deep breath, she strongly repeated: *"I CAN DO THIS!"* She took her list, and went into the kitchen to help Cara with dinner.

Cara had very little more to say, as Julia helped her finish with dinner. Knowing someone so well, even when having been apart for so long, they both knew when to give-up an argument. Or, call a halt to a discussion which quickly going-off.

As they sat down to eat in front of the giant screen TV, Julia hoped to smooth things over. "I really want you to be happy for me, and I do appreciate your concern for me. Though you know I've traveled to a lot of countries, I know it has been a while. I will be diligent in keeping-up my awareness, of things going on around me."

She glanced over at Cara who ate systematically, while choosing what they would watch from her TiVoed selection. "I doubt greatly, Tomis will be away from me very much. I do know better than to wander off, when I don't know the country or the language - though he did say most of them spoke at least some English."

"I just have a bad feeling in my gut - and don't tell me all your positive crap about feeding negative energy!" Cara turned to Julia, knowing what would soon come out of her mouth. "All I know is what I feel, I've said my piece and I will drop it for now."

Julia tried to be respectful of Cara, since she stayed in her home. At the same time, Cara did make the occasional airy-fairy comment, indicating her disbelief in what she called Julia's nuts and flakes-California feel-good stuff.

Then, almost as to piss her off, Cara said, "I'm now going to watch my 'Right-Wing' programs, as you call them. You're welcome to stay and learn something, or go to your room. I'll let you know when the other stuff is on. I'm going to bed early tonight, so you can watch what you want later."

Julia waited to see what she'd be watching, as she ate her dinner. Seeing enough, she picked herself up to move to the back bedroom. She didn't like it when they argued, but the two strong- willed women could be rather adamant in their beliefs. Julia often admitted, she knew she could be difficult in her own behavior.

Not unusual for male or female friends to be fascinated by Julia in the short term, then worn-out in the long term. She could sometimes be too much with opinions, and her open-mindedness. She filed it all away to check herself more, with her new situation coming- up.

She turned on the computer, and after checking her emails, once again googled Croatia. She found some more interesting stuff to read. Yes, she thought, she needed to get Cara to read some of this, then she'd be more accepting.

In the morning, Julia watched the clock, thinking of where Tomis would be along the highway to the airport. Only the Wisconsin- bordering counties were on Central time, so one had to adjust when traveling beyond them, which of course, Marquette and the airport. Being an hour and half drive to Sawyer, the only jet airport in the UP, meant a really early rise for the 8:45 am flight to O'Hare. Then she thought of how she'd be making the same trip in two days with Cara.

After breakfast, she began her search through the boxes in the garage, with her list of things for each box number holding them. She had brought out a laundry basket to put the stuff in, along with a knife to open, and tape to re-seal them.

Her mind kept slipping back to Tomis, and now the flight going to O'Hare. She heard a strange noise, looked out the open garage door. How totally appropriate, raining really hard, so not a good day for sight-seeing. Yes, timing had been everything in almost anything one did.

Julia began to feel very lost at not being around Tomis, and especially not hearing his lovely-accented voice with the clipped English. He'd gotten better, as he listened and picked-up words or phrases from her.

Still those difficult idioms, articles and some prepositions, which tangled most non-native speakers. She particularly liked the way he pronounced her name, with the stronger accent on the second syllable, than the first, as most English speakers did.

She stopped to count how many hours they'd actually spent together, not counting any phone calls, and came up with about thirty hours. Since most dates were shorter than their sight-seeing days, she could say they had at least ten dates, which for most people nowadays, would be a lot, before getting more intimately involved. Of course, Julia did not need to justify it, as she happily planned for it.

They had spent almost five long-days together, and had talked about so many different things. She loved how he deferred to her to explain words. Or particularly, questions about other things, both mundane or very complicated political, metaphysical and business management stuff.

Tomis would then, tell her how amazing her ability to explain it all so well. Julia smiled to herself, as her mind replayed the tapes of the places they went, and many various conversations they had. She loved how he had such pride, in what all they had done with their country since the war. And, the many beautiful places he wanted to take her to, and the things they'd do.

Then, delighted at how interested she could honestly be, in his technical engineering work, the ferryboats, and the commuter trains. He even commented on how good her questions were, as Julia told him of her experiences with them in other countries.

Several times he commented on how they might be able to do similar things with theirs. Julia had run across her resume, and though it had her San Francisco address on it, she pulled out a few copies to take with her. Perhaps Tomis might want to give it to his investors.

Then she noticed her assessment forms, she'd used for clients in Japan and Hawaii, so pulled them out. As well, several other forms and hand-outs she could probably use. "I'll get a fax number from Tomis and send these over, so they can be translated before I get there!" She thought again about her mantra of "I Can Do This." It once again applied to her new adventure.

The basket almost full, when Julia opened the box which not only had her passport and jewelry, but also the light, cotton pouch with the velcro strap. "It's perfect and should make Cara much happier."

Her late husband had bought them both the 'valuables-pouch' before they'd made their trip to South Korea. Overly-cautious, he'd heard tpick-pockets common there. She blew it off, as the negative feelings between Japan and Korea, but how he acted. Surprised she'd even packed it, so took it as a sign, it could be helpful in quelling fears, other people might have.

Julia slipped the light, thin pouch around her waist fastening the strap in the front and pulled her t-shirt down over it. "Wow! It really is invisible." She turned to look at the mirror Cara had in the garage, and felt it actually more comfortable with the pouch to rear.

She reached down for the passport, slipped it into the pouch, pushing the ribbed seal closed. She adjusted the strap and pulled her cotton panties up over it all, so the elastic waist band covered the thin cotton strap. Again she looked at it from several angles, and ran her hand over her t-shirt. With the natural dip in her back and spine, the thin pouch clung to her skin leaving no trace of its existence.

"Voila! I'm covered and covert at the same time." She immediately went to find Cara in the house, calling to her, as she continued to the back bedroom/office. With a big smile on her face, she said, "Well, what do you think?" Finishing a bookkeeping entry into the computer, Cara turned to look at Julia with her hands raised at her side.

"What, it's your imitation of a goal post?" She did not like to be interrupted when working on the bar-books. Julia walked over to her, "Can you see anything unusual about what I'm wearing?" Cara in no mood for games, but leaned in to look her over carefully, as she knew there had to be a point being made. "The waist - do you see anything different about my waist?" As Cara looked even closer, Julia added. "Put your hands on my waist and see if you can feel anything."

Now intrigued, Cara carefully ran her hands around Julia's waist, moving slowly from the front to the back. "OK, I give up. What did you do with the elephant?" She'd at least put some levity into the whole situation.

Julia pulled up her t-shirt, slowly turned around, and pulled down her panties when Cara had still not said a word. "What's that?" she asked, as she opened the pouch and pulled out the passport. "Oh My God! That's really clever." Now truly amazed at how well it had all been hidden.

Julia turned back around, took the passport and showed Cara the little chip. "Now, I hope you are satisfied you can track me wherever I am, write down my number. And, I promise you, I will always have it on when I am outside, especially away from Tomis. I can hardly feel it, and no one can see or even feel it on me. How about two points for ingenuity?" She felt really good about it, as she could see a real sense of relief on Cara's face.

"Where did you get it?" She'd written down Julia's passport number, so unstrapped the belt to look at it more closely.

"My ex, you may remember how paranoid he could be. He bought them in Japan, at some travel store before we went to Korea. I only wore it a few times in third-world countries, where they told us

U.S. passports were so valuable."

Julia took the pouch and passport back from Cara, turning to return to the garage. "I'm almost finished gathering up my stuff to pack, so now the real magic begins, as I do my trick of packing forty pounds of shit in a twenty-pound bag."

Cara laughed, returning to her bookkeeping, and being more comfortable with Julia's trip. *"Chalk one up for me,"* thought Julia to herself, as she loped back to finish retrieving the last things from the boxes. As she passed through the kitchen, she glanced at the clock again, knowing Tomis now at O'Hare, waiting for his flight on to Newark.

She stopped to wonder and question if perhaps he'd be thinking of her. When her phone rang, she stepped back to the end of the counter to pick it up. She could see Tomis' American business phone, and her heart stopped.

Her mouth suddenly dry, as her words squeaked out, "Well, Hello. And, how are you doing in O'Hare?" Though they had spoken last night, it seemed so long since she'd heard his melodious, beautifully-accented, baritone voice.

She slid down onto the bar stool, and listened as he updated her on the ferries, her flight. He repeated to call him, as soon as she landed in New Jersey, as the dock only about fifteen minutes away.

Again, he'd meet her at the baggage carousel, as he had her flight number. He checked again, she only wanted to put one suitcase in baggage, repeating he could add another one for her, if she wanted. She reassured him, she always traveled light, and knew how to pack. They both laughed, then he told her again, he'd be busy all day and late into the night, and as well Saturday.

" . . . but do not hesitate to call me, if you need to speak to me. I call you when I can, to hear your voice . . . I miss you, . . . and our lovely days together, not worrying much about business." A pause in his voice, and he added more strongly, "I see you Sunday around four

... and we have few days to again enjoy us together."

"I miss you too, and I'll keep my phone close in case you call, .

. . see you Sunday." Julia sat looking at the phone after his voice gone. She felt it truly a life-line to him.

She then remembered explaining the word 'incidentals' to him, when he had insisted on giving her the hundred dollars cash. The silly things they'd laughed at, she began to wonder just how much his business would keep them separated. She didn't get another call until early Saturday morning, as on his way to the dock once again.

Unfortunately, Julia in the shower, so only had the voicemail to replay, and keep for hearing his voice. Tomis on final inspections with small changes. The ferries were to be shrink-wrapped, crated individually and placed on the giant container ship, which sailed Tuesday morning, before they flew in the evening. She could hear his frustration and tenseness in his voice, but it lightened, again saying how he missed her company. Another call came in, so he had to go.

Julia spent Saturday at the animal shelter helping Cara at the front desk. It did help distract her from missing Tomis, and what all about to embark on doing. Cara in a good mood, kind of proud of her friend going on such an unusual trip. She told people a vacation she'd gotten from a friend.

"Yeah, she's going to my ancestor's homeland, but she'll be back in three weeks, then move into her new apartment. May as well take advantage of a freebie, instead of just hanging out at my place." Julia knew Cara feeling somewhat abandoned, but she'd moved more into acceptance of the whole situation. She'd make sure she called, and emailed as much as she could, whenever she could.

Julia finally caught up with Jeremy, and happily told him of the synchronicity of meeting Tomis, with their sight-seeing together and as many details as she could pour out for him. When she got to the job offer, she omitted the organized-crime stuff, but perhaps this would be a real romantic adventure, with a great paid vacation and training gig.

She didn't want to let on how much she liked Tomis, but Jeremy knew his mother. He wished her a great time, reminding her to email and, "And, I don't want to hear about you on the news, for causing some riot, or something." It stunned Julia, but knew him teasing her all her peace-activist stuff in SF.

Tomis called three times Saturday night, but each time they had barely started talking, when his international phone rang. He'd said it had not stopped, as they were having some problems over there, and felt he had to make the decisions. He didn't want to talk about it, and she didn't want to ask about bad news.

Julia decided to take out her nail polish - an iridescent pinkish- beige tone - to do her nails, just to kind of dress her up, for the whole event of going to New York. Otherwise, she and Cara had a quiet evening, both drinking a little too much wine, laughing at all the wild, old times and watching TV. Julia went over her lists, occasionally writing down another question for Tomis, or jumping-up to add something to her suitcase. After Cara retired, Julia tried to sleep, but only dozed to wake again, with some vision of her and Tomis together.

~ ~ ~ ~ ~ ~

Barely five, when Cara rousted her out, and she trundled off to the shower to get herself ready to leave. Drying herself, Julia leaned in to study her nakedness close-up, from top to bottom in the bathroom mirror.

"Well, you do look pretty good for a mature-Broad!" Glad she'd been doing the aerobics for so many months to keep herself flexible, and a little more tightened. As her eyes came back around from her butt, she stared closely at her crotch.

"Well, Little Muff, you may have felt closed-up and furred- over, but hopefully you'll be getting some fun action soon. I hope you do remember how; you know … 'just like riding a bicycle'!"

Julia laughed almost uncontrollably, when Cara called out, asking her what the hell going on in there. "Don't worry, I'm not using your vibrator! I don't use them!" They both laughed and Julia thought how not another person in the world, she could have talked to so bluntly, but Cara. She had done so much to get her here, and now, practically running out on her.

"I love you Cara," Julia said to the unseen face, "but destiny is calling me, and I really do need to answer. I just can't let this one go or stupidly ask, 'You talking to me?' I just know it's my time."

After doing her hair and make-up, she carefully checked and rechecked, she had not left anything in the bathroom, heading back to finish the very last of her packing.

They were already on the road to Marquette, when Tomis called Sunday morning and said he'd not had much sleep, as his phone had barely stopped all night. Julia could hear frustration in his voice, and suggested he go back to bed, since now night in Croatia. He said he probably would, as things had finally smoothed out at the New Jersey dock. He did not need to go in until later, he just wanted to talk to her before she flew out.

"We have dinner invitation, but I tell them you are too tired tonight, so it is tomorrow, if OK with you. I want us have quiet dinner, OK?"

Julia a little surprised, as she didn't know Tomis knew people

in New York, who'd be inviting them to dinner, so it must be those business investors of his. "Yes, of course, a quiet dinner *alone* sounds wonderful to me. I can't wait to see you."

"You know if really tired, I can get you your room?" A definite hesitation in his voice, asking if not sure she still wanted to be with him or not.

A little shocked, as if checking on decorum or what, Julia quickly said, "No, of course not, I'm looking forward to it. I will be fine, it's not a long flight. I'll call you as soon as we land, and see you at the baggage carousel." She then added to reassure him, "Rest up, so we can celebrate tonight."

His voice now almost cheery, "Yes, I rest up, and can't wait to see you." He had repeated her words back to her perfectly, even using the contraction. What a silly thing for her to notice. Again, she held onto the phone which had connected them, then finally stuck it in her purse. She turned to look at Cara concentrating on the road.

Catching her vibe, she glanced at Julia, but hesitated as if choosing her words before she spoke. "Everything OK in New York, or New Jersey?" She wanted to be supportive, but not easy for her to just endorse it all.

"Yes, he's just really tired, with phone calls most of the night from Croatia. He's going back to bed, since he only needs to go over to the dock to make sure they are getting the ferries crated-up right, and all of the paper work is taken care of properly.

He doesn't want to have to go back once I get there. They're shipped out Tuesday morning, and he wants to make sure of no problems. I think this is all a lot bigger than I realized. I mean I know it must be a lot of money - millions of dollars, . . . since he's got several really big investors and government-backing for it. He's totally responsible to a lot of people."

She smiled with concern more for Tomis, than the whole trip. "He also said we're invited to some dinner party tomorrow night. I guess his investors want a celebration for the completion of it all. I think they've been working on this for some time. Shit, I don't think I've got the right dress to wear for some big-money party."

"Don't worry about it, if really important he'd have told you before now you needed a dress, or better yet, let him buy you one, or something to go with it. At least he's always picked up the tab for everything, and never been cheap about the gas or anything.

This whole thing, getting you over there has got to be costing him, or whomever a couple thousand dollars, so I'll give him credit on treating you right." She cocked her head in conceded acknowledgement, but not about to start praising him, as all just too whirlwind, as far as her concern.

Cara then went over the itinerary, and had Julia check again she had all of the info - two overly organized - kind of controlling people did make for double-checking things. "Do you want me to call you from O'Hare, because I probably won't have time in Newark, since I'll be calling Tomis to meet me, and trying to find my way to baggage? I've never flown into that airport, and I'm sure it's huge."

"No, just call me if you forgot something. But you better call me from New York, and email me whenever you get the chance. I don't want to have the State Department hunting you down." She may have sounded like joking, but Julia knew she'd not hesitate, if she did not hear from her.

"If I understood you right, the American business phone number will only be good until Tuesday night, and you wrote down all the country code stuff for his international-Croatian phone, right?"

"Yes, and you've got Talia's home number and cell, right?" Julia took a deep breath. "OK, I'm Off to My Next Big Adventure!" Her mind going ten different directions, at a thousand miles an hour, and her heart started pounding. She had not been this nervous when she was flying out of San Francisco, and leaving another life behind.

155

Yes, this so much, much bigger. She remembered being almost frantic when she left San Antonio for Japan, with her husband being cool, while reminding her she could come back if she wanted. He would have loved for her to have failed, as he resented it greatly she'd been so successful there, while he could not adjust to living in a foreign country. What's with her mind, digging up such old shit NOW? She closed her eyes, took a couple of deep breaths, then visualized her Golden Light around her for protection, and White Light for direction. She continued to breathe deep, and visualized the Golden Light coming into her top crown chakra, then flowing down through each chakra until she finally had shaken the fear.

Cara glanced at her several times, seeing her eyes closed and saw her shoulders shrug, as her body relaxed. "Feel better now? I could hear you deep breathing." She may not believe or understand it, but she respected Julia's choice to believe what she did. It seemed to work for her, after so many years of being so work-stressed.

"Yeah, thanks. I had a lot of old garbage running around in my head, and I had to clear it all out. I'm good now. I just have to remember, I do know how to calm myself down, no matter what the situation." She then realized they were pulling up to the airport. "OK Kiddo! It looks like showtime coming-up in a moment. You know I love you, and this in no way changes us, or all you've done to get me here and back on my feet!"

"What," Cara laughed, "you going to jump out here, or wait for me to pull-up to the American Terminal?"

"I just wanted to make sure I told you how much I loved you, and how much I appreciated what you've done for me. And, please be happy for me."

When Cara pulled-up to the terminal, Julia had already unlatched her seatbelt and opening the door. She pulled her bag and tote out of the back to the ground. Julia grabbed each dog to give them a hug and kiss, then told them to take care of Cara. She swung her bags onto the curb and grabbed Cara for a big hug and kiss, before she could resist her efforts.

Her purse over her shoulder, she grabbed up the bags without looking back, and headed in the terminal door. Cara pulled away from the departure with a few tears in her eyes, and called back to her dogs, "OK Girls, it's just us the next few weeks. And, we'll be stopping to let you pee, once we get away from the airport."

Chapter 8
New York, New York

As being human, we have a long history
of forgetting what we have learned sometimes.
Then, become lost or confused as we cannot find,
what we do not know, or how to seek it.

As true friends, we make sure our minds do not invade
our private, personal thoughts.
But a web of mutual awareness connects them.
As if a natural process, or who we are being.

We overcome fears related to their privacy,
as are easily seen and felt in sharing them.
This allows thoughts to accelerate the creation of more
beneficial experiences between us.

It's difficult to be objective about something,
when you are immersed in all facets of it.
You often need some time away,
to allow you to see things from a variety of perspectives.

Many people perpetuate some fantasy in life,
whose fairy tale ending expired very long ago.
You must empower yourself to seek a larger truth,
of yourself, before you empower others around you.

Then you can build bridges between your thoughts,
in a way your realities of life, do not seem so futile.
In order to feel a deep truth in a person or thing,
you must know if it's your heart, who leads or follows it.

Sitting at the O'Hare gate waiting to be called for boarding the 12:15 flight to Newark, Julia read her UP history magazines trying to keep her mind calm. Not just second thoughts, but realizing what Cara had said, in she could barely know Tomis in only five days. Yes, in her 'wild and crazy' younger days, of exploring her new sexual freedom when first divorced, she'd taken off for weekends with men, she'd known for shorter periods of time.

But, they weren't taking her half-way around the world, where she couldn't speak the language. Then she thought, time is no measurement of love or falling in love - who knows, or can say how long it takes to know? Momentarily, she felt better and she went back to her reading, as she needed a distraction.

Being Sunday and the time difference, a phone call to friends back in San Francisco may not be appreciated. Since she had already talked to her son Jeremy last night, she decided to call her nephew in Chicago. He had nothing but encouragement. He said it reminded him of the adventurous aunt he grew up with, doing those wild, memorable things they all laughed about now.

Would all this become *laughable* someday, she wondered? But it did make her feel better thinking not totally nuts. In her hey-day, she'd joked about changing her men, as often as she changed her hair- do. While certainly not *that* person any more, fun to be free from having tied herself down to her career for so long. Finally reseated on the plane, glad to resume reading the inflight magazine, and ate her sandwich she'd brought with her. So far, she'd not touched the $100 Tomis had given her.

As the plane touched down, the flight attendant said they may use their cell phones once again. Julia pulled hers out, turned it on and found Tomis' business number to call. Hearing his welcoming voice squelched any hesitation, which may have lingered.

She almost gushed with excitement of being with him again. As corny, as it later seemed upon realization, before putting it away, she'd held the phone to her heart. She snickered to herself, and began the process of rising from her seat, to retrieve her tote bag from the overhead bin. Once again, she deep-breathed to deal with whatever confusion, or barrage of people she might encounter getting to be with him, and her luggage.

She began to repeat her mantra of "I can do this," as space opened-up in front of her to head out the plane, and up the jet-way to the openness of the boarding gate. First she'd stop in the restroom to pee and refresh herself. Taking a final glance, *"That's as good as it's going to get, Kiddo,"* she said to herself, and headed out the door smiling.

Julia figured it would all take about fifteen or twenty minutes, looking at what the clock behind the baggage carousel said. She glanced at the suitcases coming out, while people-watching. Friends and lovers began to greet each other, kissing and hugging with various levels of intimacy. *"I'm going to have it, too,"* she quietly said. Rather different, to have someone - a man - coming to take her away.

When she heard her name, only the way he said it, coming through the crowd, all around her went into slow motion. Then, she finally saw Tomis, politely cutting through them to her. She dropped her tote bag to her feet, as he grabbed her up and again passionately kissed her. Even for an airport kiss, a knockout!

Unbeknownst to either of them, it answered any questions of feelings they may have had. *"It is* so *good* to see you, I miss you . . . really!" A very breathy response, as they were both short from the kiss, so she just nodded. He studied her, like he wanted to be sure still as he had remembered. "Was flight OK? I want you first class, but no seats. Do you eat in Chicago?" Julia now smiled ear to ear, with the realization they were finally back together, as if apart for months.

"Yes, fine and I'm fine. Thank you for being so concerned. It's been a while since I flew first class, it would've been fun, but it's no problem. It's a relatively short flight." She then turned, remembering her luggage and saw it had gone past them about six feet. "Oops, there goes my bag, the black square one, with the blue-flowered tag."

Tomis turned away to scoot through the crowd and grab it up. She picked-up her tote bag, secured her purse over her shoulder and caught-up with him, as he slid his arm over her back, to guide her to the door. As they walked through it, Julia saw the policeman about six feet in front of the town car, with the back door and trunk open. The driver hurrying to meet Tomis, as she realized the car for them. "Oh no, I hope you're not going to get a ticket!"

He looked back at her, as he handed the suitcase to Luka, and took the tote bag from her for him also. He then glanced at the policeman, chuckling. "No, . . . it is not a problem," and helped her into the back seat, sliding in after her. As the car slipped into traffic, and away from the airport, he took her hand to kiss it, then her cheeks and finally lightly on her lips.

With Luka up front, more decorum than before. "I hope you like hotel, I stay there before when I come for business. I can suggest different restaurant for us to choose. Weather is very nice, so we can walk if you want, or take car to go anywhere. I know you said you here before, so not sure how much you want to see and do. I know we not have much time, but can do some things you want." He beamed at her, like also amazed they were together again.

"I am totally open to any of your suggestions, since it's been a really long time since I've been here." She smiled back at him, and for some reason kissed his nose, which made him laugh and she giggled. "So, the ferries all got wrapped and crated-up OK? I can't imagine fitting them in, considering how often I used to watch those humongous container ships coming into San Francisco Bay." She felt great pride in him, as she knew it had been a much bigger job than he had ever eluded to before. "You should be very proud, and I'm sure all of your investors and everyone else are very proud of you."

He smiled, acknowledging his sense of accomplishment. Glad she somewhat understood how very difficult it all had been, though not the type to reiterate the details of any big job.

"Yes, I am glad not have to return to dock, or take more calls regarding . . . update of progress. They look more beautiful finish, than photo I show you. It all take long time, but I think worth it for business and increase tourism. I have new photos in room, so I show you. I think also, big one frame at dinner tomorrow night. I hope not do too much about it all." Getting a little embarrassed, at the thought of it all being too showy for him.

"Oh, I'm glad you brought it up. I don't know if the dress I brought will be nice enough for the dinner, how dressy is it?" No way Julia could be ready for what followed, as he had never eluded to a position of power or influence.

Tomis pulled his lips in, as to take a breath, and consider his words. "Yes, about party. . . You do not worry about dress, Petar wife Jelena, make arrangement at store. Let me show you, she sends over Saturday morning." As he looked in his breast pocket, Julia more than taken aback, someone would choose a dress for her to wear to some dinner party. Did they think of her as some country, hick-girl, because of where they'd met? She controlled her own breath, as she spoke, but he quickly noted the change in her tone. He had not seen her angry before.

"Tomis, what are you talking about? Who are these people who would choose my clothes for me to wear?" Her head slightly tilted, looking at him squarely.

"No, No. I not explain correctly." He took another breath, as he began to read the paper. "Bloom-ing-dales ... 1000 3rd Street . . . "He handed the note to Julia, which had a very fancy colored insignia on top. "The woman name is there . . . "

She read the large colorful insignia: "The Consulate General of Croatia?!?! 369 Lexington Avenue?" More than shocked, she looked at him like a pleading-child. *"What are you* getting me into *here*? *Who are you*?" Julia started laughing, as a really confused Tomis not sure how to answer her questions, but at least she did not seem to be so upset anymore. She laughed, "OK, ... where is the dinner party, and how many people are going to be there?" Now going through the Holland Tunnel, so it got rather dim in the car.

"OK, I am very sorry. I not talk to you before about dinner, but really busy . . . and I forget to give you all detail. When we talk on phone, not on my mind, but Jelena ask me two times." He couldn't see her face clearly, but felt all almost good. "The dinner is at Consulate, Petar and Jelena represent Croatia here in New York. It is more business-directed, than Washington, which is more political. His . . . and her families are my biggest Croatian investors . . . what I think you call 'old money' . . ."

"You mean like they made it a hundred years ago, in some big industry like oil or steel or railroads?" Kind of joking, but wanted to make sure she totally understood who and what she would be dealing with. She began to feel like losing her footing, as these were not your average 'Joe' million-dollar investors.

Tomis looked at her trying to understand what all she'd said. "Ah, no. Their money . . . and titles and palaces go back to I think . . . 7th or 8th century. I . . . "

"*Oh, my God?!* Sweetheart, that's not old money, that's ancient money from royalty! I think I'm *waaay* out-of-my *league* here!" She snickered again. "So, this isn't *nepotism*, since you said they are investors, and in New York, it is their jobs to promote business for Croatia?" She could not have imagined all of this, and neither would Cara believe it. This destiny-thing - the synchronicity had a real sense of humor.

Still a little confused. "I am not sure I know word you say, 'nepo' but yes, they promote business for Croatia, most is tourism. We went to university together, and his brother is head of Tourist Board. And, I am not sure how many people, but maybe twenty or thirty, . . . they have party for many people there."

Back in the sunlight, relieved to see the smirk on her face. Actually, ready to laugh out-loud about the surrealism, she'd gotten herself into without knowing a clue. She couldn't help it, and loudly laughed.

All like some big joke, or being "punked" by meeting someone 'rich and famous' in the most obscure place in the world or something. "Really?! How *did* you and I - two *somewhat* international people meet in the most obscure, *people-empty* place?" Julia controlled herself in laughing, as Tomis had no clue as to the ridiculousness of her position.

"*Nepotism* means someone gets a big job, because they are related, or connected to someone, not because they have the talent or even knowledge. This is not their case, though some might think it's a bit of a conflict of interest, since they are investors in your company Never mind, let's not go there."

She doubted greatly Tomis would have gotten the contract simply because they were investors. He did have the knowledge and experience to do the job, which definitely not easy. They had followed him, as he succeeded.

"So, we, and I do mean *we*, have to go to Bloomingdales tomorrow and speak to this woman, to get a dress for me to wear for the dinner party. Are they paying?" It seemed like a logical expense they would cover. She now giggled, shaking her head at the unlikelihood of her being invited to such a gig.

Now, he laughed at her outspokenness, which brought back memories of so many times she had surprised him by it. He leaned over and kissed her on the cheek. "You are so wonderful! I never know someone like you before, and I know I say it before." He kissed her again lightly on the lips. "Yes, we both go, I have to get new tuxedo, at Jelena's insistence. She got my size and order it, I have to try on, but for you, the woman bring out dress good for the party, . . . your choice. And yes, they pay. She gave me *Consulate credit card,* to get you what you need."

He took another breath, hoping what he had to say next would not upset Julia. "If you do not mind, too much, . . . Croatian press people and other business press to take photo of me . . . and you, too, if is OK?" Jelena had asked if Julia shy, or would be OK with her picture being taken, for the publicity and promotion, back in Croatia.

She could not hold it anymore, and really cracked-up laughing, thinking what Cara would say about how expensive of a *date,* she had turned out to be. "Yes, my Sweet, it is not a problem. I did many years of community theater, so I'm used to playing as many roles as needed. I also had to do radio and TV interviews, for different jobs, so I'm cool with it. A few camera flashes won't fluster me." All too funny, and so totally surreal.

Amazed once again, "You never tell me you do theater and interviews." Chuckling how she continued to surprise him. "What else you never tell me?"

Julia laughed, doing a bad Groucho-cigar-imitation, with her hand in front of her mouth. She knew he wouldn't really understand.

"I've got plenty of secrets, *Sweetheart*. I'll reveal it all, if you say the magic *word*."

She giggled wildly, and he laughed having no clue what she said. "I also taught Western-style cooking on TV in Japan, . . . how about that one, *Kimo Sabi*?" He shook his head looking at her. "I'm going to loosen you up, Mr. Workaholic-man!"

"Yes, I think you are.   And, maybe it is very good thing." Seeing a side of her, not sure of, though she had joked with him many times before.

Since he'd already said, he'd told them it had to be Monday instead of tonight for the party, Julia felt Jelena may have preferred some young Croatian beauty to be on his arm, or even his bed.

She couldn't help herself to ask, "So, if I may ask, what did you tell Jelena and *Petar*, . . . is it, about me? How did you describe my size or shape to her? I'm just curious, as to the kind of dresses might be waiting for me." She snickered, as she knew she'd put him in a spot.

Now, Tomis who smiled, and shook his head. These were women things, as much as he could care. He also did not understand why they questioned his actions so much. Though having gone through explaining himself to Talia and Cara, he then had to explain to Jelena and Petar of his wanting Julia by his side, as well taking her to Croatia.

"I tell her you are my age, but look much younger. . . I do not know size, so she mentions several people I meet, and I tell her who look same size. I tell her you are successful business woman who can help Croatia much.

And, beautiful, with amazing eyes and lovely, not too long hair . . . and I want to touch in very personal way." He now laughed at the shocked look on Julia's face. "No, I not say last part, but true." He almost blushed, in his first real admittance of his true romantic-sexual feelings for her.

"Thank you, my dear, very much for *all* of the complimentary things you said about me. I just hope I can live up to them *all*. And, I *was* a successful business woman - past tense, I haven't worked *full time* recently."

She laughed again deeply, "Also, don't make me sound too great, I'll exhaust myself proving it. You have no idea how annoying it is to some people . . . (she wanted to add especially insecure men, but not him, so she didn't.) I must add also, I'm sure Jelena may have preferred some young Croatian beauty to be on your arm. Good publicity and all."

Tomis chuckled, "Yes, she try several time for me to be involve her younger sister. She is nice woman, divorce - two young children, . . . but no interest in her. She does not know business like Jelena background, and little I can talk about to her. I am nice to her on business trip past three years. I think . . . they think more on final trip, but I go to Michigan and meet you." He smiled broadly. "I think it is what you say, 'end of story' or something." They were then both laughing again at the whole crazy scenario.

"Well, we'll have some intrigue at the dinner party, and I hope she doesn't tear my eyes out, or my dress off in some *snit*." Julia laughed heartily, but his face looked lost.

"I don't mean to be cruel, but I am what would be called an 'experienced-woman of *substance*,' and interested in so many different things. Just as I have found you to be also. Youth just doesn't cut it along those lines. It should all be a real *hoot* tomorrow, the shopping *and* the truly 'highfaluting' party." She laughed knowing Tomis lost with her words.

"I'm really looking forward to it, and I promise to make you proud. And, I will *try* to *not shock* too *many* important people. I'm assuming most everyone there will be able to speak English. But remember, I'm not paranoid when others speak a foreign language around me." She smiled and shook her head, trying to remember when she had been put into such a situation. She'd definitely have to put her acting-chops on for this performance.

Luka had pulled to the curb, Tomis looked out, leaned over again and quickly kissed her. "We are here, I hope you like it. It is close to Consulate and many things."

He opened the door, and turned for her hand after he stepped out into the street. Julia took a deep breath, as she scooted across the seat and out. As she moved to the sidewalk, sliding her purse over her shoulder, the doorman already helping Luka with her bags, and Tomis speaking to him in Croatian.

Julia then looked up and saw the New York Helmsley Hotel. *"Holy shit!"* she said under her breath, *"This ain't no Motel 6. It's the Helmsley! Oh, my God, if Cara could see me now!"* What *had* she gotten herself into - a tight smile came across her face, and she turned to Tomis walking over to her. As Luka drove off, she noticed the Diplomatic-exempt Consulate plates, and realized why the airport policeman had been looking at the car.

~ ~ ~ ~ ~ ~ ~ ~ ~

As the bellman took them to the upgraded room on the 23rd floor, Julia held Tomis' hand, trying not to hold it too tightly. Handing the key card to Tomis, the bellman swung the door open, and it revealed the small sitting room. It had a large desk on one side and beautiful round table in the middle with a large bouquet of mixed colorful flowers.

The small couch and two side chairs were on the other side, with the French doors open to the master bedroom's king-sized bed. He had taken the suitcase straight to the rack for it in the bedroom, and placed her tote next to it on the floor.

Following him in, Tomis dropped his briefcase on the bed, let her hand go to reach for his wallet to tip and thank him. A lovely round table to one side with two nice straight-back, well-padded chairs and a settee on the other side, not far from the bed.

Julia walked to one of the three, magnificent windows to look out on the view, and delighted to see the gleaming Chrysler Building in the bright sunlight.

"Oh, I just love the Chrysler Building! Would you like to take a walk to Grand Central Station, I think it is only a few blocks away? I'm sure you've been over there, but it's so exciting just to people watch, and I haven't seen it since it's been fully restored. I just love the Main Concourse Clock, the Tiffany's clock on the façade of the building, and . . . of course, the intricate astronomical ceiling."

Julia almost giddy at the thought. Besides, she felt neither of them ready to just jump in bed. They needed a few hours to get used to being together again.

"Yes, of course, anything you want. Do you want to change or go now?" He smiled, glad she wanted to go out for a while. Standing near enough to put his arm around her and did. As he also looked out, he realized he had not once checked any view, since he had gotten back to New York on Friday. Similar to the one he had before going to Michigan, but it had only been a single king room.

"Oh, I'm fine to go now if you want. It felt warm enough, I think I'm fine like this."

"I can call car back when you want, OK?" He took her hand, and she smiled, reaching over to grab her purse to head back out the door. She talked to him about the Art Deco design, and once again of her love of old buildings.

She now added, she also couldn't wait to see some of the old buildings of Croatia. They walked and explored to Grand Central, with her usual bubbling excitement, as they entered the old, magnificent building. He rarely spoke, simply enjoying her positive energy, and how it infused him from head to toe. They spent almost an hour walking around the Main Concourse, and finally stopping at one of the coffee spots, where they could sit and people watch.

Julia had, of course, picked up several brochures and read through them to Tomis, pointing out different points of interest. Referencing the astronomical ceiling, she began to ask him of his interest in astronomy and astrology. It had been over two hours, when she realized he may have made reservations for dinner.

"No, . . . I wait for you, and if you want to go to hotel restaurant or . . . out restaurant." He had lost his concentration in listening to her talk.

"Well, have you eaten in the restaurant at the hotel, or where do you usually eat?" She wanted them to share some new experience of their dinner together.

A bit embarrassed, "It always late I come back. Luka, my driver, usually get food in New Jersey. I only eat restaurant, if business meeting dinner - investor or Petar and Jelena."

Julia shaking her head trying not to laugh. "You workaholic! How well I remember, also doing that *way too often*. OK, then why don't we just try the restaurant in the hotel. Maybe you can see if it's not too late to get a table where we can see the sunset, if one is available, or not is OK, too." He reached in his pocket for his business phone, and called the hotel, while she continued to look over the brochures.

Back in the room, Julia determined not to let the bed intimidate her, or embarrassed about changing for dinner. First times always uncomfortable. "I'm going to take a quick shower before I changed, will you need the bathroom?"

She opened her suitcase to take out her dress for dinner, and saw him pick-up his briefcase from the bed to head for the sitting room. She smiled knowing, he also avoided the inevitable consequences of them being together.

"No, I shower and change at Port before I know you call. I make phone call Croatia and give final report. Take your time. I wait for you."

She got all of her stuff she needed out of the suitcase, closed just one of the French doors to the bedroom, and went into the luxury bathroom. As much as she might have wanted a soaking bath, she knew she only had time for a fast shower.

Within thirty minutes, she'd opened back up the door to let him know about ready. She touched back-up her make-up, and puffing her hair when he came back in the bedroom.

"Is OK I come in?" She looked-up into the mirror and did not see him, so he must have waited to the side of the door. This man amazed her with his decorum!

"Yes, of course, I'm just about finished putting my face-on." He then peered around the door frame, looking with curiosity and confusion as to what she said.

"What does 'putting-face-on' mean?" Barefoot, but fully dressed, leaning over the sink with her mascara in hand, and had to pull back with the laughing.

She turned to look at him. "It is an expression women use, when putting on make-up, and trying to make themselves look so much better than they usually do. Like now."

"I do not see big difference. You always look good." She stepped over to him laughing again, raised up on her toes and gave him a kiss on his chin.

"You are wonderful, even if you are blind." His face confused again. "I'm joking, a lovely compliment you gave me." She went back to finish her eye lashes, as he watched. "Please don't watch, you'll make me smudge!" Confused again, he stepped back into the bedroom. A minute later she stepped back out. "You can have the bathroom back, if you want it now. I just have to put my shoes on and I'm ready."

He returned to the bathroom. "I think I do shaver to look fresh." He closed the door, she heard the shaver, then the toilet flush, and the sink faucet again. She liked how very neat and clean about his appearance. She slipped on her shoes, and gave herself a quick, light spray of cologne. She returned to the window to watch the descending sun over the city. Nothing like the vibration of a big city, seen from the wonderful height of a beautiful hotel room. Yes, all feeling quite magical to her.

~ ~ ~ ~ ~ ~ ~ ~ ~

Truly, not as if the sex would be their first adventure into spontaneity. Their whole connection and the continuation of 'sight-seeing' together could be considered at least impetuous.

From Cara's point of view, impulsive, in a way beyond picking-up some item shopping or saying something under the influence of alcohol. It may have been done when young, but one did not, or should not do such things when in one's fifties! But, their first act of spontaneity had fed the following consequences, as in "Why not?" or "So far so good."

For them both, it had felt good to break loose from their usual constraints of how they both usually did something. Much to be said for letting things 'unfold,' as Julia had said several times - following intuitions, feelings, curiosities, or just where the road might take them. With repeated positive results, they both released hesitations,

as trust built between them, with a sort of surrendering to each other's suggestions. Which thus brought them, to Julia inviting Tomis to join her between the soft sheets of the glorious king-size bed, in their two-room suite.

It'd been a lovely, and delicious two-hour, sunset dinner with much laughter and talk as well wine. As they took the elevator up, entwined in each other's arms, with some real kisses on the lips, building the anticipation for them both. Tomis took off his jacket, and said he needed to make one more quick call to Croatia, from the other room before he could join her.

Julia took the opportunity to change into her sexy, short nightgown, she'd brought with her from San Francisco just for fun. She slipped under the sheet on the other side of the bed. Coming in to the bedroom, his tie had been removed, and he started to unbutton his shirt, when he saw her lying in bed waiting for him. Trying not to act stunned, but he was.

She'd positioned herself onto her hip, knowing the fullness of her breasts would be obvious with the low-cut gown. Since no longer covering them for decorum, as she had most of the time the week before. So, he who blushed. Sort of the reaction of hoping for something, and actually seeing it materialized, made one's feelings revealed.

A slight breath and sigh, the knowing the desire there, yet the physical reality hesitated the capability. He pulled his shirt out of his pants, and removed the cufflinks, as he spoke softly.

"It is … really … long time for me to do . . ." She could usually tell when he had rehearsed an important line for her, and she kept a soft smile on her face. He had no idea how *sexy* his vulnerability would be to her.

Julia had also played the scenario through her mind several times, over the past few days, and lifted the sheet over in a welcoming gesture. "As it has been for me . . . It's OK, . . . Actually, it's a good thing, . . . I would not want to be with a man, who commonly-shared his bed with someone, … he'd only known a week."

The first time she'd seen his bare chest, and her heart pounded faster. "Be still my heart," she joked, and he looked at her, again not totally understanding *why* she had giggled. He finished pulling the shirt off, and put it over the chair at the round table.

Tomis laughed a little at her comments, pushed-off each shoe with the toes of the opposite foot, and bent down to pull off his socks, not wanting to look at her directly.

"No, I mean *really* long time, . . . I do not want to disappoint you . . . "

"Let's not get into dates, or how long for either of us. And trust me, you cannot disappoint me, as I've told you before. I am no longer into expectations about anything." Julia hoped her breathiness, or heart pounding rapidly not noticeable.

She watched him slip off his trousers, and put them also across the chair. He certainly got two points for neatness, as he had dropped his socks into each shoe. "It's OK, whatever happens, happens . . . we'll go with it. It's not as if we have an early morning call, or anywhere we need to be."

Julia doing her best to be casual and supportive, while a part of her screaming to get the hell out of the room, before *she* really made a fool of *herself*. Who did she think she was - some thirty-five-year-old sexpot? She tried to take a deep breath, but didn't want to be obvious about her own fears.

"You amaze me how positive you always are." Tomis walked over, and sat at an angle towards her on his side of the bed, with only his boxers on. He looked at her, smiling from ear to ear, he leaned over to her. Some things he had not been able to rehearse, were mainly controlling his nerves, along with his physical reactions.

Julia decided to play coy to break some of the tension between them, and relax their feelings. "I just have never seen the point of being negative. If something doesn't work out, then oh well, . . . we try again. To be positive and believe it will work out, may be naive, but I also believe there are lessons to be learned from the experience . . . "

Tomis had reached his hand over and under her hip, to slide her more to the middle of the bed, like scooping her to him. His hand moved up to the center of her back and gently pulled her closer-up to him, bending to kiss her lips, as she rose to meet him. The passion grew exponentially, simply from it being contained and controlled by them both for so very long.

As his lips had moved to her ears, her neck and between her full breasts, he had also moved into the bed enfolding her. She had pulled back the sheets even more in a natural movement with her free arm, as he had slipped the nightgown strap off her shoulder, just as easily.

Julia held a giggle, as the thought of it all coming back to her, *just like riding a bicycle,* when his lips had reached her breast, and totally taken her breath away.

Her hand reached down to his buttock, as she tried to slip his shorts off. Once both were freed of their night clothes, a kind of floating, peaceful non-urgency surrounded their desire. They were finally skin to skin, to totally absorb each other. Sex as though through osmosis, almost ethereal. Almost, an equal-sharing of adoration, in the touching and kissing, while then being overly pleased, at the responses of pleasure created.

Once the exploration of each other had been somewhat satisfied, the sexual energy grew into electricity, which could have caused real sparks. Pulled into the process of experiencing something new, yet familiar at the same time, few words were spoken, though long, deep eye contact kept them glued, in reassurance to move further on. With arms entwined, more than a sigh or relief. A finality of having what one had wanted so much, yet more than either had known they desired.

Afterwards, it'd be considered similar to embracing a part of themselves, who had been loved, lost and now found again. As Julia surrounded him with her legs, Tomis' lips gently caressed her eyes, lips, hair, neck and slowly down her torso. Her body naturally lifting up to meet him, when he effortlessly glided into her.

Not a powerful thrust of taking her over, but smoothly slipping in, like knowing the way from personal knowledge of her. The pulsations brought a floating lostness aloft, which returned for them both, as if no need of physical control or action necessary on their part. They were mere entities of freewill, with no memory of time or place confining them, or having any restrictions. Long after, the full release of the physical tension, by their mutual organisms, they became solid physical humans again.

They were both so overwhelmed, and awed by the extent of their love-making, they were somewhat paralyzed. As their bodies came back to feeling movement, and the tingling reality of their sexual encounter, the energy in the room still vibrated around them. Truly, the dichotomy of something being celestial, while carnal at the same time, which just didn't seem something could be.

Tomis turned to kiss Julia, putting his hand on her face lightly, then pulling her over to him for a full embrace, as he continued to kiss her face, ear and neck. She had made him feel so much more, than he had ever remembered feeling before. He then thought of what he had read, *you can only recognize your soulmate, when you recognized yourself.* He had not understood it before, but now beginning to. It would take a while, before either of them could reconcile with what all had happened between them.

Neither of them, had ever been down *this* road before. Could all these feelings, they were both having be real? Could it be true, what they had both hoped for, but never truly expected to find, have just been given to them? The whole testing of how much can one endure, and still have hope to finally be rewarded by the Universe, with the gift of each other?

For Julia, she had thought in the past year, perhaps she'd had too many men in her younger years, so she'd never find her true 'one' to really love, who loved her also. Over time and acceptance, they would both understand their union a part of a healing process, they both deserved to have, in the giving to each other.

It would take time, even re-occurrences of questioning and hesitation, if for real, or would last. He held her tightly to him and mumbled as much to himself as to her. "I do not know what to say . . . I, I never felt anything …like with you before." He released her enough to once again look deeply into her glowing eyes, which still glazed over from the incredible experience. "You fulfill my dream . . . I afraid to dream." He again held her tightly, wanting them to meld together.

Julia's eyes finally focused and she whispered, "*That* … absolutely amazing and …incredible. I felt taken over, like an out-of- body experience. I mean, I don't really know what to say either." They kissed, clinging and curled around each other, murmuring espousals of exhilaration to each other, then drifting off. Since neither of them used to sleeping with another person, their *need* to be so enveloped with each other contrary to their habit.

How long, both of them had been wanting those tender touches, neither would realize any time soon. Upon awakening from the unaccustomed position, Julia found herself still on his chest, and began to kiss it. At first startling him, and arousing him into another session, leaving them both again evaporated. With the predawn, Tomis awoke first and brought Julia back to life with his caressing kisses, for one more satiating session. This time, it had been more carnal, as in knowing the depth of each other, and wanting to explore more of it.

Neither would understand the ramifications of sharing their raptures. It helped to release and dissolve Tomis' self-imposed guilt, regarding his wife's death. By allowing Julia, to take the lead some times in their sexual relationship, it told him their passion OK to enjoy, even savor. This created a whole new world for them both.

The mid-morning sunlight, from drapes left open, gently woke them from the amazing full exhaustion of their love-making. Considering both had little sleep, and expended emotional energy prior to the sex, what they had accomplished exceeded anyone's expectations.

Seeing it after nine, and starving from all of the exercise, Julia nudged Tomis, as she slid to the edge of the bed, "Come on Big Boy, let's take a shower together, and see if we can still get some breakfast."

He caught her arm, to pull her easily back to him, kissing and holding her for a few moments. He wanted to tell her again how all parts of the night had been to him. But she saw no need for it, "I really need a shower and vertical movement." She laughed, and slipped away.

He'd let it go for now, hoping to have some clarity later, on what or how she did feel for him. Even in his early years Tomis had never known a woman so open, and comfortable with her body and sexuality. It then dawned on them both, at about the same time, they were stark-naked in the morning light.

Julia chortled, walking from the bed, "Well, the mystery is gone now - what you see is what you've already had!" She grabbed-up her nightgown, hanging it from her shoulder, as she looked back over it, raising her eyebrows and rolling her eyes, then scooting to the bathroom. While she wasn't quite letting all her inner-self be seen, she allowed him to know more than what he'd experienced before. The layers, she'd mentioned were being peeled off.

A released playfulness in him, changed his behavior more than immediately cognizant to him. He chuckled and nodded, quickly following behind her, "I like what I see Lady!" Then, they both were laughing and giggling loudly, as the water came rushing over them.

Chapter 9
A Dinner Party

Only you know what you need,
to have joy and love in your life.
No one can tell you these things.
They *are* deep within you.

Only you know, when you know,
you can no longer just settle
for the illusion of happiness.
You do deserve true, pure joy.

What other people tell you,
will not make you happy.
Your knowing comes from within.
It is a truth which does not lie.

With the awakening process -
no longer repressing your true desires,
you learn to live in the present – not
the unknown future, or faulted past.

When you love without attachment,
there are no losses to knock you down.
There will always be goodbyes,
but not blows to bring you to your knees.

Being connected to a loved one,
is not the same as being attached.
Love extends beyond all borders,
when two souls meet with recognition.

True, real love exacts no requirements,
no list of demands and no strings.
This love removes all bars - cages,
from the hearts of each, to fly free.

As the car pulled up in front of Bloomingdales, Julia could see, not the same building she'd visited years past, on her last trip to New York. Nor, similar to the Bloomingdales in San Francisco. *"And, it certainly ain't Walmart, either!"* Julia said under her breath.

At the Concierge Desk, Tomis showed the woman the Consulate note paper, to see where they might find the woman Jelena had arranged for them. Staying out of bed, had not been easy for either of them. They promised to keep the touching and kissing light, with so little time, so many obligations.

Julia tried to fix her hair with mousse, and her make-up as best she could do. She must have changed outfits six times, when she asked if Luka, their driver had called yet.

He is not rude to call, he is ready when you are ready. Don't worry about it - not a problem," using her words again. He quietly watched her change the clothes, fix herself, look again in the mirror, all upset, and pull the clothes off to dig through her suitcase again and again.

He did not understand why she needed to dress-up s*pecial* to go shopping, when she'd always looked wonderful, when going with him sight-seeing. He knew, another *woman thing*, and he'd not question it, considering the nervous mood, she seemed to be in. Also, not understanding *it*.

She loved hearing him repeat phrases he'd heard her say so often - definitely a quick-study learner with his English.

"Oh, Tomis, you should have told me. I don't like to keep anyone waiting, it's so *rude of me*. And, I do need to learn some basic Croatian, so I can say, 'Thank you, Please, Nice to meet you,' etc." She walked out of the bathroom, and surprised him at how she looked.

"Is something the matter with how I look, you seem shocked or something?"

"No, no. I . . . you are dressed-up to go shopping. You look formal, I mean I do not know how to say it." When he saw her disappointed look, he corrected himself. "I mean . . . you look wonderful. I always see you more natural - casual. . . . Are you ready?" He just wanted to escape, when his English vocabulary limited him from saying what he needed.

In the store, Julia had preferred to take the escalator up, so she could get glimpses of the different floors, and see the variety of the people shopping on a Monday. Eleven when they finally met Jelena's Personal Shopper. And, she as surprised to see what they looked like, as they were to see her. Probably in her mid-50s, and of course, impeccably dressed with perfect hair and make-up, as expected of Bloomingdales.

She showed Tomis to a couch, saying she'd call his tailor, then whisked Julia off to the back room for a bra change to a corset, and a spandex-undergarment. She saw the woman pull down several dresses, and come back with several more before she even suggested one to her to try on for Tomis. No questions to Julia, as to what she might like, even colors. She explained, Julia should *try* her suggestions first, since *she knew* what people usually wore to the Consulate dinner parties.

Julia finally spoke-up, and insisted there would be no strapless, as she did have some concern for being too exposed, though she didn't want anything, too *wispy*. The woman looked at her in a most patronizing way, and while Julia expected it, she would not be trussed into some silly, gaudy, *fru-fru* dress. She took it upon herself to look through the selection and chose one to start the process.

Julia did not really want a black dress, but it did look great on her, though she thought a tad bit too low-cut for her full breasts. When she walked out to the display platform to show Tomis, he whistled at her in a teasing manner and his tailor, measuring him turned to look at her, also raising his eyebrows. "I think it's a little low-cut for first meeting these people - you tell me, how conservative are they?" The woman started to answer, but Julia turned, "No, I want him to tell me what he thinks. I may never see them again, but he probably will   Thank you, anyway." She had added, to soften her abruptness.

Tomis understood what she asked, so he honestly answered. "Men love it a n d you, of course. But women jealous, and make it difficult for me to work with husbands." As she turned to go take it off, he added, "But you want to consider it . . . for special night when *we* go out to celebrate? I think we can get two dresses for business party here and Zagreb, and also dress I buy for you."

Julia beamed at the woman leaving the area, when he called to her. "I have to go try tuxedo now." So, also be a party in Zagreb - another surprise. OK, she 'd just keep flying on this wave.

"I would like something a little softer, like Autumn colors to go with my hair or my eyes or a coral, not so heavy on the sequins or flashiness, OK?" Julia glanced at the price tags on the dresses the woman had chosen for her, none were under a thousand, with one over five thousand.

Even when she had money, she'd never been a clothes-horse, or into brand names, much less any designer fashions. She felt she'd always gotten great things, which looked good on her, without paying full price, or label oriented.

When Julia came out again, she looked like pure Autumn in a coral and gold background, with touches of garnet and creamy cocoa. The neck just low enough, with a sexy décolleté, and enough looseness, so the dreaded corset would not have to be worn.

Julia came up behind Tomis on the raised platform, waiting for him to see her in the triple mirror. His face soon glowing at her, as he turned to look at her straight on. He slowly moved his head back and forth.

Before he could speak, she swooned. "Oh, my God. You look

absolutely *gorgeous*! I'm going to *jump your bones* right here!" The muffled snicker from the tailor-made Tomis' face bright red. "I'm so sorry, it really did slip out," she whispered, up closer to him. She kissed him on the cheek, and forced an apologetic smile.

"I not sure I know what you say, but other people do." Her face now also red, as she whispered her apology again. "I am glad you like it, but I think too small N o t easy to move around."

Julia began feeling the beautiful suit material and the shirt, while nodding approval, when she saw the label of Aldolpho of Italy. She then picked-up the jacket, to look at the fit over his lovely butt. She very directly looked at his crouch, and bent down to look at the cut over his shoes. Though it had been a long time, she did know how to dress a man to show-off all of his assets, *and* give a good presentation.

"Are those the shoes you are going to wear tonight?" When he nodded yes, she continued. "You have been working so much, you probably loss a few pounds, then being with me, we probably ate a little too much. Here come and sit down on the couch, and see how it feels getting up again."

Neither the tailor, nor the woman could believe how she had taken over the whole evaluation. Julia followed him down the steps, and watched as he sat and rose again. "How did that feel? Anything pulling, or tight when you get up? I don't want you splitting your pants or anything." Julia had not moved her eyes from him, covering every inch of his gorgeous body.

Tomis knew he could be honest with her, while he probably would not have said anything to the tailor, and just tried to lose the weight. "Yes, you are right . . . pulling tight." Tomis then leaned over and kissed her on the cheek, "Thank you." The tailor rushed over to check the seams, and see how much of an adjustment he needed.

"So, you think this is a go for tonight?" Julia had walked back up to the mirrors, checking it from the different angles. She felt really good and beautiful.

"Yes, I like color for you, . . . remind me of beautiful forest in Michigan with you." He smiled, then looking down as the tailor tugged at the material over his butt. Again embarrassed, she realized how much he did not like to put people out, or make things difficult for them. She learned things, which had never come up before between them. As in his actions with her, she'd just considered him to be more chivalrous, than most American men.

Julia almost laughed out loud and asked, "So what color do you want for meeting the President, and how low cut?"

"He loves red, but many women wear it - they know . . . and if low, you do not leave my side." He laughed, and realized perhaps the woman would tell Jelena, . . . *but now, he didn't care.* It surprised him, how she had really changed him.

When Julia came back out, Tomis had changed back into his street clothes, and sat on the couch again. The dress a light turquoise, blue-green, which matched her eyes so closely, Tomis could not believe it. The décolleté, a delicate, see-thru lace, which revealed a lot up close, but not at all from a distance.

When he walked over to her, he whispered in her ear. "It is perfect. All jealous, and we get many invitations and much business." He kissed the back of her neck, no longer caring if the woman noticed them.

Julia giggled, "This is so much fun. I had no idea shopping could be this exciting." Though it a tighter fit, she did not have the spandex on, but decided to take it to make sure.

The woman came out with several light jackets and shawls to go with the dresses. Julia chose just one she felt would work for both. They were off to the shoe department, with the tux and her three dresses to be delivered by four o'clock. The two pairs of shoes went fast, with her insisting she had no intention on wearing the really high heels, since it'd been so long she'd done so.

Julia thought they were heading for the door, when Tomis steered her over to the fine jewelry department. She rattled off, "Oh, I brought my good pearls, and I have several semi-precious, even a beautiful amber necklace to wear. Also, I'm allergic to all metals except gold and platinum." She looked up at him and whispered, "Enough money has been spent on me."

Tomis cocked his head a little, then kissed her on the cheek, just as the sales person reached them. "Fine, you wear amber necklace for gold dress. I think something blue-green to wear with same color dress, and gold or platinum to wear with black dress." He looked at the salesman, "What can you suggest for my beautiful lady to wear with new dress for special dinner party at Consulate?"

Julia touched his hand at his generosity, and said his name quietly. A little surprised, as he had never done any name-dropping before. Perhaps he finally had acknowledged his success, and all of the hard work he'd put into it, the past three years.

Tomis truly wanted her to be part of *his* celebration. The salesman raised his eyebrows, then jumped into action bringing one bauble after another to entice them both. Tomis bought the aquamarine with the Consulate card, and the incredible long platinum knotted necklace with his credit card. They would also be sent out with the dresses and shoes for afternoon delivery to the hotel. Julia, a bit overwhelmed, thought of Cara's response again, all almost too-fairy- tale to believe.

Tomis then asked what Julia wanted to do next. She picked up his hand and looked at his watch. "Well, since it's after two-thirty, we could go have some decadent dark chocolate, or a big salad or go back to the hotel for a massage. We both need to relax before dealing with all of it. *If* they could do both of us at the same time, we could then do all three." She gave him her best perky smile.

"The chocolate now, the massages in our room, and the salad. I have to eat before we party, since I can't drink on an empty stomach - I'm not responsible for what I say or do otherwise."

Tomis laughed, put his arms around her, and kissed her in the main aisle of Bloomingdales. She felt like a new kind of Cinderella - something she'd never considered even possible. All kinds of wild analogies popped in her for the fairytale.

"But . . . do you want to go to beauty store . . . for party tonight?" Only trying to be helpful, he had no idea what insinuations he may have made.

Julia's head snapped to him, "I'm sure you mean beauty *salon*, and NO. I don't *think* so. I do my own make-up and hair. " She saw his shock and immediately toned it down.

"While this really fun, . . . and obviously a once in a life-time experience for me, for which I'm quite grateful to have been afforded.

. . I'm *not* a 'high-maintenance' woman, who needs things to feel good about myself. But, a massage is good." She hoped the broad smile made up for her perhaps confusing words.

"No, I think you look wonderful. I just think women go to beauty *salon*. I am sorry what I say upset you." When Julia saw his sad, clueless look, she laughed.

"I don't know what kind of women you are usually around - probably the out-of-my-league kind - but I'm not their kind. No problem, Sweetie, I'm sorry, I DO apologize. These emotions are definitely from my insecurities. I'll need all the *help and support* I can get from you, to make it through tonight." She leaned up and kissed his cheek, giving him a big smile.

Tomis very relieved, though still lost, as to what all she'd said. "I am very glad I met you, though you do confuse me. I cannot believe how you change my life so much, so fast." He smiled.

"Definitely, it is chocolate. I remember how you talk about it in Michigan." He called the hotel to see if they could get massages together, in their room, then called Luka. "We have massage at three- thirty, I order salads for after massage."With pride he added, "And, I know chocolate shop near hotel. We need to be at Consulate at six- thirty."

By the time they made it out the doors, Luka just pulling up. Tomis had already opened the back door, as Luka got out the front, so he got back in to drive. His smile from ear to ear, as never having seen Tomis so happy before.

~ ~ ~ ~ ~ ~ ~ ~ ~

Though they were both incredibly relaxed after the massages, they were also rather ravenously hungry, gobbling down their salads with sautéed salmon and warm French bread. A real temptation to jump back into bed, but since almost five o'clock, Julia knew she needed an hour to get ready and be presentable.

She joked with Tomis about how long it probably took for the woman at Bloomingdales's to call Jelena, and tell her how they acted while there. He laughed and shrugged his shoulders - she had not seen him do that before, and it made her happy.

Like a familiar married couple, Julia showered while Tomis shaved with a real razor this time. Then he showered, while she did her hair and put on her make-up. A comfortableness with each other, made them both confident of having a perfect evening. Julia also gave credit to the wonderful massages, for them to not be rattled or nervous about it all.

Tomis had actually dozed off, and the masseuse kindly said he could come back for the table, after they'd left for the evening. She took two twenties out of his wallet and gave them each one. She didn't wake him until the salads came, about fifteen minutes later, and she'd tipped the waiter also.

"I hope you know how to tie a bow tie, because I have no clue, *and* never even any good at regular ties." She backed up to him to zip up her dress, as she put her amber necklace over her head. He kissed her bare back, up from the top of the zipper and started around her neck.

"*Oooh, noooo.* You can't do *that* now, or we will never get out of here. You turn my legs into *jelly* as it is." She gave him a quick kiss on the chin, as she went to slip her shoes on, while holding the back of the chair to pull the strap over her heels. "We'll have some-thing exciting to come back to the hotel for, Sweetie."

He watched her, as he automatically tied the tie. "Since we Croates invented tie, it is pride and honor to know how to tie several different ways." He took his jacket off the hanger, and slipped it over his broad shoulders. "Do I really make your legs turn into jelly?" She nodded and giggled at his exact repeat of her words.

"I guess *'jelly'* mean excited with me." She nodded and giggled some more. "Then, . . . I think all evening of you *'jelly'* when I bored, and people ask same question, and I give same statement. Maybe you can have headache, or I make excuse for us to leave early." They were both laughing at their inside, intimate joke. "I want right word - I must study more words to say how wonderful you look. . . . You look perfect and beautiful."

"Thank you, and those words are perfect. The tux really looks good on you, and I'm sure it feels better, too. How long do these things usually last? And yes, you do make me wobbly, like jelly. It's a good thing we make love lying down, I don't think I could stand-up."

She giggled, but also knew they better leave before their pheromones overcame them both. She'd walked over to him and picked up his hand to look at his watch - it had become a new habit she enjoyed, as it had a function, and personal attachment at the same time.

"It's almost twenty after, and I'm sure Luka is waiting patiently. I'm ready, my Sweet. Just tell everyone I'm really Cinderella, and I must be home before midnight, or I'll turn into a pumpkin!" Julie giggled again at her new life.

Tomis thinking of the Beatles song they both liked, and hummed *"Something."* He took her hand and pulled her to him, even though he knew not to smudge her make-up, and kissed her on the lips taking her breath away. Now truly sexually involved with her, Tomis kept seeing her subtle-sexuality more in things she did and said.

He then again wondered why he'd not noticed before how sexy Julia could be, and if other men saw her the same way. He knew they were *magnetically* drawn together, so the more together they were, the more they wanted to be.

"I had to do that. I do not understand 'pumpkin,' but we definite leave before midnight." He moved past her to open the door, bowed and waved her through. "Other women are still jealous." Julia beamed, and blew him a kiss as she walked out of the hotel room.

Better than Cinderella, as going *to* the party *with her* Prince, she didn't have to look for *him* anymore. Though they had only had the one night together, no question, a hell of a night. Revealed in their actions and performance, while neither of them may have had sex in a while, they both certainly still had a sexual appetite.

~ ~ ~ ~ ~ ~ ~ ~ ~

Just before they were to enter the big ballroom, Julia had to confess. "You know, as I said before, I feel *totally* out of my league here, it's been a long time. It reminds me of meeting the head honchos of Toyota, when I only knew maybe six words of Japanese. I will keep repeating to myself 'I can do this,' but it is a stretch." He gave her a quick kiss on the cheek and smiled. Her smile in return very tight, but she put her best acting chops into action, as the door opened for them.

There were about a dozen people already socializing, when they arrived shortly after six-thirty. Petar called to Jelena, when he saw them coming in the door. He could barely take his eyes off Julia, while the smirk came across his face. He immediately caught it, when Jelena came into view, and changed it to a fixed smile. He had graciously taken her by the elbow to greet them, when Julia threw them both off by approaching first.

She greeted them warmly, with the perfunctory-hug and cheek kiss to Jelena, and Petar. "I've so been looking forward to meeting you, and thanking you for your generosity in dressing me for the evening." Before the stunned couple could respond, she continued. "Doesn't Tomis look so handsome in his new tuxedo? Again, thank you so much." She put as genuine of a smile on her face as she could, moving into full acting mode. She'd decided to kill them with sweetness and kindness now, so whatever she said or did later they'd rule to alcohol consumption without really eating.

Tomis followed suit by doing the hugging and kisses with a few Croatian words, followed by a full introduction of Julia in English. At the point, where not much Julia could do to really surprise him, believing she would not really embarrass him.

He reminded himself, she did know how to handle people well, and while most of them may not get her sense of humor - him still learning - they would be mesmerized by her talent in talking to them. Petar immediately took them over to meet the Ambassador, who had come up from Washington, and as expected, talking to the New York Deputy Governor.

Having accomplished those two priorities quite well, Tomis surveyed the room and excused them to meet other guests. He glided her around the room, by either elbow or his hand gently on her back - careful of her dress - she noted in his decorum, he also knew how to perform in public.

Julia careful to not let her sly smile stay too long on her face, when she thought of some of their more intimately-sexual moments together. So very proud of Tomis' imminent presence, and could see how he could be the *quintessential,* international businessman, going easily from English to Croatian and back to English.

Prior, he'd asked her what titles she wanted him to use for her introductions, since these were mostly business people. Then, he'd also asked her to clarify her education and what areas Julia had her degrees in. Along with this, if he could mention some of her clients she'd worked with in Japan. She repeated most of it in the past, but all of it mattered he insisted, to give her credentials. She knew some of it had to do with them now being involved, but also he said, because being a woman, and some of them may have a hesitation.

On the one point, he knew perhaps her being older a good thing. He'd taken full notes, but she had no idea when he had the time to memorize it all. Again, Tomis amazed her with how well he used *her* English words, though he made a point earlier, several times to take his English-Croatian dictionary out of his briefcase, to make sure he had the right words to explain it in Croatian.

Julia knew to stick to her scotch and water, and several times simply asked to have more ice added. She'd wait until after dinner before she touched the champagne, knowing what it would do to her. Some of the later couples were American, and either of Croatian decent, or very involved in tourism or transportation.

They were talking with two heavy-monied American couples, when a Croatian assistant came up to speak to Tomis. He excused himself to step back and quickly returned to apologize again. "I am sorry, there is phone call I need to take." When Julia looked at him questioningly, he responded: "It is President, calling to congratulate."

The older American businessman laughed, "Which one, mine or yours?"

Tomis smirked back, "Croatian one, of course," and quickly walked away. Julia slightly stunned, and unprepared for the additional information.

"Well," said the businessman, "I wouldn't have been surprised if it had been ours. He's made that big of an impact in New York. The Mayor supposed to be here, but he has the flu and sent his Second instead." He turned to look directly at Julia, "That's some man you're with, he's impressed the hell out of us with what he's already accomplished . . . practically on his own. But, he certainly knows how to make the contacts, and get what he needs *and* wants. I'm glad you seem to be about equal to him. Will this be your first trip to Croatia?" No question as to the power and influence of the man, and *he* probably knew both Presidents, maybe well.

Julia now realized how low-key Tomis had been, when he had referred to 'some powerful businessmen,' who had invested or were involved, or simply supported his work. She smiled, and tried to take a deep breath at the same time, to handle these multiple revelations.

"Yes, it will be, though I've traveled to several countries around the Balkan area. I did most of my international travel while working in Japan, as a corporate trainer. I had some nice long breaks of three to six weeks off at a time. It always gave me more to share with my business-trainees when I got back. The cultural understanding, one of the more difficult topics for them to grasp, as Japan is so insular, as you may know." She felt out of her depth, and needed some fill-in material.

"I know three weeks is not a lot of time to know Croatia well, but I hope enough to get a feeling of what all I can do, to help regarding training. Perhaps you can give me some pointers or suggestions, as to what to look out for, or be aware of?"

Always throw the ball back into the other court - as most people do like to talk about themselves. Rely on pure Dale Carnegie, as people particularly like to give advice. From the smile on his face, she knew she had at least a small hook in him.

Julia glanced at his wife, over-loaded with jewelry and the other couple, not quite as heavily decked out, but were intently listening, as well judging her. While Mr.

Big's wife not a trophy-one, definitely a second, and younger than Julia, while him, a good ten years older than Tomis.

She'd not have been shocked, if he had a still much younger mistress. The other man and his wife looked like they were close in age, though she'd obviously had a face-lift.

Julia thought her dress a bit gaudy, but probably much more expensive than hers. Yet, she knew still-water often ran deep, so no way she would ignore them.

Mr. Big had been rattling-off some basic things Julia already familiar with, but she'd cocked her head, to look like she listened intently. She even raised her eyebrows a few times, and glanced at the other couple, saying "Good to know," and later, "Yes, I've read something about it."

Only when he surprisingly brought up about the Organized Crime, did she truly pay attention. She then realized, Tomis had also *not* reiterated any of these details or concerns. When Mr. Big asked if she had any concerns for her safety, she knew she'd have to address them to him. Julia started with a light laugh, as not sure if just testing, to see how much she knew, or how easily frightened she may be. She took a breath, put the perfunctory smile on her face to let him, and the others know how confident in what she would be doing.

"First of all, I am not naive, and I am originally from Chicago. And, while it may not mean didli-squat, it does give me awareness. I have more than once faced a gun, including an AK-47. I think … in Abu Dhabi airport and also in South Korea. I am also an excellent shot myself, with both a handgun and riffle." She lightly chuckled. "And that *before,* I married my second husband, a Native Texan with a large gun collection. Not only a better shot than him, I do not scare easily by them."

Noting the shocked look and gasps from the women, she'd made points of not just being a pretty face, or naive woman. "I have also had training in workplace-bullying, which again doesn't mean much, except one of my degrees is in psychology. I usually read people well. I'm also a big fan of thriller - mystery books and action movies, though also somewhat irrelevant"

She chuckled lightly, smiled and continued. "Basically, it is how you respond, or react to someone at the onset, which sets the tone of how the whole scenario is going to play-out. It means observe, read all behavior and interactions between all of the players. If you are calm, and do not show fear, they may take it as respect or disrespect, if they are socio-paths."

She took a swallow of her drink. " Of course, if they are psycho-paths, you're literally-screwed, as anything can set them off, so just be as nice to them and pray for the best." Now, Mr. Big who had cocked his head, and listening to her, rather amazed by what she had said.

"From what I understand, and I could be totally wrong here, misinformed or generalizing. I think they are bullies-run-amok, scaring people because *they* are afraid of being dismantled, with Croatia joining the EU. Yes, I know they have killed an Editor and injured other people. I also understand, some of these criminals are displaced war-veterans, so they know most of the people still have residual-fear from experiences, or memories of the war. They are frightened easily, not wanting their families to be hurt in any way. Also, because of the unemployment, it may be easy to get people to help them, or rat-out information on others for money."

She another swallow of her drink. "This is what I think is happening with Tomis' problems with the Union. Not being there, or fully involved or informed - which I don't need to be at this time - I can simply say I have opinions, which may or may not be true to any extent." Julia smiled

While Mr. Big still processing all she said, the other man noded in agreement, while both women still in shock. "So, I hope it somewhat answers your question. I am going with as few expectations as possible, as I believe it is better to let things unfold, keep all my awareness up, but learn and take the experiences as they come."

Mr. Big about to respond, when Tomis had come from behind him to rejoin the group, slipping his arm around Julia's waist. She relaxed and said a quiet *'thank you'* to herself, not only for his appearance at the moment, but also for her years teaching Dale Carnegie, so knowing how to handle pointed questions. She smiled up at Tomis.

"I apologize again, the President wanted me to thank all of you personally for your support and involvement." He looked directly at Julia, "He is looking forward to meeting you, and . . . " he turned to the others, "your return visits for business or pleasure." Since they were all still in a slightly dazed pose not responding, he asked, "Has Julia been entertaining you with her travel and Japan-experience?"

Mr. Big gave a rather unexpected, very hearty laugh. "Well, Tomis, this is some *Lady* you got there, a real keeper, if you know what I mean . . . in more ways than one!" Julia looked at him with widened eyes, and a slight smirk.She understood so much more of the connotation than Tomis would ever comprehend, and glad about it.

"Well, thank you so much," she gushed. "I'll take it as a real compliment." It threw all of them, but Mr. Big. Then he surprisingly winked at her, as she beamed in return, indicating they had shared a secret. Tomis totally lost, but not really alone in what had just been said, and happened between the two people.

"She's told us she's not worried about those bullies in the Organized Crime group, and she knows you will handle it all just fine. I certainly hope she is right."

Then a forced laugh from Julia, and she avoided looking at Tomis, as she knew he must have a shocked look on his face. "Well, it's not exactly what I said, but I'm not afraid to go to Croatia. And, I do believe Tomis, and his group will get everything with the Union sorted out, to running smoothly again."

She now had one of her plastered, big smiles on her face, when she looked at Tomis. "I'm starving, and I don't want to drink any more until we eat. Do you have any idea how soon dinner will be served?" She took his hand from around her waist, and looked at the watch. *Shit, she thought, it's only seven-forty-five and he said they probably wouldn't eat until after eight.* The smile instantly back on her face, waiting for a response from someone.

Mr. Big loved Julia not one of those women who never talked about food, and ate like a bird. "You should try some of the hors d'oeuvres, with the shrimp or crab, they're real tasty and filling. Don't want you to not be able to drink! And, I can't wait to hear more about how you came to be facing AK-47s!"

Before Tomis could question, "Oh, it will have to wait for a less formal situation, when we're all together. I've got a ton of stories to tell from my travels." Almost abruptly, "Tomis, I want to go find some yummy hors d'oeuvres and get my drink refreshed." And, again to Mr. Big and his group, "So good talking to you all, and thank you for coming to celebrate Tomis' big night. We're having the photo-fest soon, aren't we?"

She looked at Tomis directly, so he knew it now time to move on, giving his own thanks to them for coming. She bowed slightly to them all, smiled her big smile, and took his arm to head in the direction of the bar.

She looked up at him, after they were several feet away, "I'll tell you all about it later, OK?" Then she added a little defensively, "He asked me, so I responded."

Tomis leaned down and kissed her on the cheek, "Yes, you can tell me all about it later." Again, repeating what she'd said verbatim, but this time it annoyed her. They'd just gotten to the bar area and she put her glass down, when the Croatian assistant came up to Tomis again, apologized to Julia, and spoke to him in Croatian.

Tomis nodded, "They are ready for the ceremony and photos, so we will have champagne now. Are you OK to drink it now?" Not sure how much she needed to eat, or how much an excuse to leave the other people. Still really learning more about her, and it did fascinate him.

"Well, if we pass a tray of hors d'oeuvres, I would like to grab a couple, while both hands are empty." She laughed and played coy with him, "I don't want to get all mushy, as you are getting honored." He looked at her, searching his brain to understand '*mushy*.' "Never mind, just find me some snacks." She pursed her lips to simulate a kiss and they both laughed.

Julia couldn't wait to call Cara, to tell her the wild things which happened. Tomis called to one of the waiters in Croatian, and he came over with a tray for Julia, who took a napkin and one of whatever in each hand. By the time they reached the steps in front of the podium, and huge Croatian flag on the wall, she had scarfed them both down.

After blotting her lips, she deposited the napkin on another tray with a "Thank you." Though she stayed back a foot or two, almost immediately six photographers snapping photos of her, as she realized they had recognized Tomis. He turned around, and several began shouting questions to him in both Croatian and English. This again so surreal, and she began thinking she had taking him off the successful- businessman-bachelor market, just as he reached real fame. It truly tickled her, and she almost became giddy with the thought of it all.

Tomis stepped over to her, put his arm around her shoulders and smiled, "Her name is Julia Martin, and she is a professional business consultant and trainer. She has traveled extensively, including thirty-six countries, so she is quite familiar with tourism and all kinds of transportation. I met her in Michigan, but she has lived in San Francisco, Hawaii and worked in Japan as a corporate trainer for seven years. She is from Chicago, and we look forward to having her work with us. Thank you."

Julia incredibly impressed with his perfect speech about her, and wondered how long it took him to memorize it, and *when*? He then repeated it all, from the city names she heard, in Croatian. "No, she does not speak Croatian, but English is a most important language we are learning." They stood there a few more minutes with continuous photos, and Tomis laughing at some of the questions being asked in Croatian.

She had tugged on his jacket with her hand behind his back, and he looked down at her questioning face. "I'll tell you later what all they said." It really cracked her up, and again pissed her off at the same time. Him smiling like the Cheshire Cat, made her almost lose it in front of them all. "Touché" she whispered at him, as this time Tomis' turn play coy.

Petar had stepped up to intervene, and thanked them, looking directly at several of the Croatians, as he did not want the questions to get any more risqué, or translated to the American press.

"Our President called to congratulate Tomis, and wanted me to thank all of you personally for your support and involvement. We are here to honor Tomis and his company with Croatia's highest award . . ." Tomis had guided Julia over to the dais, with the head table for her to sit, kissed her on the cheek, which one of the photographers nearest to them clicked and smiled. He looked directly at the man, he knew to be Croatian from other photo-shoots, and smiled back at him. He realized they were all quite thrilled he not only had a woman at his side, but obviously intimate with, and an *American* business woman *and* beautiful. In American terms, especially New York, it would be said he hit the *Trifecta*.

Tomis stood next to Petar, with his head slightly down and a serious look on his face. When Petar had switched over to all Croatian, a male interpreter had stepped-up, and began to translate into English the praises which were being lauded on Tomis. It went on for a good five minutes, with the giant

photos of the finished ferryboats being brought out by assistants, and all of the details of sizes, speed and cost. Julia more and more impressed, applauding at each appropriate moment. Finally, Jelena stepped forward with the velvet case and opened it for Petar to remove the large, intricate and ornate square cross hanging from the red, white and blue colors of their flag.

Tomis bent his head down and Petar slipped the ribbon over it, smoothing out the large ribbon on his tuxedo lapels. After he had given him the cheek kisses and hug, Jelena stepped up to do the same, then whispered something to him, at which point he smiled. Julia rose, as most of the audience had been standing anyway, and applauded loudly. A strange feeling, to feel so proud for someone she'd only met a little over a week before, yet had come to know so deeply.

Tomis stepped-up to the microphone to speak in both English and Croatian, with the interpreter trying to switch along with him in each language. When he thanked his American investors, supporters and those businesses so involved with Croatia, he spoke English.

Likewise, he did the others in Croatian, and switched back to acknowledge the American refurbishing company, pointing out their President, its affiliates and their workers, along with the shipping company. He then switched again to mention his associates in Croatia, with the ferries and the train lines. Then he thanked everyone else in both languages for coming and supporting him on this special day.

"Finally, I want to say, we look forward to our next chapter, with our new business consultant and trainer," he looked over at Julia and motioned for her to stand up. "Julia Martin, who is joining me in Croatia, to assess more growth and improvements. Thank you again, everyone for helping me with this project."

He then motioned again for her to come over and join him, as he posed with Petar and Jelena. Though a few photos had already been taken, the moment she got to him *and* kissed him on the lips, the lights were flashing continuously.

Julia then pulled away, and smiled widely showing how proud of him. Tomis held her tightly, then leaned down to whisper, "I'm so very happy you are here with me." When he kissed her on the cheek, the photo-lights again flashed. They were both openly laughing and didn't mind a bit.

Petar back at the microphone now telling the press thank you, as the assistant passed out the press packets to all of them in both English and Croatian. They were then escorted out by other assistants.

Petar then asked the guests to please find their seats, as dinner would begin shortly. There were ten of them at the head table, with the Deputy Mayor on their end, and the Ambassador and Deputy Governor on the other end, each with their wives.

Petar delighted to be sitting next to Julia, while Jelena sitting next to the Ambassador's wife, so he could sit next to the Deputy Governor's wife. They considered it improper to have a woman on the end. There were six round tables with six chairs, and the name tags appropriately situated for those connected groups at each table.

Julia watched, as the men guided their women to their seats and how similar many were dressed. She wondered how many Jelena's Personal Shopper had served, and if they talked about her dress's distinctively-different muted colors, and less flashy style.

As they were all getting ready to settle into their seats, Julia then noticed the younger woman coming directly across to Tomis. Still at the end of the table speaking to some businessmen, Julia had met earlier.

The men stepped quickly aside, as the woman barged up onto the dais, throwing her arms around Tomis and kissing him on the lips. Though taken aback, he gently removed her arms, excused himself to the two men, and began walking her over to a far table. The moment Jelena saw Vesna, she quickly rose from her seat, and went over to her and Tomis.

He kissed her lightly on the forehead, as Jelena immediately took her by the elbow to escort her out. It did not take a psychic to figure out, it had been Jelena's younger sister who'd had too much to drink. Obviously, she'd not handled Julia's total involvement at all, with the ceremony or him.

Julia thought herself, *"The woman obviously thinks she is a real princess, considering their royalty background, but certainly can't hold her liquor."*

Tomis stopped at the table with the two men, and again apologized to them, then continued up to the chair next to Julia. He stopped briefly to kiss the Deputy

Mayor's wife's hand, as he had stood to shake hands with Tomis.

Once he got to Julia, he kissed her cheek and apologized to her before sitting down. Neither of them said a word about the incident, as it had been all too easy for her and many others, to figure out what had just happened. Julia felt to speak of it, would only give it more negative energy, and she only wanted it to be positive for Tomis.

The next moment, as Petar stood, magically the champagne bottles began to be popped opened at each table, and at the ends of their table, with the glasses being filled. Petar once again thanked everyone for coming and supporting the project, Tomis and most especially Croatia.

The Ambassador and Deputy Governor then each stood to speak, and Julia recognized they had both spoken to Tomis right after the ceremony. When they finished, the Deputy Mayor spoke, making a point to thank them for buying the Staten Island Ferries, and wished them God-speed in their new, long life in Croatia. Petar asked Tomis to speak, and he briefly said thank you to all again.

Once he sat back down, he looked exhausted, and Julia could understand all of the pressure which had been building, for so long finally over. This time she leaned over, and kissed him on the cheek. She then told him how good his English had been for his speeches, and how wonderful to share all of this with him.

"I am tired and I want to eat and go back to our room and be together. I am tired of talk."

He looked at her, and kissed her again with a slow smile. "But, I do not get tired of talk to you." Since most of the ceremonially stuff now finished, Petar wanted to talk to Julia, and Tomis happy to be quiet. Several of the servers had left to bring out the food, as others continued to refill the champagne glasses, or open the red and white wine bottles to pour them, too.

Following the dinner, they were both expected to stay and schmooze with everyone until they began to leave. If it had been up to Tomis, they would have left right after Julia got her chocolate dessert, though they did have a good laugh with it.

Once they stood and stepped down to the floor, they didn't even need to walk around, as most people were waiting to speak to them - when one couple or group moved on another followed. Julia now understood what Tomis had meant about answering the same questions and repeating himself over and over. He had held unto her hand, or kept his arm around her shoulder or waist most of the time.

In between people, she had slipped away to the ladies' room, and when she coming back, she saw Jelena speaking closely with Tomis. He seemed to just keep nodding his head for 'yes' and shaking it for 'no.' Apparently, he did not want to actually talk to her about the situation with Vesna. When he noticed Julia, he waved his arm for her to join him, and it worked like a charm for Jelena to leave. As she passed Julia, she said she said, "Glad *you're* having a good time."

They had already been on the dinner entree when Jelena had returned to their table, and Vesna never did return. Again, Tomis said nothing and Julia didn't ask. If nothing else, it must have clarified to him, he certainly had made the right decision to go to Michigan, rather than stay in New York. Amazing how synchronicity works.

Since now only a half dozen people left, Tomis decided to go up to them and do more thank you's, so they could leave. He had made sure Julia had been introduced to each and every one of the business people, so they would have no question as to her qualifications or experience. Thorough, as Mr. Big had said, very good at follow through with the contacts he made.

Almost ten, as they approached Petar and Jelena, with Julia again being the first to do the hug and cheek kisses. She got a kick out of the fact, while Jelena had tried to hold her away, Petar had made sure it a real, full-body squeeze against him.

She whispered in his ear, calling him *'a real sweetie,'* and he squeezed her again. He said something to Tomis in Croatian, and he responded only by shaking his head. As they were leaving, Petar said in English, "See if you can come by tomorrow before you head to the airport."

"I do not think we can, many things we have to do. Thank you again." Tomis took the shawl from the assistant, and put it around Julia, squeezing her shoulders lightly. Luka waiting as usual, and opened their door. Tomis patted him on the back and said something in Croatian, which made him laugh. When he slid in next to Julia, he again surprised her. "I have fallen-in-love with you, and I do not know what to do."

"Oh, my God! I have, too." As Luka's car door shut, and he drove them away, they were both silent. All Julia could think, *this was NOT supposed to happen.* All she had wanted, really just a romantic adventure. She had no plans of falling-in-love, especially not with a man who seemed much too nice, for how difficult she could be.

Chapter 10
Tourists

In solitude, I surrender myself to music,
and many songs so touch my soul.
Notes familiar or new, dance across my heart,
bringing tears of both sadness and joy.

You understand how it can be, as for you, too.
Whether memories stirred of kisses given and loss,
or chips, cracks, and dents left embedded,
from previous forays of love, and living life.

I see in you, reflections of myself –
the me who was, and the me who is to be.
Our love and happiness go hand-in-hand,
with dreams and hopes we have to fulfill.

I feel there is a part of my heart,
as a part of yours, beating in-sync.
I can think the way you feel –
having felt those thoughts, also.

Words of love you sing, I understand deeply –
having sung them, oh so often myself.
I will be your true friend, partner,
confidant, cohort and comrade in love.

Our hearts in rapture from this nourishment,
which fulfills beyond a purified luxury.
It touches a consolation of compassion,
unbound, and unlimited by any restraints.

There's an old saying, 'a bell rung, cannot be un-rung,' Thus, what we say to one another, can rarely be taken back or un-said.

A short ride to the hotel, but Julia still took Tomis' arm to put it around her, as she curled-up on his chest. He held her close, as both exhausted from the mixed emotional and physical endurance, of 'being on display' for almost four hours.

While Tomis had all of the constant English speaking to do, Julia had so many different parts to play, to satisfy so many different people. She seriously wondered if anything she said or did, would cause any problems for the business, or his investment relationships. Then, the whole embarrassment of the alcohol-induced display by Jelena's younger sister Vesna, though Julia had never asked her name or mentioned it. The situation would shadow Jelena for some time, and Julia hoped she would not be blamed, or brought into it.

When the car pulled-up to the hotel, Tomis removed his arm as he opened the door and helped Julia out, neither still had spoken a word. Luka followed them around the car, when Tomis said nothing to him, he then asked (in Croatian) presumably what time they wanted him in the morning. Julia now on the sidewalk heading toward the door, and Tomis apologized, saying he'd call him, and thanked him again for all of his assistance. Concerned by his actions, Luka then asked if everything all right. Tomis hesitated, then said just very tired, and thanked him again. The doorman held the side door for Tomis, and he slowly strode across the lobby to the elevator where Julia waited for him. They entered it together, and once the door shut, they embraced each other without kissing. Like they were keeping each other afloat, or they would drown in the emotions of it all.

Once the door opened on their floor, they released each other, but continued holding hands to solemnly walk into their room. When Tomis pulled the card-key out and opened the door, Julia walked ahead as usual, put her purse on the round table by the flowers and her shawl on the chair near the desk. "I don't think we should talk about our feelings right now. I think we are both too tired and . . . I'm feeling very emotional. I think we should start with fresh heads in the morning. OK with you?"

Tomis not sure what all she said, and perhaps his revealing of such strong feelings had frightened her off of him, and everything else. He took off his jacket and put it on the back of the desk chair, and undid his tie. "Do you want me to sleep on couch here, or get another room." He suddenly felt like a rejected, naive fool.

Julia had taken off her shoes, and ran to him almost crying, "Oh, God NO!" She threw her arms around his neck and tried to kiss him, but he would not respond. "I think, ... I just don't want to make a decision about how much I love you right now. . . Though I don't know how much more time I would need, . . . to know - to make such a decision."

Tomis sank down on the chair, and she leaned on his knee with her bare feet still on the carpet. His arms wrapped around her tightly, and he kissed her heavily on the lips, and her neck.

Julia had to pull away from him, so she could tell him the full truth. "I knew . . . Wednesday evening, as you drove away with Talia,

... I had fallen in love with you. . . honestly very frightened, because my head kept saying, ... I didn't know you long enough to know if real or not D o e s that make sense to you?" She kept looking at his face.

"Can you understand what I'm saying? . . . I feel like a frightened, little girl who is afraid to believe ... she's found the love of her life,. after knowing him less than a week."

He again held her very tightly, pulled her away slightly, and kissed her again before responding. "Yes, I do understand completely. .

. . I also feel like frightened boy ... afraid to believe he has found love of his life." They both lightly laughed.

Endearingly, she told him, "I just love it when you do that - repeat what I said!" She shook her head frustrated, but laughing at it all. She pulled herself together. "I guess my bigger concern is... I have always, A L W A Y S made it a rule, to NOT get involved with anyone

I worked with, or for. Do you understand what I mean?"

"Yes, I think you mean sex and love. You are correct. ... But you also say many times, 'Not a problem,' for many things. ... And, for me it is true - *not a problem*. You are professional, and I am professional - correct?" He looked at her, half-serious and half- sarcastic using her own words. "You also say many times, ... 'I can do this.' And, ... I believe we can."

"This does not seem like a fair discussion I can win, ... when you are using my own words against me." She did love him, and his logical, brilliant engineering-brain.

Tomis kissed her again, and said very calmly, "I love you; I know that. It is not a decision for me. We do not have to make any decision now We do not have to *do* anything about it. ...It can be

secret if you want I am very glad you feel same. I was afraid you

want me go out of your life, and for me . . ." He shook his head. ". . . very painful."

"NO, no, I'm so very sorry about my confusion, and not being able to explain it all to you. I very much want you in my life,... and to be with you, ... as much and as long as I can." She got up off his knee, "I think I better get this dress off before something wild happens to it." She turned her back to him, "Will you unzip me, please?" The energy in the room then changed and swelled exponentially.

"My pleasure!" He unzipped the dress slowly, with wet kisses following down her spine until she squirmed and danced away toward the bedroom. "Are you Jelly?" He quipped.

"Yes, I'm Jelly and you better get your tuxedo off, *you stud,* before I tear it off of you, and waste a really nice suit!" She'd thrown her beautiful dress across the settee, undid her bra, pulled off her panties and under the covers, as before on her hip waiting, when he came in wearing his boxers again.

"I am *stud now*, is what you call me?" He sat on the bed and slipped off his shorts and under the sheet, she had pulled back for him. "Yes," she giggled. "I am only doing all of this *for your body,*

nothing else - no job or trip. I only want you and you alone!"

"Good, it is mine, all I have..............no investors." The laughs were

muffled, as the kisses took over, and amazingly (duh!) they both became reenergized with the sex.

~ ~ ~ ~ ~ ~ ~ ~ ~

The international phone began ringing after midnight, in the sitting room, but woke them both. Tomis up against Julia's back, with his arm wrapped around her, and his hand tucked under her breast, holding her close. When he jerked awake, she came into a fog, barely understanding what he said.

"It must be important; they know celebration tonight." He kissed her on the forehead, "Go back to sleep, I come back soon." He grabbed his shorts from the floor, struggled into them, getting over to the phone, on the desk in the other room.

Julia slowly pulled herself up, to trundle into the bathroom to pee. Then she put on the hotel robe, which she'd not worn before, and enjoyed its comfiness. They had not closed the drapes - again, so she stopped to look out the window at the city lights she loved, staring at them all.

Wandering over to the round table, she turned on the light and noticed Tomis' open briefcase on the other chair, with several English- titled magazines in it. Then she noticed the hardcover book, and picked it up to see George Elliot's classic *Middlemarch.* Her eyes widened, he'd not only been truthful about his reading, but a woman writer of the 19th century! Duly impressed, Julia once again learned more about this man she'd fallen in love with.

On the phone, Tomis occasionally raising his voice, then quickly controlling it, and bringing the pitch almost to a whisper. Of course, speaking in Croatian, so it really didn't matter, as Julia had no clue what it could be all about.

She knew the cargo carriers with the three boxed-up ferries were set to sail in the morning, and wondered if the problem, then realized they would be speaking English. *"It is Tuesday, isn't it?"* She had to think, as the time had all been so squashed together for over a week now.

She had suggested going down to the dock to see it off, and while a thoughtful gesture on her part, he insisted really nothing much to see. He'd said, since they were each in their own protective boxes, and he had no clue where on the gigantic ship they'd be, it wouldn't matter.

Oh well, it would've been fun to her, as she'd never seen a carrier leave, which actually had something on it she knew of personally. Down at San Francisco Bay, she loved watching the going and coming, fantasizing what might be in those containers.

Tomis then trotted back in and went directly to the bathroom, still speaking on the phone. Since he had only partially closed the door, the sound of his pee made her giggle. He then flushed the toilet and she heard the faucet run rinsing his hand. When he came back through, he gave kind of a twist of a hand wave, continuing back to the sitting room. The whole scenario like a Marx Brothers' comic scene and made her giggle.

Julia thought of using his computer again to email Cara, but picked up the magazines instead. She quickly recognized them as being international-European English editions, of the top business and culture magazines. It brought back her memories of reading the Asian- Japan versions of Fortune, Time, Newsweek and others. She had often used them as discussion classes for her management-trainees.

She looked to catch the dates and cover stories, then suddenly recognized Tomis, as being in the center of a group of three men and a woman. Title underneath regarded new trends in tourism, from the budding new countries of the old Soviet Blocks. Coming up on, almost twenty years since the war had blown them all apart and free.

While the magazines were each fairly new, their main theme of tourism and joining the European Union - obviously one had a direct affect on the other. This also reiterated to her, his excellent use of English, regarding the trending terms of business acumen.

Sitting down at the table, she put the other two magazines back and naturally opened up the one with him on the cover, searching the index for the story. She flipped to the page, and began reading more about this man, she knew she'd barely known over the last week. She picked-up a few bits and pieces, but surprisingly much of what it said about Croatia and even Tomis, she already knew.

It talked about how the generational-family business, of fishing had segued into ferries. The business growing, as his father expanded into crossing the Adriatic over to Italy. But Tomis, had led the way with the new 'light-rail' passenger trains, directed towards the tourists to get them from one growing hot-spot to another.

One word jumped out at her, and not sure why. It mentioned almost too casually, "following the *tragic* death of his wife and daughter in the early years of the war, he threw himself into his businesses. . . "

All deaths in war were tragic, why was 'his wife and daughter' singled out, and how would this fit in as relevant, to the topic of tourism? She let it go, knowing not a topic for discussion at this time. She glanced at the top of the article, to see who had written it and registered the name for future reference. She had finished the article, but studying the photos when Tomis came back into the bedroom.

"I apologize for wake you and also raising my voice." Julia looked up at him, and shrugged her shoulders. She then noticed,Tomis obviously still very upset over the phone call, but she would wait for him to tell her about it.

"It is … bad news from my office. I feel they did not handle well." He shook his head, as if all his fault for not being there to take care of it. She could tell his hesitating in telling her some-thing. He knew he had to, or it would spoil their last night together, before being thrown back into the reality of his life.

Gathering the words not easy, as he knew Julia had learned how to read him. And, he recognized her intelligence when it came to business. Tomis moved his briefcase to the floor and sat down across from her at the table, yet unconsciously on the edge of his chair.

He leaned forward to put his hands together in front of him, so almost touching her knees. She closed the magazine, placing it back on the table, knowing not the time to comment glibly about him being a 'cover boy.'

"I tell you before, we have problem - the unions, and is usual

… from success - they want fair share, and OK. But problem is Organized Crime get involve, . . . see it way to get easy money and control. They . . . interfered worker groups . . . "

Julia interrupted with "infiltrated?"

He thought a moment. "Yes, better word, infiltrated and pay protesters to stir up . . . and threaten workers to join *their* union, not one our government support - one worker join for many years." He took a deep breath, knowing this could be convoluted and confusing, so not sure she would understand all the ramifications.

"It is very involved, but bottom line, some workers, tourists and local by-standers . . . " He looked at her to make sure he had used the right word and she understood him. She nodded.

"Some get seriously hurt. Tourist season almost over, not worry too much . . . internet word-spread. We must clean-up … and straightened- out before Christmas holiday season here." …

Here came the kicker he's not wanted to tell her. "I am sorry, but soon we get there, I must leave to go and straighten out . . . my brother, Ivo . . . made promise to them." Tomis shaking his head and squeezing his hands together, obviously very angry.

"He thinks he avoid trouble, . . . but you cannot … give-in to these people . . . the demand have no merit or support from majority of workers. Also, need to know worker involve and why. . . . I mean, if families get threaten, I must get State Police involved. I do not want to

. . . they are violent also, 'shoot-to-kill,' I think is phrase. So, if no family fear, only take pay-off money, … I need to fire worker We hire many new people in tourist season, and they know get laid-off for slow time, … so may be open to bribe, or easy listen Organized Crime-union people."

Too quickly, Julia rose out of her chair and walked over to the bed, pursing her lips as she turned back towards him. "How incredibly stupid are these people? Do they really think they can put-off the inevitable, by their ridicules strong-arm tactics? They are stupid, *archaic, atavistic* bullies, like leftovers from old B-gangster movies!" Standing there shaking her head, with her fear blowing them off, as if ignoring them would make them go away.

Tomis quickly rose from his chair, striding over to her and strongly placed his hands on her shoulders. The physical act took her aback, as he had never touched her so hard. She then saw a frightened look in his eyes, as in a forewarning of her ignorance being dangerous, in ways she had no idea of.

"*Julia, Please!*" His words were begging her in a way she did not understand, and the fright grew in her eyes.

"I do not understand all you say, … *please* do *not* under- estimate these men, they are … criminals, very organized, they are *not* threatening bullies. They *kill* people for say things against them . . . and *kill* who try to stop them. … They care nothing for human life - men *or women* . . . they think they get control by physical - brutal force. ... PLEASE do not get involve, ... you must be careful *what* you say . . . *people* you say things. ... Many informers on payroll everywhere . . . and *now* in my company union." He didn't want to think how they'd react to her.

"I don't understand. Are you saying a group of sociopaths or psychopaths, just go around extorting money from businesses and get away with it?" It seemed incredulous to her; such a thing could still be happening so openly. "Do you mean you have a group of Russian-Soviet mobsters running around trying to control business in Croatia?" Julia back to shaking her head, not wanting to fully believe him in the danger he predicted. She felt him just being way over protective, her independence rose-up to argue, as no shrinking viole,t or dainty girl who needed protection.

Tomis released her shoulders, shrinking in apology for the rough gesture and retreated to sitting on the bed. "More than Russian mobsters or psycho-paths. I think you read about Croatia . . . you know organized crime violence is major concern. Our government very serious . . . problem threaten EU membership. Court sends mobsters to prison, more group rise-up. This is why State Police shoot- to-kill, show government serious to stop mobsters."

He sighed deeply, knowing he must make her understand the whole picture and his involvement. Tomis patted the spot next to him on the bed for her to sit down, so he could calmly give her details.

He knew Julia frightened, but did not want to admit to it. She walked over and sat down with his arm gently going around her, pulling her to him. He pursed and pulled his lips in, gathering the words he needed to get her to accept his concern, as well his need to protect her from them and herself.

"There is much history to all … beyond our civil war, and is…. complicated. I know you can understand, if I can explain . . . we call them Soviets, they are not Russian people." He breathed deep.

"We call them *left-overs* from Soviet control - Slavic …countries and more. These people - many generations - never know respect except

… brutal force and power. They never know happy living - love or family or think of future happy. Life end," he snapped his fingers and Julia actually flinched.

"Any time - turn against other to move-up group … for more power. Look for people weak spot - addiction, you say to exploit - gambling, drugs, liquor or sex - and control or make do …what they want or turn on people to destroy and get more power. Most people very afraid … after long war … but weak, so keep silent or worse, inform gangsters. … They think they safe, or not get hurt. Not true, gangster hurt many . . . they finish job, … so no need now."

Tomis put his other arm around her and drew her closer, so he looked directly into her eyes. "People like this in America, … long time ago. And, now in your Southwest - Mexican drug-gang . . . kidnapping, ransom and many innocent people die. All about money and power." He moved his hand to her neck and chin. "I love you, and care about you very much. … I never forgive myself if I bring you to my country … and you get hurt." He moved his finger to her lips, as about to speak up in protest, still not wanting to believe in the reality of it all.

"You must   *Must* promise me you NOT *do* or *Say* thing or talk to people *joking* this ... " As her eyes were questioning, he clarified. "I mean make fun, or laugh at them be *bullies*. … I know." Kind of smirking himself, "you do have a way of '*spurting things out*,' as you say. Jelena say to me, she hears you are *impetus* - I think is like outspoken, and you say this too. But not joke . . . and cannot apologize ... what you say about them. Do you understand?"

She glanced down and nodded her head in agreement. "*Julia*, you must say *out loud* - promise me you take seriously, and not say or do thing to anger them or . . . I send you back to Michigan *now!*" He wanted to shake some sense into her, with *fear-feeding his* anger.

She pulled back away from him, a little upset about being treated so naively. She pressed her lips against her teeth, resenting how he looked at her so seriously and sternly, but she also knew he meant it. She tilted her head down, so any good face-reader could have known, how much she did not want to say what she knew she had to say.

"OK, I promise I will take all of this seriously. I won't joke or make fun of them, or say things to other people about them. But, why are they targeting you? What have you done; they are trying to extort money out of you?"

Tomis released her and slumped back a little. "First, 'Thank you' for promise, and I *remind* you, if I need to." He got up and moved back to the desk to pick up the magazines. "It is all '*my rising success*,' involved in tourist business - 'our *fastest growing business*' and . . . 'connected to government,' because of it."

He took a deep breath. "Any business person who support our strict government law against crime, organized crime, is target. We very much want to join EU. To join, mean we *equal* to other European countries, and very good for business. EU made clear; we must clean- up all organized crime. My growing business ... *vulnerable* to vandalism, we have some small bombing of my trains. Because my new ferries come, they try to exhort money from ferries ... business, . . . and try to take control union and people work for me." He slumped into the chair.

Real fear beginning to cross Julia's face again, but for him, not his trains or ferries being damaged. "I do not mean to frighten you, I have security - government and private, I hire last year. . . . Maybe I need to think more about this, … and not bring you back with me." He put the magazines down, and stared at it all in front of him. "You add… 'new element' to security risk, they tell me Maybe it safer … to

send you back now, … and come back in six months" His mind

now off, figuring what would be safer for her.

"No!" she almost yelled out, with his head turning to see her really upset. "I *can* do this, I promise, *really* . . . I promise, I'll be good, and not piss anybody off I *can* bite my tongue and pretend to

be nice to them all   and pretend everything is OK."

She stood up and walked over to him. "Please don't send me back, I *want* to do this, I want to be with you. I love you and really

care deeply for you also, and . . . I just want to be with you. . . .

Remember, we are '*meant*' to be together, and whatever happens … is meant for us to be together … as it happens."

The word had a commitment, which brought so much more than they could handle into the picture right then. She reached him, as he rose from the chair. They kissed with a passion neither of them wanted to admit, filled with so much love, tinged by fear if losing the other.

When they had paused to breathe, she pulled back slightly, and looked him directly in the eye. "Remember when I told you, I used my affirmation of a Golden Light around protecting me, and a White Light in front, guiding directing me safely on any of my trips?"

He nodded, but his eyes were questioning how words could help them. "I want you, to *promise me,* you will use it for yourself. And also, direct it towards me, whenever you think of me, and I will do the same for you. We can live through the fear, as long as we don't *live with it* - . . . which means not be thinking of it."

Tomis looked at her once again with amazement, as to how she could think of such a thing, after all he had said to her. "Again," she emphasized, "remember - '*anything you keep thinking* of, you *feed it* your energy,' so don't think about fearing them, it gives them power. Only think, *remember* we are both protected, as we are the *good-guys* here, with a purpose." She smiled.

He wanted to believe her, but he had seen the brutality they had done, and the lives they had destroyed - including his own during the war. Being positive *would not* be easy, but being negative did not get him to what he had accomplished, so he did know to believe. Just her presence with him, these past few days had made his life already, so much better and happier. He felt relief, she had so insisted on going on with him. But, he'd also gotten a pinch in the back of his neck, when he thought of what a vulnerable, loose canon she could be.

Tomis thought of the visualization of the Golden Light she'd taught him, and seeing the White Light guide him. Yes, having her around did make it easier to remember to be positive, and believe they were protected. He must believe it for her sake. *But,* he would also get another security detail just for her.

"Yes, I promise I think of it, but it takes more than words. I get more security, too." He tried to put a smile on his face for her, but not easy.

Julia shook her head, ignoring what he said, actually slipping into her Pollyanna stage. "Now, lets get back to bed. We are supposed to play tourist tomorrow and sight-see New York, before we leave. We are *not* going to talk about this again, promise? I made my promise to you, and now you make this one to me." She put her forefinger in her cheek, and twirled it, smiling.

He shook his head a little, letting it all go. "I promise." She threw her arms around his neck and kissed him deeply. Julia then pulled him over to the bed, where she tossed herself across it, and untied the belt of her bathrobe for him.

"These are really nice robes; *we* should get one for *me*." She laughed, rubbing the gold insignia. He sighed deeply, at how hopelessly-silly she could be sometimes, yet knowing one of his favorite endearments about her. He slid down beside her, kissing his way up from her belly, as they once again began to enjoy each other.

~~~~~~~~~

Julia mentioned to Tomis not to hesitate to make any calls he needed, especially in the morning when they were getting organized. She just wanted him to give her an idea of how long they would be, so she could either call Cara, or do her emails on his laptop.

This way, she said they could both get their necessary personal things done, without the other waiting. Going to be a rather simple day, with a ride out and back on the Staten Island Ferry, then a poignant visit out to the 9/11 Memorial Site. Julia hoped they'd also have time for a long drive through Central Park, to have some colorful, tree-time before needing to come back to finish packing.

Long before they went down to breakfast, she called the front desk for his tux, her dress and some laundry to be done, then bagged for the trip. Tomis had said their exit time, regarding traffic, should be around four o'clock, for the seven o'clock flight out.

The day before, Luka had picked up a garment bag, large enough for the three dresses and his suits. He'd drop her passport off at the Consulate to get the Visa put in, and they'd pick it up on their way back to the hotel.

Julia into her semi-casual-professional look, more because it *was* New York, and also because she planned to wear the outfit on the plane for comfort. She planned to shower and change clothes in Paris, so she could arrive fresh in Zagreb, for the people meeting them there. Her colorful top, fresh underwear and frilled skirt fit easily, rolled-up into her tote bag. She had bought the brightly-colored outfit, on a whim at a super-sale in San Francisco. She then had something special to wear for her artist friend's last show. When deciding to bring it to the Upper Peninsula, she doubted she'd ever have a chance to wear anything like it. Something had now told her, *the* perfect outfit for arriving in Zagreb.

She had her passport in a small manila envelope, and took it out of her shoulder bag for Tomis, as they approached the car. He handed it to Luka, holding the car door with some instructions in Croatian, as Julia slid into the back seat. While Tomis talking to her about riding the Staten Island Ferry, she noticed Luka had spoken into a two-way phone shortly before they pulled up to the Consulate.

The moment they stopped, a man came out and around to Luka, to take the passport envelope, and immediately returned into the Consulate. Just as quickly he had sped the car off, gliding through traffic to the humongous Whitehall Street Terminal pier, in lower Manhattan where the ferries were.

Tomis helped Julia out, as Luka came around speaking rather directly to him, and Tomis kept saying 'no' several times. Luka looked upset, as Tomis calmly gave him some instructions. He placed his hand on Julia's back, and guided her toward the entrance to the waiting hall. Momentarily, she thought how different now from the laid-back man, she'd toured with in Michigan.

Julia then looked around at it all, as she'd not been there since its renovation in the mid-90s. The panoramic views, of the downtown Manhattan skyline and waterfront from the rooftop viewing decks, were magnificent. They had a twenty-minute wait, since off-commute hours, so they sat on a granite bench, after walking all around. The art installed on the benches entitled "Whitehall Crossing" and depicted Indian canoes crossing New York Bay.

Being such a beautiful fall day, Julia wanted to sit on the open deck for the short twenty-five minute-five-mile ride. She talked about her first trips on the famous Star Ferries, which made the crossings from Hong Kong to Kowloon twenty-four hours a day. Ferries had always been a fascination for her, and Tomis talked also about other ferries he'd ridden.

Julia then commented how she loved the "Old Style" appearance and ambiance for the new ferry. When she read each new boat had a price tag of about forty million dollars, rather shocked. "I read the Ferries were constructed at Marionette Marine in Wisconsin, so they are made in America. In case you don't know, it's just south of where Cara lives."

She continued to rattle on, "These ferries certainly do have quite a history, dating back from the Civil War, to helping transport people after the 9/11 attack on the World Trade Center, and one ferry even being made from the its steel girders."

Tomis smiled at her, but polite enough not to tell her, he knew all those facts and probably a lot more. "OK, I'm sure you know all of it. Still, I can't wait until I get to ride on your new ferries. I must admit, I like your national colors better than these Safety Orange ones. But this really is a wonderful, if short ride."

"I do not think they go in service before Christmas holiday, but you can see them arrive, if you want." Trying to be in a good mood, but a concern on his face. He'd given her a quick smile and returned to looking out over at the perfect view of The Statue of Liberty and Ellis Island. "I know the Statue is source of pride for all America. Talia talk about crying when she see it, and know she is safe in United States."

"I know you are enjoying your ride, but you seem concerned about something. Everything OK with Luka?" She knew he heard her, but he continued to look the other way. "Luka isn't just your driver is he? He is also security here, . . . am I correct?"

Tomis looked down, as he slowly turned back towards her, and put his arm around her shoulders, squeezing them a little. Almost a snicker, with a little shake of his head when he finally looked at her.

"Sometimes you are too smart, even you do not speak Croatian." He took a short breath and watched, as the St. George terminal on Staten Island grew closer. "Yes, Luka is one of my security details. He receives many phone calls from Croatia, and he did not want us to travel on ferry without him. But, I want alone time with you."

His smile still trying hard not to be forced. "There is very nice Tropical Fish Tank at St. George terminal, we can look before we return to New York City." He got up and took her hand to walk towards the front, to get the view of the docking. He began pointing out the different steps and procedures, the pilot and his men on each side we're going through, to get the giant ferry into its dock. She wondered then, how many years he'd done the similar job in Croatia, but still loved watching it?

While listening to Tomis talk about whatso familiar to him, succinctly and calmly, she thought how he continued to protect her, and not want her to be frightened. How silly and naive she'd been thinking she - they - could go untouched. Glad she'd not been dumbed enough to ask if Luka carried a gun, obviously a moot point of discussion, when dealing with Organized Crime. Visions of telecasts of the Mexican Cartel flipped through her brain.

Most of the tourists had vacated the ferry by the time they exited, and headed over to the two 1,600-gallon salt-water fish tanks. Julia still determined to perk Tomis' feelings up, so she began to tell him how her son Jeremy had always loved fish, and even had a 125 gallon salt water tank he'd made himself.

"When growing up, I tried to make it a point to take him to places which had aquariums on our vacations, or the various places I lived he visited. My personal favorite has always been jellyfish, and the Monterey Aquarium in California. How about you?" She smiled brightly at him, and he became more than willing to have her take him out of his funk. This probably their last casual tourist time for a while.

"Yes, of course, I like aquarium. Talia takes me to see big round-one in Chicago when I visit, very nice and interesting."

"It's called the Shedd Aquarium, and I took Jeremy there several times before we moved to Texas." As they stood there quietly looking at the fish, Tomis again put his arm around Julia, and lightly squeezed her. She soon picked up his wrist to look at his watch.

"Did you want to catch the next ferry back or hang around here some more?" It then dawned on her, he may have seen the 9/11 Memorial being built, and the whole thing may be rather depressing to him. "You know if you've already seen the 9/11 Memorial, we can take a pass." Again, before he could answer, "I know, have you ever eaten at a *real* Jewish Deli? We could go have some pastrami sandwiches and yummy potato salad!"

He looked at her and laughed, not really sure if just all about trying to cheer him up or trying to do as many things as possible before they had to leave. "Yes, I see the Memorial building last trip, but interesting to see progress."

Then he leaned down to kiss her nose. "And, no, I do not think I eat at Jewish Deli, sandwich sound good. We have time to catch next Ferry." He dropped his arm from around her and took her hand, walking slowly, looking around at all of the people, concessions and decorations. Since his work now done, he'd not be returning there any time soon.

Julia asked him if he wanted to get any souvenirs, and he laughed, saying he had gotten some several times before on visits there. Once they were on the Ferry, he called Luka and he waited at the gangplank.

They talked walking over to the car, and he whisked them over to a particular side at the Memorial, Tomis felt had the best view of the whole project. While he didn't get melancholy, Julia surprised herself by tearing up. Then she told him, she'd actually been waiting for a ferry, when ithey all found out what had happened.

"I guess I will never understand why some people have to be so hateful, and destructive of other people and things. Don't people understand peace is equally?!" Then seeing a policeman, and tears still in her eyes, she asked him if he knew a good Jewish Deli close by. He pointed them in the direction of one only a few blocks away.

Only after she'd thanked him and walked away, did she realized how totally callas and inappropriate she had been. "Oh my God, Tomis!" She surprised him and he stopped short. "I can't believe I just did *that - here*?! How insensitive am I. Or just want to get away from my pain memories?"

He stood looking at her, trying to understand her own confusion. He finally put his arm around her and guided her to the car. Luka again whisked them the two blocks over to the Deli. As they got out, Julia stopped short, leaned back in and asked Luka if he'd like to join them for a sandwich.

She had almost startled him, and he simply shook his head 'no,' then said "thank you." Tomis chuckled and shook his head again at her - she never ceased to amaze him.

While they were eating their sandwiches, which he did enjoy greatly, Tomis explained it to her. "It is nice you invite Luka, … but it is *not professional* for him to eat with us. He can not be distract from his job. He is very dedicated and . . . not sure of word. Want to do best job?" He looked at her and realized she had just taken a bite of her sandwich. "OK, do best job."

Julia later gave him the word 'diligent,' which he liked and used. As they were finishing up, he thought it best to tell her: "Luka will be flying back to Croatia with us. We are in First Class, and he is in Business, where I usually fly. But he only disturbs us if emergency. OK?"

Julia happy to have her mouth full again, and just shrugged her shoulders. None of it her choice anymore, and something she would have to get use to accepting. Once they got on the plane her new world would change again. Her choice to go, though all these consequences hadn't dawned on her prior.

While not a long drive through Central Park, Luka did make a slow pass through, and they both enjoyed it immensely. Again he made the quick stop at the Consulate, with a man run out, but this time he had a large, legal-sized, black leather portfolio. Tomis lowered his window, as he approached, handed it in to him and they exchanged information, then pleasantries before raising the window.

Julia had started to recognize a few words, though not ready for any lessons. He opened the two strap combination locks on the portfolio, and took out a square white envelope with the Consulate insignia on it and gave it to Julia. "Your passport is inside, fix for you." She took it and put it directly into her purse not opening it.

Only a little after two o'clock when they arrived back at the hotel, so they did not have to rush at all. Julia hoped Tomis would open up a little more about his concerns, but she also knew they had plenty of time on the flight over. She then thought of their long day, when they drove to Porcupine Mountains and Lake of the Clouds, and how it had brought them closer.

When their clean clothes arrived from housekeeping, he helped her fit them into the large garment bag. It also had room for those extra things she and Tomis were no longer able to fit into their suitcases. "Tomis, I have never had so much luggage before, except when I moved back from Japan. This is going to cost a fortune in extra fees, I hope the Consulate understands all of the expense."

He laughed, as he closed up his suitcase, and walked over to her, as she kneeled down to fit a few more things into the garment bag. He lifted her up by her elbows, and put his arms around her to kiss her passionately. The whole act, so overwhelmed her, she teetered, and he had to catch her butt to balance her. It may have broken the moment, but not the meaning.

"I love you *My Jelly*, even when you upset me and *not* listen." He held her at arm's length. "I love to make love to you one more time, … but no time. I want to stay here in this room with you forever, . . . but we cannot." He kissed her again, and she held him so tight, even she couldn't let go. "It is OK My Jelly, we OK. As you say, together we *meant to be,* so OK   And, the Consulate is very happy with you, and with me. We do great job for Croatia. They are happy to pay for us. Do not worry, as you say, … *the small stuff.*"

This time,a luxury van out front with the Bell Captain helping Luka and another man, dressed identical to him, to load all of the luggage into it. Julia had her tote bag with her change of clothes and other needed items, along with her purse. She and Tomis had not changed, as he would also freshen-up and change at the airport in Paris, too.

He helped her step up into the van, and Luka resumed driving with the other man sitting in the front seat with him talking. They arrived at the International Terminal of JFK in a little more than thirty minutes, and the luggage quickly taken in to the First Class and Business.

As they headed to security, Tomis guided her to the far lane, the pilot and crew usually used. When she hesitated, he simply said, "It is OK, take out your passport."

Since she only had her driver's license out at this time, she quickly dug out the white envelope and opened it. She took out her passport, and handed it to the TSA person, with her ticket Tomis had given her. He looked at her photo first, and inside at the folded paper stapled to one of her pages with the stamp underneath it. He unfolded the paper with the Consulate insignia, and she saw her name listed as a 90-day Diplomatic Attache', then followed by the dates allowed for its use.

When she caught her breath, the TSA person looked up at her

to see if a problem. Tomis then put his hand on her shoulder, "Is everything in order?" The TSA person nodded, and marked her ticket, then checked Tomis and Luka's identical passes.

Dumbfounded, Julia continued to follow Tomis, with Luka right behind her. The same situation happened at immigration, as he steered her over to the special lane, and they again zoomed through. As they continued to the gate, Julia turned toward Tomis.

"Gee, it's the first time in years I didn't have to take my shoes off, or worry about setting off some beeper." Tomis chuckled and kissed her on the forehead, as he continued down the walkway leading them to the gate. Yes, the responsible one, he'd been so for a very long time, and others depended on him to continue.

Chapter 11
Another Country
Underestimating Women

We are not the women of twenty years ago,
Much less those of fifty, or a hundred before.
Our sense of humor has buoyed us.
We've changed radically, men have rarely.

Resilient from surviving so much,
And letting go of those small minds,
Who have been shocked and rocked,
After underestimating us so often.

It is more than basic education,
Which has made us less innocent.
Or, no longer ignorant of the world,
Nor myopic of who we can become.

We're 'the Queens of multi-tasking,'
As we guide family, career and even
Contribute well to the community,
While barely-breaking a sweat running.

We are neither fragile, naive nor afraid
Of taking on the issues of adulthood,
While looking to embrace age … as a
Gift to use our experience and wisdom.

Tomis had gotten the last row in First-class On-Air France, not only for the privacy, but so he could stretch out his long legs, without concerning himself about someone behind him. Luka, in the first row of Business Class, diagonal from Tomis, since seated on the aisle, also. This gave Julia the window, and also no interference, if Luka needed him.

They were both sipping on glasses of pinot noir, with Tomis reading files from the portfolio, as Julia flipped through the inflight magazine. She soon stuck it away, and pulled out one of the international business magazines, she'd taken from his briefcase. She'd not been reading long, when she decided to ask.

"May I interrupt you, to ask a few questions about your business structure?" Never to be one to beat around the bush, he knew she had some direction going with it. He took off his glasses, she'd not seen him wear before, and put the papers down.

He picked up the wine glass and took a sip. "Of course, you are Business Consultant." His face calm with a slight benign smile, knowing some serious in her tone.

"I have only heard you mention Ivo, and you are the President of your company, and you have said he is your assistant. But you did not mention his title, but he funnels information to you, and now you are upset with his decisions."

She paused to get it right. "Do you have a CEO or COO or Vice President or other decision-maker? Or even, someone else who is in charge under you, or when you are gone, or for handling the day-to- day activities?" She had thought it over, and time to ask.

Another mouthful, but she knew it, so had spoken slowly and carefully. He knew too, she probably assumed the answer to all of her questions. But, he knew it had been a subject, several of his investors had wanted him to address, and change some time ago.

So, perhaps, this a good time to do it, though not sure how to proceed without hurting Ivo in the process. She would be meeting all of his people soon, so she may be able to suggest a strategy.

"You are correct, . . . and some investors agree, I need to have CEO or COO. Ivo is my brother, but I know he is not good to be in charge. Now ferries finish, I stay in charge to clean-up problem.   After I fix problem, I find OK job for Ivo. He knows he make mistake

… and very sorry."

Tomis paused and sipped his wine. "I have some good managers and make one COO, and Ivo understand." His lips were pulled in again, as he didn't want to tell her any more than he had to. He stared at her for a moment, and knew she wanted him to make more of a commitment, but he felt he had - somewhat.

"You promised your father before he died, you would take care of Ivo, and give him a job or active part in the company, didn't you?" She now pushed the *consultant* thing.

Tomis shook his head a little back and forth, then ran his tongue over his teeth under his lips, trying not to clench his jaw. "You are very, very good.   Yes, I promise my father because he give me company. I work with him many years, go to university and work hard do many company jobs, and Ivo   "

"And Ivo is, as Talia said, 'lazy, and looking for some easy- way to make money without working.' It's why he gambles, he's looking for the make-it-rich-quick scheme." Julia now the one shaking her head and pursing her lips.

"I'm not really blaming you Tomis. You feel guilty for being smart and ambitious, as well the need to be loyal to your father. But, Ivo does take advantage of it, and you know it, and it really burns you, but you still defend him because of your promise." She looked at him more directly.

"You cannot move forward with him, *and* when your investors find out he's the one who created this devastating problem, they are going to jump all over *you, not him*." He hung his head down, nodding in agreement.

"So, what kind of job do you think you can give him, he can handle? I'm sure he doesn't care what it is very much, as long as it is easy." Julia had softened some to what she wanted to say, but she could see Tomis still not happy.

"Something you might want to think about, which would not have been a concern before. You are the one bringing *me* there to help others, so *you must* be *an example* of good business management. The best leaders always lead by example." She could see his brain churning, and more acceptance coming on his face.

"I try many jobs for him, and he did not do good … enough. Many complain from co-workers and even some customer. Maybe I try have him work with tour company. He love our country and know many thing on many places."

Tomis quiet for a moment, and Julia knew to wait for it. "I know, . . . I have him help you on tour, you ask many question, so he can see how important tourist is . . . and how he can help tourist learn Croatia." He smiled at his idea.

Rather directly thinking again of what Talia had said, "What about my English limitation? What if he can't understand the question, or explain the answer in English?"

Tomis now smiled bigger, he'd thought of it and made arrangements, he just had not told her about it. Not as if to be a surprise, but he didn't want her without an English speaker around.

His smile from ear to ear. "I already *have this one covered*. I have excellent translator waiting for you, … and she travel with you, too. Her name is Inka, and … very good experience in business English … in New York with … Consulate, and go to translator school."

Julia smiled back at him, knowing he had been waiting to spring this one on her. "Well, listen to you and your *colloquial* English

- '*I already have this one covered.*' My own personal translator, I'm impressed." Yes, much would be cleared on the long flight.

He looked at her questioning, "What is 'colok' mean?" "*Colloquial* means speaking in common, conversational form, like a native speaker. It is what using your phrases or idioms do for your speech. It's less formal, and makes you sound more natural in what you are saying. It is very good. I'm proud of how much you're always picking-up new words and phrases. Soon you'll have to teach me, or perhaps Inka can teach me to say a few common words or phrases in Croatian." Julia quite happy, and smiled broadly at him.

He gave her his devilish smile, "Well, maybe good and maybe not . . ." He started laughing at his joke, and she poked him with her knuckles, and he feigned pain. She shook her head.

"Yeah, like I'm going to get any kind of fluency in three weeks, and understand what you are saying!" She laughed, leaning over to kiss him, as he leaned down to meet her lips.

"OK, if Inka is so good, maybe we can shape Ivo up in the three weeks, so I'll have him traveling down the country visiting all of the tourist spots. You better warn him, I can really ask tough questions, so he better be able to explain them to Inka, if not me."

Tomis put his glasses back on and picked up this file folder to continue. "Yes, Boss, you shape us all up." She poked him again. "Ooooh, you hurt best student, *again.*"

After another glass of wine, dinner and after dinner drink, she said she announced about trying to take a nap. Without her asking, he called the flight attendant to ask in French for a pillow and blanket.

Julia merely said a "Merci" smiling, slipped on her footies to keep her toes warm, curled-up her legs and propped the pillow against his shoulder. She just started to doze, when she heard the whispering; opening one eye just a little, she saw Luka bending over talking quietly to Tomis.

She may as well get used them, not having any kind of extended privacy. Yet, having some of him, better than having none of him. She closed the eye and dozed back-off.

It must have been a sound sleep, for when her body recognized the change in the plane pitch, she automatically woke-up. Before she moved, she realized she had stretched across his leg, and him asleep leaning over holding her.

He'd extended both seats fully back, to stretch out, but how he managed to move her, and not wake her, amazed her. Or more so, how Tomis able to sleep in his position, which spoke of how tired he had been.

The cabin lights started to come on, and the lovely voice of the Air France flight attendant began waking-up her passengers, in the three languages. She sweetly let them know, they'd be arriving within thirty minutes, adding the current time and weather in Paris. Other attendants were coming around with hot towels, and passes for the airport, First Class lounge to freshen themselves, if continuing on to another flight.

Since the one, starting at the back standing there, Julia used Tomis' aisle arm rest, to pull herself-up. She to took two passes and two towels. She caught the momentary stare, stuffed the passes in her bag on the floor, and said "Thank you."

Not as if his fly open, but she'd been in a rather precarious position on his lap. She continued to push on the arm rest with one arm, moved her legs down at the same time, then catching him, before he slumped further. She began to whisper his name in his ear, and lightly wipe his face with the warm towel.

As Tomis came awake, she began to kiss him and his body began to stretch with a deep breath. She knew his stiffness would be worse than hers, as she handed him his towel, and she used hers on the back of her neck.

"Good Morning, I'm glad you got some sleep, but I'm sure not very comfortable. We land in thirty minutes, and I have the passes for the lounge and showers." She kissed him again. "You look so sexy, when you are so vulnerable."

Tomis wiped around his neck and face again, then stopped to look at her. "That make no sense to me." Way too early, to try to figure her out.

"I know, it just is." Julia watched him, thinking of what an intriguing man.

"I never sleep on plane." He leaned over and kissed her. "You are very good for me. I feel good, and I need rest, very long and busy day today. *I can do this.*" He smiled and kissed her again. "Yes, We *can* do this. You are right, I stay positive." They laughed.

"Soon my love, you will learn - *I'm always right!*" They both laughed again.

"Yeah, Right?!?!" He said, as sarcastically as he could.

"Touché!" She said, giving him kudos for his response, and they again laughed.

~ ~ ~ ~ ~ ~ ~ ~ ~

Luka and Tomis were waiting outside the women's First Class lounge, when Julia came out all perky and refreshed. She had on her special, bright rosy-coral scooped-neck top - just low enough, with a flouncy, floral-print skirt, which came just to the knee. When both of their eyes popped, she knew she had chosen well. "Do I look OK?" She asked as *demurely* as possible, for her, as not one of her acts she did well.

Luka still staring, while Tomis smiled from ear to ear, "You look perfect. And, I tell you before the President love you, and jealous of me." He let go of a delighted chuckle.

Julia swung her purse over her shoulder to take his hand, as she had her tote bag in the other. He had shifted his carry-on strap to his other shoulder, and carried the portfolio in his other hand. "We need to get to gate, plane leaves at 9:45am. It is only two-hour flight. So, coffee on plane, OK?"

"Sure, it's not a problem. So, will the President be there at the airport, or do we go see him? She hadn't really asked for any details, since it didn't matter to her.

"Press be there, so President there, too." A little snicker, as Julia knew he didn't like all of it, but knew a part he had to play, for the support he needed. An inconsequential flight, except Luka sat in the aisle seat across from Tomis. As only Business class or Coach, so with the two seats across, Julia again by the window.

Once she finished her second cup of coffee and cinnamon bun, Julia back looking through the international business magazines, as he continued reading the files in the portfolio. Luka reading the Zagreb newspaper, he'd gotten from the flight attendant.

He leaned over to pass the folded-over paper to Tomis. He put down his file to take it, laughed and passed it on to Julia. A full page of photos of them from the New York celebration in the business section, and two pages in society section. "You can get Inka to translate, or can figure out easy, I think."

The photos had been taken Monday night, which Tuesday morning in Croatia. So, either they didn't have time to make the Tuesday paper, or knew Tomis returning Wednesday morning. Better to print them then, to announce his return, like the Prodigal Son, at the same time. No wonder the President would be at the airport, what politician would want to miss this kind of positive photo-op, when other problems abounded for them.

"Oh, my God. You really are a celebrity! How many women are going to scratch my eyes out now?!?" Trying to keep her face straight, but started to giggled. Tomis looked at her sideways, and shook his head, then took the paper from her to give it back to Luka.

Julia now giggled uncontrollably, so he had to stop and join her. She could make him laugh, even when she upset him.

"I am very glad you handle all with your 'bent sense of humor.' Press and photos is some time … annoying to me, but you know it is necessary for business."

"Yes Love, I do. And, you know I am a very secure woman, so you do not need to worry about me being jealous, of all of your adoring, female fans." She giggled again, and he had to chuckle. She did make him happier than he had been in a very long time.

They zoomed quickly through immigration and customs, with one inspector actually saying a 'welcome back to Tomis, and welcome to Zagreb to Julia.' It impressed her, knowing he had obviously read the newspaper.

The moment the doors swung open for their luggage carts, into the unsecured area of the airport, two men dressed identical to Luka, and two women approached them. The younger woman in a pants' suit of the same color as the men, and the older woman in a skirt with a blouse and jacket.

Tomis stopped to put down his carry-on, and one of the men instantly picked it up, as he greeted the woman with a hug and cheek kisses, as their luggage magically disappeared.

He then turned to introduce Inka to Julia, and they shook hands. As she quickly began welcoming Julia in excellent English. Tomis turned back to the older of the two men, introducing him to the young woman.

After shaking her hand, he guided her over to Julia also. "Excuse me Inka, Julia this is Marijana, she is your security, and she is with you, when I am not." Julia looked at him pointedly, and he returned the look, *"I told you,"* raising his eyebrows.

Julia put a smile on her face, "How do you do Marijana. Am I saying it correctly?" Inka answered 'Yes,' then spoke quickly to her, with Marijana replying in Croatian. Then Marijana spoke her somewhat-limited English, but did understand more than she could speak.

"No problem, Marijana, I understand completely. Please do not hesitate to ask me to repeat something for you, if I need to. Thank you, I appreciate your protection." Inka repeated it.

Marijana carefully asked, "May I take your bag for the greeting?" Julia understood she needed her hands free to meet the President, and greet the press.

"Yes, of course, thank you." She handed her purse and tote bag over to Marijana.

The press, though being held back behind the expansion tape, had already been shooting photos. Then two side doors opened simultaneously, and two more men dressed similar to the others stepped out. Then came the President striding over, calling to Tomis what Julia figured a big welcome.

They did their greeting, and Tomis turned to Julia, but again before he could say a word, she walked forward and gave the President the same hug and cheek kiss greeting. The cameras were flashing like crazy, with him jubilant. He then held both of her arms, and smiled, as he kept repeating "Welcome to Croatia!" "We are so happy to have you here!"

The President could not take his eyes off of her, and even turned toward the press to show her off to them. Tomis holding in his laugh, letting Julia do her *wowing* of them. Again, he thought of how he'd not even considered how there could be this other side of her, those first few days they had met. She still amazed him, with her talent to change often, so much.

Finally, the President turned to pull Tomis into the picture, but did put him on the other side of Julia, so he could put his arm around her. While Julia could recognize him speaking Tomis' name, she had no idea what all going on about her.

At last, he released her a little, so she put her arm around Tomis under his jacket, and looked endearingly up at him. The President had asked the press for any questions, and several of them were calling them out.

He and Tomis took turns answering the questions, and the President turned to one of his non-security assistants, and waved his hand. He quickly began passing out press packets to them. He then began to thank them, and the entrance doors were opened out to the sidewalk, and the police began waving their hands to encourage the pressmen to leave. One more question called out to Tomis, and he said a definite 'no,' and something. Julia looked up at him, "What did he want?"

"He want to interview you and I say, 'no, not now.'" He turned to the security head, and asked a question and got his answer. "We leave now at special exit." The President had turned back to them, and gave Julia another big hug and cheek kisses.

"I see you Saturday night at Celebration Party. . . . and we dance together, OK?"

Julia put another big smile on and kissed him again, "Yes, of course, I wouldn't miss it." He headed out the side doors with his staff and security, and they followed shortly behind him with theirs.

Julia giggled at the thought of being in a circus parade. This time they were in a slightly-stretched Mercedes Benz, with the only difference being, the President's had two flags and insignias on his. Inka rode in the second car with two security, and Marijana rode up front with Luka in their car. Julia assumed all their disappeared- luggage had been put in both vehicles.

The surreal-nature of the whole scenario, not only mystified her, but made her feel she like in a bubble, which could burst anytime, and the joke would be on her. The only way she could handle it all, she had to laug. "So, the party Saturday night is also going to have dancing? How fun! We haven't danced yet, so you better have your dancing shoes on, so I don't have to look for a substitute, *fella*!"

He looked at her and laughed. "I do not understand - I dance. Is what you ask?"

"I love to dance, so I hope you dance with me, or I'll have to dance with another."

Tomis looked at her, but she couldn't tell if searching for some smart-ass remark, she'd made in the past, he could use. *"I don't think so!"* He barely got it out, before he started laughing and she roared, giving him another 'touché' kudo.

"But, I just promised the President, I'd dance with him, and I don't want to hurt his sweet feelings." She loved playing their games.

"But, if he squeeze you too much, wife get jealous, and not good for him or my business."

They had finally gotten out of the busy area, and Julia looking around at the houses. "We're going to your house, aren't we?"

"Yes, we be there shortly. . . . And, you know . . . I have to leave right away?"

"You mean as in 'right away' you have no time to make me Jelly?" It had become a proxy for any talk of making love, and his term of endearment, when he called her "My Jelly." While they had 'slept' together on the plane, no time or place now.

He looked at her with yearning in his eyes. "You know I love to, but many people wait for me, and I do not want just *sex* with you." He took a deep breath. "Friday I return, I promise . . . by dinner, and we stay in bed until party Saturday."

It sounded wonderful to them both, but they both also knew it probably wouldn't happen. "You see Zagreb with Inka and Marijana, so you learn much for your business consult. I think Inka has plan and appointment for you. I have phone and laptop for you . . . you can call Cara and send email. I call you and we talk at night. I love you . . . we can do this, yes?" Tomis watched her face and eyes carefully.

Her eyes got all watery, and he got very upset. "No, no" he whispered, "please do not do that. . . . I am good, safe. … I am OK. Please do not worry. Be positive . . . Golden Light, and White Light, remember. *We can do this* . . ." He pulled her to him, holding her tightly, when Luka called to him from the front, as they pulled into the driveway. He mentioned about the new security gate, the State Police had installed and finished just that day.

It surprised Tomis how big, but did not want Julia to know new security. Marijana put in the security code, which she said would be changed daily, and be used from the left-hand side passenger seat. She pointed out the cameras, and new system connected to the dock and to the house, which would have a 24/7 person to watch them.

The gate opened quickly, and she explained the sensor knew how many cars were in the driveway, so it would close quickly also.

Julia had gathered herself together, but sensing something different, and they were talking about it. "What is it?" She started to pull away, and she felt Tomis hesitate for her to move.

"Oh, I am sorry. They are concerned about gate, nothing to worry about." He released her, and tried to act calmly, but knew how she read him. "We are here, so you can meet staff and talk to Inka for plan this afternoon."

Since not looking at her, she knew something had jolted him. She looked at the huge gate, but of course, none of their talk made any sense to her. She had no idea, some of it because of her, they got a brand new, state of the art security. The car had stopped in front of his house very nice, yet not as large as she'd expected. But then, never nothing ostentatious about him, in any way.

She learned later, a four bedroom, and the staff of two part- time older women, did not live there. Ivo did live there sometimes, and now Marijana would, when Tomis gone. He had a studio apartment at the docks, he stayed in when he had to be there. With almost a three- hour drive to the port, not a quick commute. And, while he could use a State Police helicopter stationed there in an emergency, he'd never taken advantage of its availability.

Tomis opened the door to help her out, and Luka already at the trunk taking out their bags. Marijana had taken out her suitcase, in assisting him with the others. Julia then saw her tote bag in Marijana's hand. "Oh, thank you, I'll take it." Tomis had gotten his carry-on and portfolio, then headed to the door with Julia. The door opened just before they got there, and he gave hugs and kisses to the two older women, happily waiting for his arrival.

He introduced them to Julia, and they scooted out to help with the luggage. Then, the yard-maintenance man came through to be introduced, and also headed out to help. Julia could see large, heavy furniture in the living room, as she followed Tomis up the wide stairs, and into the master bedroom at the end of the hall.

Julia looked around at the large, lovely room which stretched across the far end of the house. It had a nice balcony, off to one side with a view of some woods, beyond the yard fence. "Oh, this is lovely Tomis, and some nice privacy."

A door slightly ajar, which connected to what he'd made into his office. Then another opposite it, went into a nice large bathroom, with a footed-tub on one side, and a large, glassed-in shower on the other.

The toilet, sort of in an alcove, and the vanity sink quite large. There were shelves for the towels, and a lovely plant in the large window to the side of the tub. "That's a wonderful bathroom, I can't wait to take a nice, long soak in the bathtub. Everything is really so comfortable, your ladies take care of it well."

Tomis had already emptied his carry-on out on the bed, and repacking it to take with him. "Thank you, and I think of you soaking in bathtub, and it keep me happy." She sat in the chair next to the large dresser, to watch him methodically, put back in clean shorts, socks and tee-shirts. Definitely a man who had taken care of himself efficiently for some time.

He certainly knew how to pack. He took down two pairs of khakis, and three shirts similar to what he'd worn when they'd been sight-seeing. He folded and rolled them, knowing how much would fit into the bag. By the time they'd brought up all of the luggage to his room, he had finished. They asked where the garment bag to go, and he walked into the office. "Julia do you want garment bag in closet here?"

She followed him into the room, as he stood with the almost empty closet doors wide open. "If I can hang the dresses and your tux in here, just have the bag put on the bed. I'll unpack and hang them myself."

"They want to help you. They do speak some English and Inka can give instructions if need." He looked at her, not wanting to interfere, but also not wanting to leave her with things unsettled. "Let them do it, so you go with Inka."

"We'll work it out, I'm not used to people doing those things for me, but it's OK."

Tomis gave them instructions, and picked-up his small bag. "Come down with me, so I can leave." He picked back up the portfolio and waited for her at the bedroom door. She looked back at the two women opening his luggage, and headed out the door with him behind her all the way down the stairs.

Inka waiting there for them, her briefcase at her feet. "Please give Julia her cell phone and laptop. Thank you for your assistance." He then added something in Croatian, as he continued to the door.

"Yes, of course." Inka waited by the stairs, as Julia continued to the door.

Tomis put his bag down, and leaned the portfolio against it. He took her in his arms and gave her a very passionate kiss. "I love you My Jelly, and I call you tonight."

He kissed her again on the forehead, picked back up his bag and portfolio, opened the door as he said, "Have good time with Inka." Tears were welling in Julia's eyes again, as she mouthed out the words, *"I love you, too."* "I know" he responded, closing the door behind him.

Julia walked over to the side window, and watched as the man holding the passenger door open, took his bag to put it in the open trunk. Tomis slid into the back seat, just as the man closed his door, then got into the front seat with Luka, who immediately accelerated out of the circular drive.

The senior man got into the passenger side of the second car, and the other man drove off following Luka. They were like an assembly line, working in perfect symmetry with each other. She hoped it meant they could keep him safe.

Julia wiped the tears from her eyes, as she turned around to have Marijana standing there in front of her. "To let you know, I sleep in room at end of hall. You may not see me, but I am here. I am walking ground now, to get familiar with it all. Camera-man is 24/7, so always here."

A little taller than Julia, and those were defined-muscles on her tight body. Probably in her late twenties, and quite dedicated to what she did. Julia wondered if she had one of those new, light-weight, super-strong, bullet-proof vests on? She figured she probably did, as well a gun somewhere accessible. All way too much a real, reality check, she didn't want to think of.

"Thank you Marijana. I'm sure you know I'm not used to all of this, but I do know how to follow instructions, so I will listen to you." Marijana slipped away, as quietly as she'd come, so Julia walked over to Inka, who had picked-up her briefcase in readiness. "Well, I don't even know where, to ask you to sit down to talk about our schedule. If you know the house better than I do, maybe you can give me a clue." Inka probably in her mid-forties, almost pretty, and while she seemed competent, she also seemed rather uptight.

"As a matter of fact, I've been working with Tomis for over five years, and even more so the last three with the ferry project. We usually work in the conference room back here." She took Julia passed the stairs to another set of double doors, and opened up the one on the right.

Inside wall to wall books, another desk, and a huge rectangular table which could probably seat ten. The house much larger than it seemed from the outside, and obviously used much for his in-town office. Julia immediately walked over to the rows of books, and ran her hand down the various leather bindings. Almost all of them were English titles, and certainly classics of all ages. Duly impressed from the start, he'd been sincere as to his love of books.

"Did Tomis happen to mention to you, this is how we met - him buying classic books?" She continued to walk around touching the books, until she ended up at the head of the large conference table. Julia glanced back at Inka to see her staring starkly at her.

"No, he didn't. I simply heard he met a woman, . . . uh, you in Michigan visiting his sister. I thought maybe you were Croatian, or Italian, or simply a friend of hers, introduced to him."

Julia cracked-up laughing. "I bet you were shocked to see my photo, and see I'm close to his age then?" She felt the real revelation.

Inka a little taken aback by her directness. "Oh, no, . . . of course not. When Jelena called last week to ask me if I could set-up some appointments here, and be your translator, she mentioned you had worked as a business trainer."

"Hey, don't mind me, I'm very direct, and I have a rather *bent* sense of humor. Tomis is learning to understand my jokes." The surprised look on her face said much. "Yes, he mentioned you'd gone to school in New York, and worked at the Consulate. Just a fluke, or are you related or connected to Jelena and Petar in some way? I mean, I know it's a small country and all, so people are supportive of each other."

Again, Inka surprised by her direct question. "Well, yes, I am Petar's youngest sister. But, I worked for several corporations involved with Croatia, not just the Consulate. Did you want to start going over the schedule? I did have an appointment set for today." "Oh, yes, I'm sorry. I just like to get to know people when I'm dealing with translations. I always used *my own translators*, when I worked in Japan, because they knew me. And, how to interpret what I said, you know the *innuendoes*, *flavor* of my *intentions* and of course, my sense of humor."

Julia could only imagine what all Jelena had said about her, and she did want to clarify how she felt about being interpreted correctly. "So, tell me about the company we have the appointment with today, and their expectations of me."

It had not taken Julia long to stump Inka. "I'm sorry, I'm not sure I know what you mean by their expectations of you? You are going to be training them, aren't you?"

Julia felt like saying "Gotcha!" But then Inka could only do, as much as she'd been told. And, if it came from Jelena and not Tomis, then she'd have no clue, of what all they had talked about. "OK, maybe you should tell me what all Tomis or Petar talked to you about these first preliminary meetings. We had talked about some rather definite proposals, and areas in which I could do consulting and training for them, depending on their kind of business." She breathed, trying not to show any disappointment.

"That's why I wanted to assess them, you know about their business, its needs and their expectations, of improvements from my helping them. I always did a full assessment of the company, so I knew who and what I'd be dealing with, how to make it better."

Inka had a blank look. "I am sorry, I did not get the information correct. Actually Jelena who talked to me, not Petar or Tomis. This is much more than I thought. I apologize, maybe it is a mistake for me to do this. I am not prepared."

Bingo! All Julia wanted, as it clarified everything. Now, she'd save Inka's ass, and know she'd be on her side, and not have any more of Jelena's snide resentment clouding what they needed to do. Julia took an obvious deep breath, and put a smile on her face.

"Inka, no problem. We can work this out, if you work with me on it. Your English is excellent, it is just your business acumen is a little *shy*. Why don't you go into the kitchen, since you're familiar with the house, and get us some ice tea, or even just ice water. I'll run up stairs and get some forms I brought along with me, since you don't have a copy of the assessment. OK?"

"Yes, of course. And, I do apologize." She started to get up from her chair, dazed from what just happened, and what an incredible fool, she'd almost made of herself.

Julia pushed her chair out, "Oh, what time is the appointment?" Inka dug out her appointment book, to open to today's date.

"It's at 3 o'clock."

Julia looked at the large grandfather clock about to strike two. "OK then, I guess we need to get a move on. I'm figuring it's downtown, right? How do we get there? Does Marijana drive us there, or do we get another person from here, or do you drive? I don't know how this is to be done. I'll find Marijana and ask her if you aren't sure." Inka's eyes were about to pop out of her head, as she had not planned this well at all, as Julia so *totally different* than Jelena had said.

Julia walked past Inka calling to Marijana, and up the stairs to their bedroom. The ladies had unpacked Tomis, what they were familiar with and had unzipped the giant garment bag. Julia picked-up her suitcase, pointed to it as the ladies watched, and she said "NO." She then crossed her hands in an X - universal for NO, and pointed her index finger to herself. "I open and unpack my bag, OK?" Both ladies nodded and said OK.

She started digging through the side pocket of her suitcase, and pulled out a half dozen of her files. She decided to take them all and go through them later. She picked-up her tote bag, emptied the contents on the dresser, turned to the ladies and repeated her whole NO and X routine, they again agreed OK. She put the files in the tote bag, grabbed her purse, started for the door as Marijana came in looking for her. "You call me?" Running up the stairs, her voice breathy.

"Yes, thank you Marijana. Inka and I need to go to a business appointment. Are you to drive us, or does someone else drive and you go along, or how do we do this?"

It took her a moment to translate it all. "I drive you." She turned to the ladies, and presumably asked for the car keys of whatever car she could use for Julia. The younger lady answered, and Marijana followed her out of the room with Julia tagging along after. When they got to the bottom of the stairs, Inka coming out of the kitchen with a tray and two glasses of something iced. The lady leading the parade, asked her what she'd done, and Inka answered, as if with authority to do so.

Julia stopped in front of Inka. "How long will it take to get to the appointment?"

"About twenty or twenty-five minutes."

"OK, we better leave now. Marijana is going to drive us, and I'm not sure how well she knows it all. Besides, I like to be early, and she may be nervous doing this." Julia balanced the tray with one hand, and picked-up a glass with the other, to take a big drink, then replaced the glass. "Thank you, this is really good."

Inka stood there for a moment. Julia turned back toward her, as she headed out the front door. "You need to grab your briefcase and come on so we can go." Inka took the other glass, and a big swallow.

The older lady coming back through, to go back upstairs to continue the unpacking. Inka handed her the tray, with the glasses, saying 'thank you' in Croatian, as she quickly walked into the conference room to gather up her appointment book and briefcase.

Marijana just pulling up, Julia opened the back door and climbed in moving to the far side. She motioned to Inka to climb in next to her. The moment the door shut, Marijana speeding off. Julia thought they'd all been trained identically. "Inka you need to tell her where we are going, and where she should park." Julia took a deep breath, feeling herself move into her element.

Inka still trying to grasp the whole situation, and how Julia had taken charge to save it from flopping. She re-opened her book, she hadn't bothered to put away, to read the name and address to Mairjana. She then ask if she knew it, or needed directions? Marijana thought she knew where, but wanted to make sure where she should park. Inka clarified the information, as they were all off to a new adventure.

Julia had taken out her files, and flipping through to find the assessment forms which would be best for this client. She found the one she'd sent to Tomis to have translated, which she used for service businesses and handed it to Inka.

"This was *supposed to* have been translated at the Consulate, or sent to you to translate. Sorry about it, *whatever* happened, or *whoever* didn't do it, doesn't matter *now*." Julia explained its purpose and ran through the questions, clarifying certain points of importance.

"Read it over, and make sure you understand *all* of the questions in detail, *please* ask me whatever you don't totally understand. I want you to be *totally comfortable* with it all, as *you* are going to have to explain it to the client, so we can get it filled out correctly. You'll need to make two copies at the client's today, as you'll do one in Croatian and one in English. Tomis also wants to make sure, all those involved up-grade their Tourist-English."

Inka looked at her a little stunned, and smiled. She had never really been given such a task before to handle on her own, and it made her feel very important. A little early to talk about it, but Julia would later explain, a prime example of the *power of empowerment,* and how it made an employee a better worker.

With several questions, Julia took her time to explain the words, so Inka knew how best to translate them into Croatian. She took out her English-Croatian dictionary, to make sure of the words to choose from.

Inka then mentioned to both Julia and Marijana, they'd need to stop at the bank after, to set-up Julia's account, as her pay would be deposited for her every week. Julia impressed, and thanked her for it. Inka quickly said, it had been Tomis, who'd made the arrangements.

Of course, thought Julia, "But, *you* are the one in charge of *follow-through*, the most important part." Marijana did a great job of maneuvering the big-ass Mercedes, and they were soon back downtown. She checked with Inka where best for her to turn, and she found the lot to park with ease, close to an elevator for extra security.

Before Marijana could open her door, Julia had done so, and climbed out with ease. She then immediately complimented Marijana on her excellent driving, and getting them there so quickly. Julia noticed she'd put on a light, vest jacket, which sure only worn to cover up the gun, she carried behind her.

Julia began talking, as the three women stepped into the elevator, and when they stepped out on the floor of the client - the largest tourist agency in the city, and probably the country - she'd finished sincerely praising them, and the two were changed women.

Julia smiled, specifically letting them know how they'd all managed to also be just as synchronized, as the men in getting to this first appointment, with their organization skills all clarified. To Julia, it's all about praise and appreciation of any employee, key factors in any successful business relationship, and what Julia preached and trained most often.

Inka began to realize what had so attracted Tomis to Julia. Truly, just like him in taking over, and getting it all moving smoothly. No job too big to handle, or too small to do right. This a woman who'd treat her like an equal, something Inka had rarely experienced.

Marijana smiling with pride, too. And, while some of the men had thought it a fluff-job, she knew it would be more. Besides, *she* alone the one in charge, and responsible for Julia's safety. She'd also been empowered without realizing it, and she felt so good, already doing a better job. Julia knew personal responsibility and involvement always key.

She and Marijana also bonded later, over Julia doing her aerobics. She'd seen her the first night, when she came by to check her room, and asked if she could join Julia. She then told her about her belief in the importance of her arm and leg moves for total control. She said she did the ab-crunches in the morning before her shower, so Marijana welcome to join then, too. Together exercising always so much more fun.

So it continued for the next two days, the three women going on several, quite successful appointments a day. With Tomis as the intro in, how could anyone really refuse, when they trusted his own success. Inka had them stop at different restaurants, to teach Julia the various foods, and even take time for a few tourist experiences. Julia pointed out examples of good service, great brochures or displays, and even collectible souvenirs.

And, while Marijana usually in the observant mode of diligent watchfulness, she learned much from the conversations she overheard between the two women.

In the natural unfolding, Julia shared how she and Tomis had enjoyed the different sites, while both a tourists in Michigan. As well, she continued to drop bits and pieces of her extensive resume, and experience in travel. They both looked at her in a continuous light of marvel.

But Inka, quickly realized Jelena had tried to sabotage Julia's success, being so jealous Tomis did not want her younger sister. He called each night as promised, and while he shared parts of his day, she shared the successes of hers. He had expected nothing less of her, but still so proud she handle it without him.

She never told him of how Jelena had interfered, but did mention how devoted Inka had become. Julia repeated how all about acknowledging her talent. Likewise, he'd said nothing of the snipers they caught, and one even wounded. Tomis now had to wear a bullet- proof vest, whenever he left his office. They also now had to check for car-bombs of any of the cars they used, after having found one.

Julia also never let him know, she'd figured out he and Inka had been involved for a short time, probably four or five years ago. In the few days, she and Inka had been together, easy to see why it had not worked-out. Inka not funny or quirky, or unique, but sadly uptight, but competent and dedicated, yet without creativity.

Ina would have made a good wife, but not a great partner or lover. The kind of woman who'd never challenge a man. Tomis needed an equal, and he'd certainly found one, who kept him on his toes in more ways than one. Julia truly, and genuinely surprised how happy she had become in it all. But then, nothing like work to fulfill a part of her, which nothing else could. She'd recently learned the rewards of limited contracts, so no longer afraid of her workaholic-addiction returning.

~ ~ ~ ~ ~ ~ ~ ~ ~

Publicity definitely a two-edged sword, in which it may give you fame and glory, or business without advertising. But, it could also create jealousy, or an easy target. Julia's first client had seen how her arrival to work in Croatia, the opportunity for free publicity. What could be better than to have the country's new darling-foreigner, promoting for him? Though he had the largest tourism company, always room for growth.

She and Inka were barely out the door, when on the phone to his contact at the newspaper's business section. He happily told how he'd been chosen first, and duly impressed with the assessment, which resulted in Julia's suggested consulting and training - blah, blah, blah.

Yes, all true, but no one else would be able to claim the title of *being the first,* to sign up for *the Tomis endorsed*-training program - not really true.

Therefore, Thursday morning found the ladies, Katya - the younger one and efficient housekeeper, and Babbush - as Julia called her, since she could not pronounce her name - the cook, were each reading copies of the paper. Not only had Julia and Tomis made the front page with the President - they actually used the photo of Julia in the front with the President's arm around *her,* and Tomis in the back- ground.

But, in today's business section, more photos of her, with the tourism company owner, proudly smiling in his own photo. The caption read about him being the first to sign-up for the new business program. Inka smiling ear to ear, when she came in with her copy of the paper, as they had actually mentioned her name several times.

So, all day, each of the other tourist businesses were anxious to get their photo *with* Julia, and be written up in the business section. By Friday, Inka's phone ringing-off the hook, and she could barely keep up with the voice mails or calls. The Press had now taken up a "Julia- Watch" - not quite the paparazzi, but figuring out where she might be next, with most businesses letting them know. She'd become *the news,* having been in the paper the   last   four   days.

Julia's   only   response   to   laugh hysterically at it all. Certainly not San Francisco or the UP! Unfortunately   for   them,   Tomis   tore   through   the Organized Crime's web of contacts and connections, firing people or the State Police arresting those proven to have participated in extortion or other crimes. Since well protected with the new security system, and extra physical guards, the Crime Lords only had to look to the daily paper, to see a more advantageous target.

By Thursday afternoon, Marijana had reported to her supervisor a suspicious car had been following them. She also spotted it parked not far from their last two appointments. Within twenty minutes, watching from the reception window of the third client, while Julia and Inka did their thing, three State Police vehicles surround the car, removing the men in handcuffs. Still, she knew it would not be over, and criminals would be more stealthy next time.

For their Friday appointments, Marijana had sent the list over to her supervisor, and she recognized the two unmarked State Police cars positioned, as she pulled up to drop her charges off. Of course, not a word had been said to either lady, at Tomis' instructions. His statement had been to his security detail, "Not in my city, or on your watch can anything happen to them." Now two State Police cars were also stationed outside of his house, which had now become a secure compound, until he returned Friday evening with his security detail in tow. They were close to exposing the head Crime people, and Tomis knew he'd get it done by next week. Julia scheduled to go down the Coast to the key, hot tourist spots, with them meeting up in Dubrovnik. So at least then, he thought, she'be away from their grasp of hurting her in the city.

Chapter 12
My City
Know Enough

Time is no measurement of love, or falling in love.
Or rules, *with enough time*, you will know love.
While love may not come instantly, its budding may.
If I feel I know you enough to love you, then I do.

Will I know if my love will grow? I don't know.
It may be a momentary thing, a blessing, a gift,
To know for a short time, I loved - was loved.
Perhaps if looked at it without expectations, it will.

Love may be shy, and need time to unfold.
Never rush Love, or have a completion-by-date.
Just because you have a long time together,
doesn't make a love more or less than another.

Love is mine to give, receive without judgments.
I know you enough to love you, it's all I need.
Time blesses us, to see it, feel it and it grows.
It gives us memories, to keep beyond time.

No guarantees of time, or love or happiness.
My love is with me through-out whatever life,
no time limit set by life, or when it's lived.
If we're meant to be together, we will be.

Their last appointment on Friday with the full Tourism Board, and not easy. Julia knew dealing with Boards never simple, and she'd learned to give them as much information ahead of time as possible. This helped to cut-through the chase, of who planned or tried to trump whom, and where the loyalty, or sides would be drawn.

She'd given Inka the 'homework' on Wednesday night of doing a full translation of the assessment and agreement forms into Croatian, so the clients would have all what they needed to aner. Inka then faxed them to the Thursday and Friday clients, with copies also to each member of the Tourism Board.

Julia took the time to be introduced to each of the seven members, then let them know her time limited. She told them she had a five o'clock, last minute appointment she needed to do. She then added, she'd not be in the city next week, but working her way down the coast to other tourist cities.

Putting a timeframe on something usually worked, and they had no need to know her appointment for Tomis' return. She decided to have each member take one of the assessment questions to answer, so involving everyone had given their *tacit, specific support*. It worked, and even after all the photos taken, they were out of there by a quarter to four.

Tomis and his detail were to leave the docks by four, and it should take between two and half or three hours for him to get to her. She should have time to soak in the bath, prep herself and also make sure his special, favorite dinner ready, before the ladies left for the weekend. She'd requested to have the house to themselves, and Tomis had agreed - excepting, of course, the security detail who stayed to the back and basement areas.

On the drive back, Marijana had gotten the call saying they'd left the dock. She called back to Julia and

Inka the good news. She'd talked a few moments longer on the phone, but did not relate any of the other information. When they exited the car at the front door, Julia gave Inka a big hug, thanked her again for all of her hard work the last few days. They'd meet again first thing Monday, to plan the specifics of the port meetings, and those down the coast.

Marijana pulled the car into the garage and headed to the security office area, as Inka got in her car to drive home. As Julia came into the house, she headed straight to the conference room, which she'd taken over as her office. She loved being in the room surrounded by Tomis' books, and feeling him there. Dropping her stuff on the giant table, she sorted it with the other clients from the prior days.

Everything a client had in their own pile of reference materials - brochures, schedules, or whatever they used to promote themselves. Until she got files made-up of them all, this would be the best organization of them.

She walked out closing the door, and headed for the dining room to check the place settings, at the end of the giant dining table, which could also hold ten. She called to Katya and she came rushing out of the kitchen. "I just wanted to thank you, for the beautiful flowers from the garden, and how perfectly you set the table."

Since she pointed, then waving her hand and arm with a big smile on her face, Katya got the gist of what she said. Julia then walked into the kitchen, with Babbush busy fixing all of Tomis' favorite goodies. Inka had explained to them what she wanted in detail, including the chocolate dessert. Julia bent down to smell each thing and gave 'oohs and awes' for them.

She then picked up the wine bottle, they had already opened for her, and poured a half glass. She again said 'thank you' to them both, in her fractured Croatian, and kissed each cheek, smiling.

She looked at the clock, and pointed-up to tell them, she'd go get ready. Julia trotted up the stairs into the master bedroom, going first into the bath to turn on the water for her tub soak, then turned down the bed, followed by laying out her clothes she'd wear. She stepped over to the CD player, and pushed on the discs he had in there, she'd been playing each night.

Julia then went back, and poured some lovely, smelling bath salts into the water and stripped-off her clothes, dropping them into the hamper. She placed her wine glass - after another sip - onto the little marble table next to the tub, then stepped in, gently sliding herself into the water. She adjusted the water temperature slightly, and leaned back to cover herself in the massive bubbles.

After another long sip of wine, she leaned over to turn the water off. She slid further down into its warmth. She swished back and forth against the back of the tub to relax her back. Absolute heaven, as she began to relax, thinking of Tomis kissing her all over.

~ ~ ~ ~ ~ ~ ~ ~ ~

Just as Tomis and his team gathering-up their stuff to leave, a call came in from the President. He wanted to be the one to give the State Police report to Tomis. (In Croatian) "Two other cars were followed and pulled over, with the men arrested on grounds of 'suspicious behavior.' I am concerned Tomis for Julia. They must know your schedule - when you are leaving the dock and what time you and the men will arrive. I think you should take the helicopter, and get there before they can plan anything else. It will get you there in forty-five minutes, and just a fifteen-minute drive to your house. Please do this as a gift to Julia, for the great job she has done for us this week with all the tourist companies."

Tomis quietly listened and agreed, thanking him for his concern. "I will tell her, it is a gift from you for her good job. I do not want her to know, she has become their next target. Once we get her out of town, I am sure she will be safe."

"I totally agree Tomis. I will call now to get the helicopter ready, so you can leave as soon as you get to the military post."

Tomis, Luka and another security man flew up to Zagreb, while the supervisor and two other men drove the two cars back over to the house from the port. The President had sent one of his cars over to the airport, so once they arrived to take Tomis and his men to his home. Once picked up at he airport, Tomis ask the driver to pull-up into the back area, and they'd all go in through the back entrance of the house, so he could surprise Julia.

They smiled and agreed - they also had seen her in the newspaper each day working hard. All who knew Tomis from their year together protecting him, were cheering and applauding. This famous, but caring workaholic had met his match, a woman worthy of him. What they didn't know, how his work passion could be redirected to his woman.

The men headed to the basement, and Tomis went in the back kitchen door, holding his finger to his lips, as the women gasped with happy surprise to see him. He then asked about Julia, and they said taking a bath. He smiled and Babbush giggled. He then asked them to finish what they needed to, then leave for the weekend. When he saw what had been prepared, he smiled, kissed and thanked them both. They quickly told him Julia had requested it all.

Tomis carefully walked up the stairs, the music playing covered any noise he may have made. He took note of the bed being turned down, and her clothes at the foot of it. He slid-off his shoes, shirt and pants after closing the bedroom door. She had closed the bathroom door slightly to keep the warmth in, and her eyes were closed while she lay in the tub lost to the outside world.

He carefully slipped her Helmsley Hotel robe off the back of door, quietly walked over to her, holding it open and whispered. "Hello My Jelly, are you ready for me?" He saw a smile come across her faces if dreaming, which she thought she must be. Then she felt the energy of his presence, and her eyes popped open.

"Oh, my God, Tomis! How did you get here so soon? Did I fall asleep?" But she felt the water and still quite warm. "Oh, no, I'm not ready for you."

He held the welcoming robe out to her, "Yes you are." He smiled, then chuckled at it all.

Julia shook her head and started to pull herself up from the tub, with him reaching to give her a hand. He had stepped back far enough, for her to get her feet on the bathmat, so neither of them would fall down on the slate-tiled floor.

She turned to slide into the robe, as he secured the belt around her, and turned her back for him to kiss her. The passion too much for them both, so he scooped her up and carried her to the bed.

Once in the bed, he used the robe to dry her off and undid the belt. She then surprised him, rising out of the robe, shedding it to move-up on him unencumbered, and roll him over. She then began kissing and licking his bare chest. "No, I need shower . . ."

"No, you don't. I'm only going to get you all sweaty again. We can take a shower later ... together." If she didn't care, he certainly didn't. It felt too good having her take him over. She didn't spend too much time with too many kisses before she turned to pull his shorts off, toss them to the floor, and mounted him. No woman had ever done that to him before, and amazed at how it felt. When she leaned over him with her full breasts, he naturally reached up for them to kiss, and she exhaled heavily.

She then began to give him a real roller coaster ride, he hadn't known his capablity of doing. She never ceased to amaze him, or what they had deeply awakened in each other, almost too much to imagine its depths. They were both flying again, like their first session, and time melted away from them.

Julia certainly kept her promise, as they were both sweating so heavily, a paramedic would have been frightened for them. She'd collapsed on him, and literally slid off on their mutual sweat. Her head between his neck and shoulder with her one arm still on his rapidly beating chest.

Both of their bodies would be getting chilled before either of them spoke a word. She lifted herself enough to reach for a sheet or blanket to cover them, but found her robe instead. She spread it over the main part of their bodies, and sunk her head back down on him. Both finally came back to life, as the Beatles CD played. He smiled, and chuckled. "What did you do to me, Jelly?"

She raised her head. "Me? Well, *You* carried *me* off to your bed, what did you expect?"

They both started giggling, and she moved up to kiss him. And, *"Something in the Way She Moves"* played, and they both began to laugh heavily. "Honest to God, Tomis. From now on … whenever I hear that song, I will think of this Jelly-Session."

"Yes, I will think of it, too Jelly. And, I think I play it over and over!" Their giggling grew louder, and they both said together - "Touché"

She'd gotten enough clarity in her head to ask how did he get there so fast? "It is gift to you from President, for great job you do this week. He saw you in newspaper every day. He said to take helicopter, so we get here fast. So, thank you."

"Well, I'll just have to give him a big kiss when I see him, and tell him what a great time we had." She gigged again, then quipped, "Nice having important people in high places!"

"No big kiss. I tell you before, jealous wife is not good for business." They laughed, and held each other talking, kissing and caressing. And, while they'd shared during the few days apart, now more details, especially Julia talking about the food, and some of the sites she'd been able to see. Still, both kept back what they felt the other had no need to know - him for protection of her, and her for non- invasion of his past life. But, the whole Jelena-thing, she might, yet.

"Perhaps tomorrow we could go and do some sight-seeing before the party. I'd love to see what your favorite places are, and your favorite restaurants, could we do that?" He thought for a moment what places would be safest, or the detail could go out ahead. Concerned for them, as much for innocent bystanders wanting to site-see some famous place, or a restaurant.

"Sure, I can do that. I think of what place to take you." He kissed her forehead. She leaned half way on his chest, while he gently stroked her breast. "I want to tell you … I learn new word about you - *sen-su-ous*…"

Julia moved-up to look at him in pure curiosity, as she really wanted to hear this. He glanced down, with as much of a smirk as he could. "I remember first time I realize you sexy, Wednesday after dinner in UP - and wonder why I not know before."

He lightly chuckled, considering what they just shared. Now Julia even more intrigued to hear it. "So I use dictionary to look up *sexy*, and find … you call syn-on-yms." Not wanting to interrupt, she nodded. "And, I find *sensuous*, which I think is more you. As is *sense* to touch and feel things more and deep. It is more like you Jelly, than only sexy, I think."

Tomis looked so deep into her eyes, tears began to form there. No man had ever said anything so incredible to, or about her before.

Her direct reaction almost frightened him. "Did I say some thing wrong?"

Julia rose-up shaking her head, "No, it could not have been more perfect. I've never had a man say such a touching, personal, and loving thing to me before. I truly love you, so much! I can't believe I've found such an incredible man, as you are!" She rose further up to kiss him passionately on the lips, with him returning it. "You know, if you keep playing with me, I'm going to have to jump you again."

"Is that promise?" His devilish smile said it all.

"Wow! You're really getting good at this colloquial speech." "That is not all I get good at." This time he rolled her over under him. He then began at her neck kissing with his tongue, as she had on him, and went slowly all the way down her body until Julia squirming almost off the bed. "I truly love you, my Jelly." A quick-study learner at more than just his English.

The shower refreshed them and they barely dressed, only in case any of the security needed to find him. With it now dark outside, they made their way to the kitchen. Tomis showed Julia how to work the stove, as well explaining what had been cooked for their dinner - which he thanked her for requesting. She then opened the refrigerator to show him, her requested chocolate dessert.

After their long, slow dinner, she took him into the conference room to show him her work and explained it all. Julia then told him how much she loved being surrounded by all his books. "I brought the books from the library-sale down from your other desk." He picked them up and looked at each of the titles - Fitzgerald's *The Great Gatsby*, Hemingway's *For Whom the Bell Tolls* and

Steinbeck's *The Grapes of Wrath*. "Those are three of my favorite writers." Their whole synchronicity bounced in her head.

"I look forward to read this winter." He smiled, "What do you want to do . . . now?"

Julia felt content. "What do you do evenings, when not entertaining clients, or a lady-friend?" He shook his head, but knew she had to tease.

"I read, watch television - movie or American show." Kind of strange, since they had not really had any ordinary evenings together.

"Oh, OK, let's see what kind of movie or show is on. We can pretend we are just regular people - you not a workaholic-engineer trying to transport people, and me not the superstar business consultant." They both had to laugh at their reality. She followed him into the living room, for him to stretch out on the massive couch, with her curled-up next to him. Tomis found a movie they had both seen long before, but good to see again.

A little after eleven, the security supervisor came, and apologized for disturbing them. They spoke momentarily, then Tomis said he needed to check some information, and would be back shortly. Just as at the docks, with regular, outside perimeter checks, they'd found a man with a rifle.

The interrogation revealed the same information as the others, so the State Police came to take the man away. Trying not be be disturbed at how correct the President had been, Tomis also talked to the supervisor about what places would be best for them to sight-see, and how it would be covered. Julia watched the mantel clock, as Tomis gone almost a half hour.

He paused to take a deep breath, before walking back in, hoping she'd not read too much into his actions. "We all set for tomorrow. We can leave when you want, but must come back by four o'clock to get ready for party, OK." He sat back down, and put his arm back around her. Of course, he said nothing of what happened, but she didn't want him to lie if she asked.

"I show you my city tomorrow, and Sunday too, if you want. We have fun together." He squeezed her shoulders slightly, like all alright, but she knew it wasn't.

She couldn't hold it any longer. "You are such a terrible liar. You know how good I am at reading you. I swear I'm going to learn Croatian, so I'll know what you are saying!"

"I don't know what you are talking about, . . . and by the time you learn Croatian, everything over anyway." He looked down at her with his devilish grin, at having repeated her words so perfectly. She poked him in the side, for again using her own spoken words against her. And again, he feigned-pain from her poke. He knew she knew him so well, and yes, they both pretended everything fine, . . . and as for the moment, perhaps.

The movie soon ended, so they went up to bed, both exhausted from long, busy days. Sexually contented, they slept soundly, curled around each other. It still amazed Julia, she could sleep so well with Tomis. Honestly, she couldn't remember the last time before him, she had actually spent a whole night with a man.

In the morning, another story, as they once again found fun and satisfaction with each other. They later headed down to the kitchen for Tomis to show her more of it, and make breakfast together. Not the greatest breakfast either of them had ever eaten, but they had fun putting it together.

Still drinking their coffee, which to Julia quite strong, Tomis going through the morning newspaper and found the latest story on her. He was translating as he read. "You come out Tourist Bureau and say your meeting success. You say you only want to help make Croatia most popular country to visit, . . . so everyone can see her beauty, . . . glorious history and wonderful people." He moved the paper to look at her, "This is very nice of you to say."

He went back to the paper, "When ask about Croatia joining EU, you say - 'It is very best thing for Croatia to grow and expand, more jobs . . . and to bring more tourist easy, because . . . access to other EU countries.' You say, 'Just like United States, and each of fifty States, . . . all are different, but equal and . . . independent with own law and . . . cultural taste or umm . . . flavor."

He looked at her again, but his smile had gone, but he continued. "Same true for Croatia when join EU, it have equal . . . to other countries, but also have independence, laws and . . . own cultural flavor." He put the paper down, and picked-up his coffee to drink before speaking.

"What's wrong? Everything I said is true and what you also know and believe. What did I say wrong?" No way, he knew how to tell her. She'd definitely put a target on her back. Perhaps, in some ways, an even bigger or easier one, than what he had on his.

"Yes, you are right, but your time to say is wrong." He paused to get his words correct, yet the damage done. "We are very close to catch head-men, but . . . I do not want them come after you . . . because you support and . . . encourage others to support join EU. I must go talk to security . . . are you ready to go to the city?"

"Yes, I am ready, I'll go get my tote bag and hat. I'll be ready whenever you all will be." She did not want to pout, as so childish. Yet, some how she thought she'd done the right thing.

When she got into the bedroom to get her stuff, digging through her suitcase she ran across her passport-pouch. She'd totally forgot to tell Tomis about it, and it would make him feel safer for her. She'd be sure to use it, when they left to travel down the coast for her appointments.

There had two cars traveling to the city, with Luka and Marijana in the front with them. At first Julia felt like she'd created a hassle, and she thought, *fuck it. If this is what it takes for us to spend some time together, then this is what we do.* Tomis in a better mood, so she took her deep breaths and put on her happy, smile-face. She would ghave a good time and be positive, no matter what happened. Really curious, as to where Tomis planned to take her. Sure, Marijana had told them where they'd already been. Once out of the gate, she started reading to him about his City, from a tourist brochure, and what she wanted him to show her.

"Zagreb's main orientation point and the Spiritual, if not the geographic heart of the city, is 'Trg Jossip Jelačića'" - he corrected her terrible pronunciation. "Ban Jelačić the 19th-century ban, or viceroy- governor, who led Croatian troops into an unsuccessful battle with Hungary, in the hope of winning more autonomy for his people.

The statue of Jelačić" - still pronouncing it wrong, and he now laughed - "'standing in the center of the square stood there from 1866 until 1947, when Tito - the Yugoslavian dictator ordered its removal, because too closely linked with Croatian nationalism. Unity of the group of Soviet countries, what the Soviets pushed. One of the first acts of the new government in 1990, to dig the statue out of storage and return it to the square.' This is so cool; I just love it."

The cars parked in a special no parking zone, but their tags exempted them. Tomis led Julia to the middle of the square, with Luka and Marijana staying back about twenty feet on either side. She had no idea where the other security had gone.

There were perhaps thirty or forty people roaming around the area. As they walked around, Tomis had continued to tell her about the buildings, as most of them dated from the 19th century, and pointed out the reliefs were by noted sculptor Ivan Meštrović ... Since she'd told him how much she loved architecture, he explained and answered her questions about the buildings. They walked over to Banski Dvori, or the Ban's Palace, once the seat of Croatian viceroys, and now the Presidential Palace.

Julia wanted to go in for a tour, but Tomis pointed out a sign saying no tours today. "They are all too busy get ready for party tonight. But we can . . . maybe do it tomorrow, if you ask the President tonight."

He suggested they could come before noon to see the regal, guard-changing ceremony. She got really excited, and said she definitely would. Tomis started laughing, as he could see the President the morning after a big party, trying to show her around with a hang- over.

As they continued to walk around the building, he explained actually composed of two baroque mansions, which housed courts, archives and other government offices. He then mentioned, as the war started in October 1991, the Palace bombed by the federal army, an assassination attempt on the President at the time. Julia saw remnants of the war still remained, for a reminder.

They then went over to the eastern side of Markov trg - square, which mainly filled by the Croatian Sabor, or Parliament and center of Croatian politics. The site of these baroque 17th- and 18th-century townhouses were in a neoclassical style, and built in 1910.

The secession of Croatia from the Austro-Hungarian Empire proclaimed from its balcony in 1918. Their history seemed to keep repeating being taken over, and fighting to get their independence back. They were such a resilient people, who had been through so much for so long.

"So, who is the bad-guy politician in the Sabor, who is fighting so hard to keep Croatia from joining the EU? I mean, it always comes down to power and money grab." Suddenly, Julia could feel some intrigue, and wanted to know all of the players.

"What do you mean?" She'd lost him, he didn't know what she had been talking about.

"Tomis, in any great thriller, crime-mystery, the two main suspects are always, who has the most *to win,* and who has the most *to lose.* The 'most to win' would be the politician fighting against joining EU, because he wants to be President, and run Croatia like a dictator - *power and money grab.*"

Julia looked at him pointedly. "So, who's the President's biggest opponent? And, who has the 'most to lose,' would be one of *your competitors* in the ferry-tourist business. You have three new, famous ferryboats coming, and you are supported by the government. He will *definitely lose business,* if not go out of business. He has probably been doing *shoddy*-business deals all along." Julia looked at him directly. It sometimes took an outsider to see it clearly.

Since she seemed to have him hooked, she continued. "Now, usually *these people* don't like to get their hands dirty themselves, so they gang-up with the *notorious* gangsters. Those people who are already into drugs, gambling, prostitution and loan-sharking. So, if they get rid of you, me and the President, they can run the country the way they want.

They probably have some *honcho,* you know big guy, up in the State Police, who keeps them informed of what's going on, where we all are, etc. So, they can *skip-out* by ferry, just before getting caught." Julia on a roll, feeling like her favorite Agatha Christie character, Hercule Poirot!

She'd left him rather stunned. "You know you can check the phone records, and bank records to see how they are all connected. Who's paying whom, and who is doing the dirty work, and will benefit from it all." Tomis shook his head, once again totally amazed at her, and what all she'd said so succinctly.

"You think *this* all right now?" Julia smiling broadly and nodding her head. "My security team work on this for more three months. Wait for final proof Monday or Tuesday. But not find State

Police informer. You always amaze me." He kept shaking his head, but smiling this time. He leaned down to kiss her on the forehead.

"But, Tomis, the *State Police informer* is the most important piece of the puzzle, and will blow your whole investigation up. They all have *No Moral Compass,* as to any feelings except for themselves. Check bank records, under his wife's name or relatives. As I said, they will be escaping by a ferry of your competitor, and going to one of your prior joint countries - Slovenia, Bosnia or Serbia, because they all still resent you for leaving them. They may even have a part in all of this, because you - your country has become so successful, and they have not."

Tomis now shook his head 'no.' "I do not want to think they support killing more innocent people." In return she shook her head, 'no' as to him being totally wrong.

Just then a woman and her daughter walked up to them. Instantly, Luka and Marijana were at their side, but Tomis put his hand in front of Luka and said 'hello' in Croatian to the woman.

"Excuse, please. Julia sign," and she began to reach in her shopping bag. Now Marijana reached over for her hand, but Tomis put his other hand in front of hers. The woman presented the morning newspaper, folded to Julia's photo and story to her.

"Tomis does she want my autograph or something?" Shocked, looking at the woman and the newspaper now in her hand.

"Yes, you have fan." He reached into his jacket pocket and produced a pen, handing it over to Julia for signing.

"Tomis please ask her what her and her daughter's names are?" He asked and spoke them, spelling them out to Julia. When she handed the paper back to the woman, and she saw their names, she began to bow and touched Julia's hand, repeating 'thank you' in both English and Croatian.

Luka then said something to Tomis and he said, "Yes, I totally agree." He looked at Julia. "You are bigger problem than we think." The woman had scooted back to her friends in the square, calling to them what she had received. Several then picked up their newspapers and came running over. "Julia, I think we must leave."

"No, let me sign for these people first. What I said, did mean a lot to them." The other two security men and State Police were now in the crowd and watching the people closely. Julia signed six more newspapers, and she waved good-bye to them all, as Tomis lead her back towards the car.

Just as Tomis helping her into their car with Luka and Marijana flanking them, a news cameraman came rushing up in his car. He snapped a few shots, and someone from the crowd called to him saying what Julia had done for them. He rushed over to get their story for the next day's paper. So, she'd make the paper another day to piss them off even more.

In the car, and a little after noon, Tomis told Luka to drive up to the southern side of Mt. Medvednica just above Zagreb. The medieval fortress the most important monument in the city. Built from 1249 to 1254, erected to protect the city from Tartar invasions, and itself well-protected by high rocks.

The fortress owned by a succession of aristocratic families, but fell into ruin as a result of an earthquake, resulting in general neglect. Restoration began in 1979, but pursued with greater enthusiasm in 1993 and 1994 when the country looked to honor monuments from its past.

Once up there, Julia could see the rebuilt thick walls and towers, next to a small chapel with frescoes. Also the Shrine of the Homeland, which paid homage to those who died for a free Croatia. Since a beautiful, clear autumn day, Tomis held his arms around her, as he pointed out many of the views of Zagreb and surrounding areas below.

"This is a remarkable city Tomis, and you have remarkable countrymen and women. I can easily see how you take such pride in it and them." A growing inner-satisfaction with it all for her.

"Thank you, I am glad you can see it. A wonderful thing you're doing for them." As they wandered around the hilltop and through the fortress, none of the security out of site. "It is almost three o'clock. We can stop and get some lunch, if you want. I know you do not like to drink at party when you hungry."

Julia laughed, "I told you before, if you want me to keep it together, I can't drink on an empty stomach. Yes, I would love to have some wonderful, traditional food, nothing fancy, just Croatian everyday food. Could we do it without causing too many problems."

Julia paused for a moment and added. "You know, a very brave woman to bring her daughter up to us. It is never easy to be first." Tomis spoke to Luka, and he nodded as he headed back to the car contacting the others, as he went.

Definitely, a 'mom & pop' small restaurant, as she'd requested, with maybe a half dozen other people inside. Speaking their English quietly, the owners had not recognized them, until the food being delivered to the table, by the waitress who recognized them.

The 'mom' then came out of the kitchen, and over to their table. As Tomis tried to stand-up, the large, older woman put her hand on his shoulder, and shook her head, saying something, so he sat back down. He introduced Julia, and the woman insisted they eat before it all got cold. She nodded, and thanked him again, heading back to the kitchen.

The several items, he had selected, sure Julia would like from what he'd seen her eat before: Burek - a delicious pastry filled with heavy cheese, and another with meat. He explained this one of the main dishes for farmers and fishermen, which he often ate at the port - breakfast, lunch or dinner.

She laughed, "So almost like a fast food, but better than McDonald's." The Cevapcici were spicy meatballs made of beef or pork. And, Raznjici, basically a shish-kabob, Croatian style. The local wine, also very delicious!

Just when Julia telling Tomis she's getting stuffed, the woman came back out with a huge tray filled with a variety of pastries. Julia did her 'ooh and awes,' but could only take a bite of each, and got him to do so also.

She then asked if they could take some food for the security team. They were all standing around the outside of the restaurant, so rather obvious. Tomis concerned it would be too expensive for the owner, as he doubted from what the woman had said to him, she would let him pay.

"I think those are her grandchildren, give me the money and you go talk to her and her husband, while I give it to them." He looked at her surprised.

"You are always so clever." He turned to the side, so they would not notice and pulled out a wad of cash and passed to Julia. She slipped it into her bag, and started to get up.

He walked over to the older couple, and their son brought big bags of food out to the security detail, who put them in the trunk. Julia, in the meantime went over to the young children sitting at a table where the father had sat, while she and Tomis were eating.

She found an envelope in her bag and pulled out the contents stuffing the money into it, as flat as she could. When sure the couple weren't looking, she slipped it into the newspaper they had been reading. Then for fun she turned to the page of her photo and story, to put the envelope under the next page, so they would find it easily after she and Tomis left. After speaking to the children, she rose to join Tomis, his signal for them to leave.

He gave the couple both the hug and kisses, as Julia did likewise to their surprise. As they were heading out the door, Julia turned back to see the young boy pull the envelope out of the paper. They were getting in the car, when the boy gave it to his grandfather, who saw it as real manna from heaven and sealing their feelings. Before taking her shower, Julia decided to model the passport-pouch, the same way she had for Cara, to see if Tomis could see it. The routine almost identical, except he wanted to play more with her body. When she pulled her blouse off, he thought definitely getting his wish, but she turned her back to show him the pouch and told him to open it. "It is like magic, very clever Jelly." But still distracted by her body.

"Hey, I'm more than happy to play, you know that. But you are the one who said we had to be there by six o'clock, because we are in the reception line." She had turned back around and lifting up his head, as he had started to kiss down her back.

"It is the new passport which has *a micro-chip* in it, so you can find me. But, you must not tell anyone about my secret weapon, *no one at all,* because you do not know who the informant is. Do you understand, just you and me will know about it. And, I will wear it, when I am away from you. OK? You feel better now?"

He nodded and smiled. She undid the velcro and bent over to throw it in her suitcase, before heading into the shower. But he scooped her up, while still bent over. So they were about ten minutes late getting to the Palace. But, as Tomis said, since they were the guests of honor, they really couldn't start anything without them. "Touché" she said, "you really are loosening up."

~~~~~~~~

Even Marijana looked lovely in a black, simple evening gown, and never more than six feet away from Julia. She had teased Luka, as the only one of the detail wearing a tux, and had actually opened Marijana's car door for her.

From the back seat, Julia had giggled at how cute they looked, when Tomis shook his head, she answered back. "I know, they are still working, and it looks better for them to be dressed. I can't imagine those thugs trying something at the Palace with so many State Police around. By the way, will my 'nemesis' be there? I'm curious, as to what kind of a hypocrite he is?"

"Nemis, what is it mean?" He knew she'd behave, but he wanted to make sure what she her mind up to.

"*Nemesis* means someone who is determined to defeat or destroy you. And, *hypocrite* is someone who says one thing, but does another. So, he'd be pretending to be supportive, but he is not - yet he wants to learn as much as he can, to use it against me or you. Kind of like a spy, or one who sells-out their talents to the highest bidder."

He looked at her closely and processed all she had said. "You are correct what you say, and he probably be there, pretending, as you say, to be supportive."

"Also," Julia then added, "I'll bet he's a sexist, or even worst a *misogynist* - a man who *really* hates women. Most think the bigger the boobs, the smaller the brains. They truly do underestimate women like me." Now laughing, and as Tomis had understood what all she'd said, he was roaring with laughter.

"Yes, very big mistake to underestimate you." He leaned over to kiss her cheek. "I do not any more, . . . I do not *think* I do, anyway." Still chuckling at her description. He then remembered, "Do not forget, wife of President speak less English, OK?" She nodded with a smirk. Tomis narrowed his eyes wondering what she'd do.

Julia, of course, stunning, as she entered in her aquamarine dress, with the elegantly simple matching necklace. Once she'd given the President her kisses and hug, with him taking notice of the décolleté of her neckline, he forgave their being late.

"I'm so sorry we're late," saying as introduced to the President's wife, "But Tomis kept having difficulties tying his tie. I had to help him with it." Tomis glanced over at her in the middle of greeting the President. He almost laughed out loud, at her very *un- sexual* reference of why they were late. He knew, she knew neither understood.

Once they were in line, with Julia next to the President at his insistence, Tomis leaned over to whisper in her ear. "You are very funny tonight, My Jelly." She beamed at him, with her most mischievous smile, and he knew it would be an entertaining evening.

With the Prime Minister's wife next to him, then the Prime Minister and heads of the Sabor. There would be more than one hundred in attendance, and most would be from the tourism industry, with some coming all the way from Split and Dubrovnik.

Those Julia had already met, greeted her like a long-lost friend, and those she'd be meeting with next week, were enthusiastic at the opportunity. There would be much less English, and what spoken, she knew would be more broken. Inka to arrive shortly, and would be at her beck and call, if Tomis not around.

All of the Sabor-Parliamentary people supportive of their EU bid, or associated with tourism would be there, too, or simply curious about meeting the American, Tomis discovered.

At this point, in strutted the American Ambassador in *front of* his wife, who both spoke fluent Croatian. "Welcome! You've made quite a *name* for yourself, in a *very* short time. From what I've *heard*, you're *supposed to* help all the tourist companies, be more competitive with other European countries."

Julia gave him a big smile, yet her 'thank you' more perfunctory, as his statements seemed rather patronizing to her. Perhaps he had expected to be consulted with, or at leased informed about her coming.

Tomis glanced at her, as they stepped away, surprised she had not engaged them in more open conversation. She later told him, the man arrogantly-patronizing, and especially the wife seemed wimpy. Tomis had learned before, Julia did not like powerful men who married weak women. She then asked Tomis, if the Ambassador had helped with any business contacts in New York, when he said 'no,' she knew the Ambassador jealous of their success without him.

The orchestra had been playing from the start some lovely music, and a few people had begun dancing. After forty-five minutes standing in line, it slowed enough the President decided to get on with the ceremony, so they could party. Most people had already stopped over at the extensive buffet table with large plates, or at the stations around the room with alcohol and small plated appetizers.

The same ferry photos were mounted on the wall behind the dais, but these had much more elaborate frames. As the President called Tomis up to the platform, the security opened the doors for the television cameras and news reporters, into a sectioned off area for them in the enormous ballroom. The ceremony much the same, and Julia stood to the side with Inka translating.

Virtually nothing spoken in English, until the President mentioned her, and the designated title of Business Consultant-Trainer. Patient Tomis repeated his performance, and bent his head down to receive the tri-colored ribbon with a larger, more elaborate medal.

This time, the ribbon clipped to his lapels, so held firmly in place. After the applause, Tomis spoke for only three or four minutes, then called Julia up to platform, which accelerated the camera flashes, and the TV camera concentrated closer-up on her.

Again, he only spoke a minute or two, all in Croatian. When one of the news men called out to him, he leaned over and kissed Julia on the cheek. When Tomis spoke to them again, she did understand him saying 'thank you' and probably no more questions at this time, as before. The President thanked them all, as security ushered them out, many still covering Julia and Tomis.

Following, the President invited everyone to eat, drink and celebrate the wonderful occasion, or so Inka said. Tomis had immediately been surrounded, so Julia asked Inka to go with her to get some wine. They had barely moved, when Julia surrounded also by some of her tourism compadres, but she guided them over to the booze with her. They had already been drinking, but she had not been able to do so in the reception line.

Julia suddenly wanted it to be over, so she could just relax and cuddle with Tomis. But she knew it would not happen for several hours, so proceeded to make the best of it. Before she had more than two swallows of wine, the President at her side asking her to dance. Actually a rather good dancer, though he did hold her a little too close for comfort.

She made a point to put in about the tour on Sunday, and perhaps watching the Guard change from his balcony. He said his wife or special assistant were more proficient at the tour, but he'd love to join her on the balcony. Immediately, she added - "Oh, Tomis will be so happy. He's never seen it from there."

To compensate for his fallen ego, she kissed him on the cheek, and he responded with a big smile. He added anything she wanted; she should not hesitate to call him on his private line.

She almost swooned, "Oh, you are so kind. I'll be sure to ask Tomis for the number." She made sure not to catch him peering down her dress to her cleavage, and just kept smiling at him.

Just as she finished the second dance with the President, Tomis came over to rescue her. "Excuse me, Mr. President, I request next song for orchestra to play for us." Julia had no idea, but she had been looking forward to them dancing, so delighted. The President bowed, and kissed her hand, turning it over to Tomis.

Once in his arms, the music for *"Something in the Way She Moves"* started, and Julia's eyes welled up in a rush of sentimentality. "For you, My Jelly," he whispered in her ear. "I love you, and you look so beautiful tonight. I am very lucky man to have you with me." He felt her almost loose her footing and caught her, pulling her tightly to him.

He kept dancing, and slowly moved back to look at her face.

Tomis saw Julia almost in tears, which shocked him. Totally lost, he had no idea how he had hit such a vulnerable part of her. To Julia, the steel coating on her heart had finally and completely dropped away, and the unprotected organ lay open to exposure. This definitely no longer a 'romantic adventure,' or just romping-sex with a younger man. He softly asked, "Jelly are you OK?" Really difficult for him, how she could be so strong, then tear-up.

No way Julia could explain what had just happened to her. She'd sworn to herself she would never let herself be so vulnerable to a man again. And yet, Tomis had broken through with his honest love of her. She truly felt like her heart wide open, and arrows were going to come flying into it any moment.

She took a really big breath, and let it out slowly to get composure. Yes, she knew this in some ways almost too good to be true. While part of her desperate to cover her heart back up, the other part visualizing it being handed over to him, and he kept kissing it gently.

Julia came back to the real world with Tomis kissing her on her cheeks, nose and forehead. All acceptable places, considering all eyes were on them, since everyone had stepped off the dance floor for them. "Oh, my God Tomis, everyone is watching us!" He simply smiled and nodded. She took another breath.

"Yes, I'm OK. You just sweep me off my feet, with the wonderful things you say to me. *I* just can't believe how much I love you." She moved in to put her head on his shoulder, and everyone began to applaud them.

Chapter 13
My Country
Crazy, or Not

A zillion tiny pieces of nothing and everything,
are zapping around in my brain, at all levels.

The minutiae flit in and out of the reality realm,
like leftover notes floating through the universe.

They have searched out every crevice, corner
and interim mezzanine of thought-blips or emotions.

How many are day/night dreams, or actual happenings?
I have no idea, as they fall on me like pigeon-droppings.

I may as well be tossing coins in every fountain I see,
as for the results, or efforts to be real or virtualized.

I know time passes, whether I do anything with it or not.
Yet time is a plague, if I cannot clutch fulfillment for me.

Nothing last forever, after the warm sun comes the dark.
But does not have to be cold, if we bundled up against it.

While happiness wraps around me, it's not permanent.
Like everything, it's my choice, decisions I choose.

Within my experiences, I love my free-to-be craziness!
Within craziness, my truly closest friends choose me.

Julia never did meet her nemesis, though he did come in and saw them dancing. Once the other people had pulled back from the floor, and applauded them, he left quite disgusted, as well furious. Only one way to handle them, especially her - they must be destroyed. He rushed back to his office, full of revenge with phone calls and arrangements to be made. If it couldn't be done in Zagreb, he knew the perfect city for it all to happen.

On the ride home, both exhausted again from being 'on' for more than four hours. Yet, Julia had some questions for clarification. "I'm trying to understand, why so much adulation - you know praise and appreciation for me. It's almost like they worship me, but I don't really mean *worship*. They are real fans, asking for autographs. I know, especially the tourism people, they see and deal with lots of foreigners, lots of Americans. What is it?" She then started to joke, . . . "Are they so very happy you finally have a girlfriend?"

Tomis gave her one of his looks, about saying something so ridiculous. "Yes, most people last few years see many foreigners, especially Americans. And, they spend money and most are nice people.   But, you Julia, you want to *help* my country be better, … and you *support* my country to join EU. And, you tell them *they are wonderful*, and *country is beautiful*. It is not just cheap, good time. You *want to be here*, not just money or job. You like them and their country, my country. They never see it before. You are special . . . and maybe autograph give them something to remember you."

Tomis got very quiet, perhaps realizing *what would he have* to remember her? She had not even been there a week, but now scheduled to leave at the end of three weeks. What would he do without her? Once again, he could not truly remember his life before her, like not even *A* life before, but merely an existence.

What he said all true, but it had not started out as he said. Could she even tell him? Julia pulled her lips in, and looked out the car window to see the last of the city lights fade behind her. She loved this man and knew he loved her.

Real love, supposedly the sort of thing all about honesty, and either he'd accept her as she was or not. She turned back to him, putting a leg under her to get closer up to him. "Honestly Tomis, it started out more like the typical American, than the altruistic person you have now painted me as being." She watched his face intently, in the soft light of the car interior.

"I've told you, it *had started* as a romantic adventure, and me NOT supposed to fall in love with you. With bonuses of some *generous money*, and *a free trip* thrown in to a country *I had wanted to see* for the past few years, or so."

A deep breath to continue. "But it all began to change in New York, emotions I did not think I'd have. Then, it really changed when you left me, so I *had to* make a go of it with Inka and Marijana. Then I saw how much your tourism people wanted to be better, and how fascinating your city *is*, and *was* in its majestic, yet tragic history."

Julia took another really big breath for the finale, not sure if she'd get it all out correct. "I truly can't believe how much I love this place, more than anywhere I've ever been. And, also how much I love you, . . . more than anyone before."

She had not meant to actually say the last part, it just seemed to naturally slip out. Quickly biting her lips again, as her heart out of her chest. Seeming to be waiting for the arrows to be flung at it. She finally broke eye contact and felt her eyes welling up again.

Tomis reached over and lifted her face back up to him. "Look at me Jelly." She took another breath before she could, and now when he saw the tears forming, he understood. *The exact way* he had felt several times over the past week.

"I know. You change and I change . . . *a lot*. Love changes us, love can do that and it is scary, …as you say. But it is OK, … it is good. It is really great, and we are happy together."

She began to move up on him, and he kissed her, but moved her back down to the seat. "We almost home, OK." When they arrived at the gate, two of the security men were on either side of it. As Marijana put the code in, the one spoke to her and the other to Luka. Once the gate opened, Julia could feel the car going faster than usual i nto the drive, and Luka said something t o Tomis.

He calmly turned to her, "We go in back door, not front, OK?" She knew better than to ask any questions. They were barely in the house, when shots were fired away from the house. With-out turning on any lights, Tomis took her to the stairs with Marijana following, "Please go up and go into bathroom with Marijana. Wait for me please. Do not come down, OK?"

He watched to make sure they'd done what he said. Then he went back through the kitchen, taking the stairs down into the security room to watch what had happened on the cameras. They already had a man tied to a chair, and gagged with his hands-cuffed.

In doing the now thirty-minute, outer-perimeter search, two of the security had found two men this time with rifles - one had been captured and the other had gotten away. They knew the scenario would be to shoot, as Tomis and Julia were going into the house.

They had stealthily continued to search for the other man, knowing he might be in hiding, until someone gave him updates, as to the car's location to the house. Since he'd have to come out to shoot at them, they were ready to pounce themselves. They knew it'd be a close cat and mouse game, but no other way to flush him out, and they did. State Police had been waiting for the second man to be caught, before they rushed in to arrest them both, and take them back into Zagreb.

Just as before, they were men who had worked part-time for Tomis. The one man, single had gambling debts, the other married had borrowed money from a loan-shark, with his family being held by them. State Police at the docks were given his home address, to rush over to rescue his family, so he'd talk. More pieces to the puzzle, and both men had been called earlier in the evening to do the deed to pay- off their debts. When asked, they admitted they were to shoot both of them.

The older man, who had been caught first, began to cry, apologizing and saying he had to do it, because of his family and his debts. The younger man remained quite arrogant, and un-remorseful. Tomis said to the State Police to be sure to punish him to the full extent of the law, but the other, older one more leniently for his financial circumstances.

The security computer man had been doing his thing, searching all calls from Zagreb to the Rijeka area code at the docks. Once again, he narrowed it down to a repetitive number calling to other repetitive numbers. They had nailed Julia's nemesis, as she had called him. Now, they just needed a little more proof, as to his cohorts in crime, including the ferry owner who had been working with the Organized Crime group for some time.

Marijana had kept a watchful eye at the bathroom window, with Julia lighting a few candles. Meantime, she'd, taken off her lovely gown, hung it on a hanger, slipped on her Helmsley robe, and sat on the toilet seat nervously listening for Tomis' steps on the stairs.

He then called her name, as he came into the bedroom, and she opened the bathroom door rushing into his arms. "It's OK, no one hurt." He turned to Marijana and thanked her, with Julia adding her thanks too, as she left the room.

Tomis took Julia to the bed, and got her to sit while he took off his tuxedo and hung it on the back of the chair. Neither of them talked, while he finished undressing down to his shorts, and sat next to her on the bed. "I am so sorry I get you into my mess." This time Julia put her arm around him, giving the gentle squeeze he usually gave her. "I want you to think about *'resilience,'* do you understand? It's when you take negativity, or adversity and turn it into something positive. It helps you to become stronger, and . . . more resourceful, to know you are actually building to a healthier, better future." She watched him watching her speak.

"It's not simply coping with a situation; it's turning the difficult times into a positive growth experience. You ARE doing it, but not acknowledging what you're doing, and accomplishing. Every time you catch another criminal, or find a bit of revealing information to get you to the 'head-honchos,' you are proving your strength and resourceful- resilience. You are all smarter, stronger and more determined to beat them, destroy them, from ever hurting anyone else again. You need to acknowledge what you've accomplished. You are *resilient!*"

Julia got her sense of herself back, as she'd watched him, and determined for the evening not be ruined by a few gun shots.

"You don't have to apologize again, and no, I'm not going to be sent back to Michigan, so don't even go there with your guilt."

She chuckled, but a bit forced. "You know I had no idea success and tourism - such an *innocuous* industry - could be so dangerous. . ." She then took another deep breath, squared her shoulders, and put a perky smile on her face, to go into her 'Susie- Sweet-breath' act.

"Did I ever tell you, I had a *Yakuza* living next to me in Japan? And, more afraid of me than I ever could be of him. Of course, a very low level, just ran a bunch of Pachinko Parlors - the pinball-gambling- machines - and *tity-bars*. Such a joke, I made fun of him to my friends."

She laughed, "Sure, these Japanese Yakuza rarely have guns or bullets." Tomis looked at her with the most amazed stare, as to how she could say some of the most intelligent, then bizarre things sometimes. Still, he could not resist himself. "Why he afraid of you? What did you do to him?" Julia cracked-up laughing, as she'd hooked him.

"The Japanese don't really have a clear sense of timing on movie stars. James Dean, Marilyn Monroe and Audrey Hepburn, to name a few, they believe still alive and well, because they watch their movies all the time. He fear of me, because originally from Chicago - you know, Al Capone-fame, but mostly since I *wasn't afraid* of him, snickering often." She laughed again.

"Everyone else, even on the streets, Japanese people would stop and give way to *any* Yakuza, who may be walking by. Gaijin - foreigners - didn't, they saw the Yakuza as fools, and just bullies. I purposely would yell at his dog, when it barked at two o'clock in the morning, when he came home. People were shocked, and he thought I *must* be connected to the Mafia, or I would have been afraid of him, . . . thus afraid of me"

Julia took another deep breath, "It is all about *perception*. I told you before Tomis, weak people give other people their power. These gangsters have no *moral compass*, but still only get away with what they can - *are allowed to*, when a weak person does what they want them to do. The weak ones, especially with addictions, give up their power to them. You are very strong, not weak-willed, I am also."

She continued on her roll. "We will win. I cannot deny, I have a concern for your safety, as you do for mine. But you have a good, diligent security team, and the key will be when they can also *nail the insider* in the State Police."

Listening to her, he pulled himself out of it, as he laughed at her. Turning on her, as if wrestling her down on to the bed. "So you are really Mafia-girl from Chicago? So, I need to be afraid of you?" He had surprised her, but she quickly got into the game, vigorously wrestling with him, and trying to get on top of him. "Hey, I'm the one who does the aerobics, so don't try to pin me down *Mister*. This body should be a registered weapon!"

At that, they both ended up laughing so hard, they could not continue. They laid side by side kissing and caressing each other, until arousal built-up in them both. No, a few gun shots would not ruin their night of bliss.

~ ~ ~ ~ ~ ~ ~ ~

Their foray in the kitchen better on Sunday than Saturday, but still not what Julia would have liked to prepare for him. Again, Tomis translating the newspaper to her of their evening before, including their dance together.

"I'm sure some people must have told the press of our dance and everyone applauding for us, since they weren't there then." He laughed at her naïveté.

"OK, Duh! Everyone wants to curry-favor with the paper, so they get some publicity, too. I don't mind, but a very personal moment. Though, not sure why they applauded, . . . or even left the floor for us."

Tomis put the paper down. "I tell you before Julia, they like you very much. It is . . . their way to say how much, I think. We need to leave about ten o'clock to get to the Palace and walk around before the tour. I never saw tour, just room with the President."

Julia burst out laughing. "Now you are the Duh! Most people just get the tour, not get to actually be in a room *with* the President!" "Yes, . . . you are right." He picked back up the paper and she pulled it down.

"Of course, I'm right! You are starting to learn, as I told you, I AM always right!" Laughing, as she got up from the table to begin to clear the dishes, and he grabbed her to pull her into his lap. He began covering her with kisses, and in between saying,

"Yes, you are right, . . yes, you are right! . . .Yes, You are Right!" He then leaned her against the table. "Explain to me - how can you be so smart *and* so silly?"

She looked him seriously in the eyes. "I really work at being silly, it makes everything better. My sense of humor has gotten me through much." She leaned in and kissed him fully. About to move to another level, when a knock from the kitchen area.

Tomis broke it off to look towards the sound, and there stood his brother Ivo. About five-ten, so much shorter and stockier than Tomis, with receding hair, making him look older than his late thirties. "Ivo, Hello! I did not expect you until later this afternoon." Ivo said something in Croatian, and Julia knew immediately, he'd not understood the English. She pulled herself out of his lap, as Tomis lifting her up to her feet. He rattled off some Croatian and proceeded to introduce Julia in both English and Croatian. "We go sight-seeing, but you are welcome to join us."

Again, almost upset, Ivo said something, and Tomis turned to Julia. "Leave dishes on table, it is OK. And, get finish ready to go, OK?" His jaw had tightened and his eyes had darkened.

Julia knew this not good, but not her relative. She could only think of what Talia had said about her brother. She leaned-up and kissed Tomis on the lips. "I'll be ready in fifteen minutes and be back down, OK?"

He nodded, and waited for her start-up the stairs before he cut into Ivo. Julia could hear the control in his voice, then how it would slip, get raised, and controlled again. No way, this could be good. Julia then certainly hoped Ivo would not join them sight-seeing, and with thought, she didn't even want him to go down the coast with her. She could see the resentment in his face, and he didn't really look at her when introduced, just a quick glance and nod.

Julia grabbed her hat off the dresser, then for some reason, she decided to stuff her passport pouch away in a pocket of her suitcase, and closed it up. Something very unsettling about Ivo, and she didn't trust him at all. *No, she thought to herself, you know it's not how you handle those kinds of people, you kill them with kindness, so they feel guilty for not liking you.* The only problem, he didn't understand much English, so it might not be easy to do..

When Julia came back down, Ivo gone and Tomis had finished clearing the table, to put the dishes in the dishwasher. "Sorry about that. He go to see friend here, and back at six o'clock, so we talk about trip down coast then." He washed his hands, and grabbed his jacket, as he guided her out the back door to the waiting cars.

He then rattled off information for her. "We stop at Lotrščak Tower from Zagreb history, built middle of 13th century to protect southern city gate for over hundred years cannon fired every day at noon to celebrate we chase Turks away from Sava River. You can climb tower for good view, but not today." Julia cracked-up, but Tomis not interested in the joke.

After the quick gate stop, on to the Palace with the President's special assistant showing them the various public and private rooms. He answered everyone of Julia's questions, regarding the architectural- detail on the exterior and interior of it. Tomis only had to interpret for her a few times.

They ended up on the balcony at a quarter to twelve, and watched all of the people gather around below for the Guard Changing Ceremony. The President got there only five minutes before, and as Tomis expected, quite hung-over. He only did a few waves to the audience, then stepped back towards Julia. Tomis thought it very funny, but Julia kissed and pampered him, feeding his ego.

From there they moved on to Algoritam, one of Tomis' favorite shops. Off Trg Jossip Jelačića, and had a wide selection of books and magazines in English, French, German, Italian and Croatian. After savoring it, they then went back out to the book market in the square, and walked around slowly. He showed her some of his favorite sellers, and their selections to browse. While no one asked for any autographs, several people did recognize Tomis, and came up to shake his hand on the celebrated accomplishment of the ferries.

Julia felt very proud of him, and though the security had instantly appeared not uncomfortable. They then went inside the Hotel Dubrovnik, as it could be accessed through a separate entrance of the bookstore. They sat to have coffee and Julia had a glass of local wine, while munching on a slice of kremšnite - custard pie. "I just love the beautiful blue trams, trundling along the city streets, it so reminds me of San Francisco and their streetcars."

From there, Tomis took her to Dolac Market stalls, which had the very best Zagreb souvenirs. Once she had finished picking and choosing ones to buy, St Mark's Church from the 13th century next. Its famous steeple and roof of mosaic tiles were decorated with the Medieval coat of arms of Croatia, Dalmatia and Slavonia, with the emblem of Zagreb on the right side. They took their time going inside looking at all of the sculptures, and Romanesque window on the southern side.

Back out on the streets, Julia loved looking at corner balconies on the building facades. She pointed them out to Tomis, "Now these remind me of New Orleans, as it combines several different cultures and styles, too." More as a joke than anything, Tomis decided to take her to Kroata Crayata. "Since necktie invent in Croatia, very good souvenir gift, and this is best place to get one." Julia surprised him by buying a tie for her son Jeremy, though she doubted he would wear it much, if at all in Texas. Still, if he needed one, he'd have it.

She'd noticed him look at his watch several times, so not sure what surprise up next, but something timed. When Tomis walked into Regent Esplanade Zagreb, a world-class hotel, Julia stopped him saying she'd not dressed for such a polished-dining room.

"They have very good food and it is OK, we have private room. I am sorry, but security supervisor not want us to eat in open area." The Maitre' D must have been watching for them, as he approached immediately, and greeted them both in English, addressing Julia as Ms. Martin.

Tomis had remembered her mentioning lamb not readily available in the Upper Peninsula, so he had taken the liberty to have three different dishes for her to choose from. She, of course, chose the Croatian style, with his description sounding delicious, and the štrukli - baked cheese dumplings with it and a salad before. He also had a bottle of French Pinot Noir open, and waiting at the table.

He lifted his glass to her, "To us, My Jelly. You make me happy, so many way." He smiled in having it all go so well.

"Thank you, and you make me so very happy, too." Then she had to ask, "Is this all for our second anniversary?" Smiling, she then saw the blank look on his face.

"Second Anniversary? I do not understand." Curiously lost, once again.

"We met two weeks ago today. Our first dinner about this time. I thought thiss why you wanted this special dinner for us." She tried to smile over his confusion.

"We meet two weeks ago? You are sure?" His mind racing, trying to remember, as he sure she had to be wrong. "It must be … more than two weeks."

"Oh my God, Tomis," she laughed. "We have been a whirlwind. Last Sunday I flew into New Jersey, the first time we made love. We haven't really even known each other a full two weeks, as you flew out on Friday, so we didn't have Friday or Saturday. But we can count it from the day we met, at the book sale to today - two weeks ago. It's really all about books."

"That *is* amazing. I feel I know you much more than two weeks." He began to think how could so much have happened in such a short period of time? "I am very sorry, it is now for our second anniversary. We have happy anniversary!" Smiling, but still lost.

"Was there another reason you wanted us to have a special dinner?" Now, her curiosity, since he had obviously gone to a lot of trouble to have it arranged.

"This very nice place, we can be alone and safe. … Monday busy in Rijecka at the docks, and not have such nice place ... to be alone and safe. Tuesday you go to Zadar, ... then Split Wednesday and Dubrovnik, ... but I see you Friday, not Thursday."

He smiled to continue. "I fly to meet you ... for weekend. Then we take ferry back, ... and stop at some islands for swim. Does it sound good ...for you? If we can finish soon ... at the docks, I come soon ... to be with you, OK?"

"Yes, my love, it all sounds perfect. We will talk every day, but I will miss you too, very much. So, we have this wonderful dinner together, and savor each moment to remember when we are apart." Truly, all about catching the bad guys and how soon they could do it, so they could be together freely.

"Best laid plans of mice and men," popped into Julia's head, but left unspoken to him.

~ ~ ~ ~ ~ ~ ~ ~ ~

They got home a little after six, but Ivo not there, so Tomis went to check with security downstairs, and he had not been back. When he came into the conference room, to tell her he didn't know if Ivo would be showing up or not, Julia could see Tomis quite upset. She felt she had already put her two cents into it, on the plane coming over. One thing she would not do, rub salt into a wound, especially when it involved family. She decided she'd simply move on with her organizing for the coming week and kept working at the table. "I'm sure it will work out. I'm going to get what I can ready and call Inka. What time should I tell her to be here in the morning?"

Tomis looked at her, grateful she had not lectured him again on Ivo, or placated with a 'don't worry.' He came up behind her, looking through her piles and wrapped his arms around her. "Thank you, Jelly for no comment   We leave at six o'clock, you know is long drive. I know is early for you, with only two appointments - my companies and the other large one."

He had let her go and moved to standing next to her. "I introduce you to my two managers, for ferry is Jossip and train is Antun. I am interested in what you think." He now hesitated, and Julia turned to look at him, knowing some-thing else he had to say to her. He felt her reading him, so no need to put it off any longer. "I need tell you, security supervisor make me wear bullet-proof vest … when I go out." Tomis watched her face, it didn't show a flinch. Then he realized she'd figured it out. "We had two gunmen with rifles, they found and shot one, he just wounded."

Julia moved to him, and now put her arms around his waist. "You must also wear vest … if you go out into dock, do you understand?" She nodded her head into his chest, and squeezed him a little tighter. He breathed easier. "We have much security there, … and they know to watch you very close. I know you not listen to not go . . ." She pulled back from him and laughed. "I have concern for you and Inka, OK?" She leaned up to kiss him and he met her lips. At that moment again, staring Ivo knocked on the open conference room door. He said something in Croatian, which made Tomis' head almost snap around. Julia felt his body tense-up immediately, so she let him go. As he turned to face Ivo, she went back to sorting through her client's stuff on the table. They were already talking intently, when Julia interrupted.

"Hello Ivo. Excuse me Tomis, I'm going upstairs to call Inka. Let me know when you are ready to talk about next week." She walked past them and went up to the other office. By the time she got up there, she could no longer hear them, except for when one or the other raised their voice.

About twenty minutes later, Tomis called her from the bottom of the stairs to come down. He waited at the stairs for her, and smiled at seeing her. She carried a stack of manila envelopes, she had taken from his stockpile.

"I borrowed some envelopes. Everything OK now?" She tried to be as cheery and perky as possible, but could see his controlled face tight.

"Yes, it … OK. I tell him job with you, … but you need to talk what you want." In reality, Julia didn't want anything from Ivo, or even to be with him, but somehow Tomis thought Ivo could be a tour- guide. Or, maybe he just wanted Ivo to get to know her, and accept her into their life - whatever - Julia had no real clue. She took her usual deep breath to deal with it all, and be positive of the outcome.

"Hi again, Ivo. I'm looking forward to getting to know you and spending time with you." She waited for him to respond, as sure Tomis had asked him to try to speak some English. Tomis then said something in Croatian to him.

"Yes, I look forward, too." He had several of the brochures of the cities and sites along the coast in his hand. "You have brochure, … why need me?" Julia then noticed he'd been looking through the client's stuff, and several of the brochures were no longer on their own stack. She walked over to reorganize them, but did not say a word about it.

Julia then turned to look at him smiling, but he still didn't do more than glance at her and look away. "Tomis said you know a lot of information, background and history, since you spent more time down the coast, and on the islands. I would like to know those details and see what has been used on brochures and what has not. We may want to do new brochures, giving more history and interesting cultural information."

She had no clue how much he had understood or

not, so tried a different tactic. "I think you may know Inka, my translator, and if you can talk to her, it would be helpful. Traveling with us, when you see a place, it may bring some ideas or memories to you. Does that clarify it all somewhat, how you can help me, ..us?"

Julia again waited, looking at Ivo for a response. He glanced at her and over to Tomis. He then made some remark to Tomis, not hiding his smirk. Even without knowing the words, she recognized the smart-ass tone.

Since his anger had been barely controlled under the surface, it erupted quickly and Julia watched, as Ivo's smirk grew bigger with Tomis' angry words.

Ivo had played him. And while, certain Tomis may have known it, he could be way too emotional when it came to Ivo. And, especially lately, with all of his screw-ups.

It suddenly dawned on Julia, Ivo had been quite self- destructive to see just how far, or how much Tomis would put-up with him doing.

Now, she felt sorry for Ivo, but also had no intention of rescuing him. Tomis had been unfortunately, doing it for way too long. Julia then felt she should again physically remove herself from them, but not out of the room. She picked-up the brochures Ivo had put back on the table and walked around to the far corner of it.

She busied herself with putting them in one of the envelopes, which she then marked, closed- up and put down. Then she reached over and pulled out the English brochure from each pile - as she had planned to check the English on each. She then put all of them in one envelope, marked it, closed it up and put it down. Tomis had finished his exasperating dissertation, with Ivo making probably foul retorts. Tomis ended it by telling him to be there before six in the morning, and ready to go. Ivo left without any remarks to Julia.

Julia walked back over to Tomis, took his hands and put them around her waist, as she patted his chest to calm him down. "It's OK, breathe deep and let it go, OK?" He nodded his head and took a deep breath.

"Again, another deep breath." She waited until he'd be ready to respond, but held any of her psychological assumptions. "Perhaps I can talk to Inka, and have Ivo speak to her directly, so no English to deal with. She can also ask him questions, if he doesn't come forth with any info on his own. How does that sound - easier for all of us?"

To a certain extent, Julia felt as if Tomis simply trying to get Ivo away from the bad influences of his gambling and drinking. He'd tried to offer him one more chance to change, thinking Ivo would like being out among the tourists.

"I do not know what to do. I try to help him *over and over ...*" *That's the real problem,* she thought, but said nothing.

~~~~~~~~~

Although Rijeka hardly a 'must-see' destination, it did have some real assets, such as Korzo - the pedestrian mall, a tree-lined promenade along the harbor, as well the imposing, hilltop-fortress of Trast. Lately, the bar-club capital of northern Croatia, making it almost more interesting to visit by night than by day.

Despite some unfortunate, postwar architectural ventures in the outskirts, much of the cityscape contained the sort of ornate, imposing public buildings one would expect to find in Vienna or Budapest. They were evidence of the strong Austro-Hungarian influence, exerted on the city's cultural and economic life in the 19th century.

But, Rijeka such an important port and transportation hub, almost impossible to avoid. The buses, trains and ferries connected it to Istria - the heavy, Italian region, and Dalmatia with Zagreb and points beyond, all seemed to pass through the city. As Croatia's largest port, Rijeka full of boats, cargo, fumes, cranes and the kind of seedy- energy, which usually characterized most port cities around the world.

However, because of no beach, the resources for visitors were scarce. Trast Castle, built in the 13th-century, high on a hill overlooking Rijeka and the Rječina River, gave it some majesty. It occupied a position of immense strategic importance, and may have been a Liburnian hill-fort in prior aeons, but the Frankopan dukes of Krk, who built the present castle, to protect their holdings in Vinodol, further east.

The Konak, an enclosed yard with a cistern, the best-preserved part of the original structure. From the 13th to the 15th century, Trast belonged to the Frankopans, or their relatives, but seized by the Habsburgs at the end of the 15th century.

Julia and Inka would be dropping off Tomis at the office first, and making a quick stop at the Castle, as their appointment not until ten o'clock with Jossip. This gave Tomis time with his manager first, to go over business and other happenings from the weekend.

There had only been a few points of interest, Tomis took the time to point out to Julia on the way there. He had mainly been going through his print-outs of the weekend, he downloaded from the office. So, it had been a rather uneventful ride out, with Tomis and Julia in the lead car with Luka and Marijana, followed by Inka and Ivo in the second car. Inka had her instructions, as to how to handle Ivo, and ask questions when he didn't volunteer any.

In all honesty, she didn't particularly like him either, but knew she needed to be nice to him for Tomis' sake. And, he may be able to help Julia's efforts, for improving all the tourist information.

So, Ivo had joined them on the trip up to Trast Castle, choosing to ride alone in the second car. The security detail knew to keep a close eye on him, as his tendency to wander-off. While no longer married, he had a child, but he'd chat-up the young, female workers, distracting them from their jobs.

To say he took advantage of his position and relationship to Tomis, a grand under-statement. The security supervisor felt it relatively safe for them up there, as few tourists would be around so early.

Julia did make a point to have Inka ask Ivo if he could add any specific details, and he actually did. She told Julia later, she'd been trying to give him some background on her and what all she'd been doing to help Croatia, especially with the tourism industry. Inka then mentioned, he asked about Julia's relationship with Tomis, so she told Ivo, truly the first time she'd seen him happy in years.

"Thank you, Inka. Though I don't know if it's a good thing or not, as Ivo is so envious of Tomis. At least he knows, I'm not some bimbo, just after him for his money or this trip." The look on Inka's face reminded Julia, Jelena had said much the same about her to Inka. "That's OK, Inka, thank you, as always for your support."

Julia found Jossip, the manager, to be well-organized and most anxious to use his budding English - though basic, but he really tried. With the slower season coming on, he'd be going for more classes, he happily told Julia. Probably around Tomis' age, a little shorter at around six feet, but seemed to be in good shape. Julia noticed his diploma and other certificates on the wall, as well a *no smoking* sign in Croatian.

One thing she had Inka ask all the clients to note, how much they had traveled and to where. Jossip enthusiastic to share how many countries, including America and Asia he had traveled to, either alone or with his wife. Particularly he liked to go to countries which also had large ferry systems, when he mentioned Hong Kong, it caught Julia's ear. She asked him several questions, as to if before or after nationalization with China.

Happy to share a few tidbits, which s thrilled him. She could see why Tomis' first choice to be the COO - Chief Operating Officer. Inka then began to go over the details of the assessment with him, as Julia looked around the offices and picked-up every brochure she saw available. One thing she felt most important were the restrooms. Then she saw Ivo, "Oh, Ivo could you look in the men's room and see if anyone is in there?" When he pointed to the ladies's room, she explained. "Oh, I want to look at how clean it is, and the layout." He shrugged his shoulders, walked in and called to see if anyone using the stalls. When he shook his head,

"Would you watch, so no one comes in while I'm in there? I'll be just a minute." He stood by as she went in to check, and back out shortly. "Thank you so much, the restroom is very important to many people." He actually looked at her then, and even gave her a slight smile.

"Please feel welcome, if you want to come in to listen to our presentation,. I would like your input on it too, if you will do so." He s tared at her, so not sure how much he understood. When Julia went back in with Jossip, Inka just finishing up.

They began their presentation routine, which they had gotten pretty good at doing together. He had a few questions in both English and Croatian, before signing the agreement for the training of his people. Ivo had not come in, so Julia thought the next time, she'd have Inka talk to him.

When they left the office, Marijana waiting for them. It always amazed Julia how she could appear or disappear like a ninja. Since the ferries, trains, and buses were all interconnected, they would not be out in the open and vulnerable. But Marijana had scoped it all out, to make sure no one lurking around. Julia had actually noticed several other of the security detail momentarily.

They had about fifteen minutes before the meeting with Antun, at the train station office, so she asked Inka if she wanted some coffee or something. Marijana then turned to her, "It is better to go to train station office and drink coffee there." Julia understood and agreed, thanking her as usual. When they walked into the office, Inka told the receptionist they were early, but would appreciate some coffee, if she had it. So happy to see them, she started to get-up and walk away with her phone headset still on.

They had just gotten their coffee when Anton came out to greet them, also using his best English. Younger, a little shorter than Jossip, but also looked to be energetic in his demeanor. He insisted they bring their coffee in, and seated them at his couch with the coffee table. He pulled up a chair from in front of his desk and sat down with his own coffee cup. Julia impressed at how well he had handled it. While Inka gave him some basic information, Julia glanced around the office. She noted, he also had a diploma and other certificates on his wall.

When they got to the travel question, he had not done much outside of the region. But, proud to say he had actually taken a trip on the Orient Express, when they were doing the promotion a few years back. Catching the name, Julia spoke up to ask him how far and what cities, so also delighted to give her more details.

Once Inka began to go over the details of the assessment, Julia again got up to wonder around the lobby area. Again, she picked up every brochure she saw available, glancing at the English ones. This time Marijana had been waiting for her, and stuck to her for the bathroom inspections and all. Julia had her large manila envelopes in her tote bag, and stuffed the material in each designated one, she'd already marked.

Again, she returned as Inka finishing, and checked for any questions before having him sign the training agreement. Once they were out of the main offices, since almost noon, Julia asked Marijana to check if Tomis might have time for lunch or not. She called, and told 'no' by the security supervisor, as Tomis deep in union meetings. He added, he should be finished to have dinner with her.

Julia disappointed, but knew Tomis really needed the cooperation of the union, to keep the factions at bay. "Well, could Inka and I at least go to Korzo, the pedestrian mall, with the tree-lined promenade along the harbor?"

Marijana got back on the phone to the supervisor and reported back. "Only if you both wear a vest." Julia looked over to Inka, and she vigorously shook her head 'no,' while her eyes almost popping out of her head. Just then Ivo showed-up, with no excuse for his absence, he asked Inka about lunch plans. She then explained to him about Julia wanting to go to Korzo, but they had to wear a vest to do so. He laughed and rattled something off, and Marijana came right back at him with information which made Inka gasp, and Ivo say something along with a 'no.' Julia began to laugh, realizing Ivo had no idea of the attempts on both of their lives, but especially on Tomis'.

Julia decided to see his bravado. "You want to wear a vest and go with me Ivo, over to Korzo?" He just shook his head, now knowing Julia a target, and walked away. "Marijana, is there any where we can go for lunch, where we can at least see the water and the boats, if not be outside?" She turned to Inka for some English clarification, and she explained it. She got back on the phone to the supervisor, and handed it over to Inka to translate to Julia.

"OK, we have a place . . . you can use lunch room on . . . second floor. It has windows and . . . terrace, but you . . . must sit inside and . . . in corner." Julia then went around the corner to call back to Ivo to join them, they had found a place for lunch.

"Something is better than nothing. I just hate being on the water and not being able to enjoy it." Marijana back on the phone and let the supervisor know they were all going to the second floor lunch room, so he could get some more security over her way. They all followed her, and by the time they reached the lunch room, several security people had passed them, to go through-out to the terrace area.

While Julia didn't want something, as seemingly simple as lunch to become a major problem, she reminded herself, the whole situation temporary. They had until two o'clock before their last appointment, with Tomis' next biggest competitor - but not the one they were suspicious of collaborating with Organized Crime. Julia told Inka to feel free to go and walk Korzo without her, but at that point, Inka preferred to stay around the security.

Their last appointment a 'mom & pop,' who concentrated on car ferry service, but had seen an increase in tourists during the season. They didn't want to miss-out on being better, as their oldest son had come back from college, so now interested in the business. They said he spoke much better English, but doing the nine-hour ferry-run down to Dubrovnik. They were really sweet, and Julia kept sitting there smiling at them, as Inka translated back and forth. There were no diplomas on the wall, just photos of their children, and she could see the ashtray where 'Pop' probably smoked. But 'mom' happy to make the business better for their son.

Julia did get-up when Inka started on the assessment, and went over to pick-up several of the brochures. Right away, she saw several English mistakes, but said nothing putting them all in the designated envelope, with their name on it. Julia excused herself, and when she exited the office, Marijana right there waiting to help with the restrooms check.

They walked around a little and Julia asked if she had some lunch, which she had. Julia then went back into the office. They had several questions, especially if the training going to be in Croatian, or just English, and Inka assured them it would be available in Croatian.

When they signed, 'Mom' insisted on giving Julia a hug and kisses. She rattled-off something smiling and Inka said, "She is very grateful for all of your help, and God bless you." Julia kept saying 'thank you' in English and her fractured-Croatian, as tears began to well up in her eyes. She made a point to shake hands with Pop, and he kissed it. Her exit of them almost too quick, but she did not want them to see her cry.

These people, Julia thought, after all the horrors they have been through, and they still keep going. She'd dug a tissue out of her purse, and wiping her eyes when Marijana reappeared. "Can we go back-up to the lunch room to go over our paperwork, and get something to drink?" Julia turned to Inka to make sure Marijana had understood her? Marijana asked what had happened with Julia, and Inka told her, but not sure. Marijana called again to the supervisor, and he agreed to send more people again.

They had at least an hour before Tomis would be finished, so they may as well get some work done. Out of the clear blue, Ivo showed-up again, and for some reason, much nicer to both of them, particularly Julia. She couldn't imagine what had happened, but she'd soon find out. Unfortunately, Ivo not nearly as smart as he thought. But plans had been put in motion, and lives would be changed forever.

Tomis had wanted to get a hotel room for he and Julia to have more privacy, but the supervisor had said 'no,' since not sure t some covert activity going on. They had already picked-up two men in separate areas, with handguns this time. Since not the most upstanding neighborhood, the supervisor had no proof they were in any way related to Tomis and Julia's safety.

Dinner would have to be brought in, and she'd have to share his small studio with the double bed. Julia laughed, "It's not as if we take-up more than one space anyway, and the point is to be close."

Still, she could hear the men once in a while in the hall, and also below their window in the bedroom. The quietest sex they'd ever had. And, each time one or the other got the giggles, or started laughing, the other would go to cover their mouth, and just laugh more.

Julia whispered into Tomis' ear, "I feel like we are *lab-rats,* being observed for our sex activity." It had all made her feel so clandestine, she got the giggles.

He looked at her in utter mystification. "You scare me some time Jelly, . . . how you *think* of such *strange* things." They then both got the giggles so bad, they put their pillows over their faces. Finally falling asleep, probably one of their most fun nights together.

Chapter 14
Kidnap/Rescue
Chapters & Books

The longer we live it,
Sometimes the more cognizant
We are about life,
And our choices in it.

We might look back on it
As chapters, or even books,
Like a trilogy or series.
Not stuck in just re-reading it.

While each book or chapter
May have its own "Revelation,"
How we use the experience,
Is again our choice.

With time and/or space,
Even painful relationships
Can attain insight for growth,
Not repetitive wrong actions.

Love, companionship or friendship,
Can once again be approached,
Like new chapters to a new book,
Reading/Writing pages, slowly/thoroughly.

Age/experience does give us,
The perspective of not rushing.
Time has become a friend –
Satiating in moments, savoring details.

More Second Chances are out there.
We simply have to be receptive,
To the here and now of it all.
Not fables in our age of enlightenment.

One has a second lease on life -
Or third, fourth etc., goes with a price.
It's really not over till we choose.
While no promises, but always choices.

Reading a good book, we must admit,
Not nearly as exciting as writing one.
Yet, *living* each chapter and page,
Ultimately, fulfills a great conclusion.

In the early morning light, Tomis walked Julia to the garage for her trip to Zadar, further down the coast. Ivo riding in the front with Marijana, and Inka already in the back behind her.

Tomis didn't seem to want to let go of Julia, *and the back of his neck kept pinching.* No way he'd remember the last time he felt it in New York, when first concerned for Julia's safety. They were driving down without an escort, since another State Police car meeting them in Zadar, next to the tourist office in the town center.

The supervisor had felt they'd be fine on the highway, with just the one car. Though it would be almost a three-hour drive, as the road follows close to the coast. The curves back around the long bay.

"I will see you Friday in Dubrovnik, . . . enjoy Zadar, it is very old city and . . . Ivo have many good facts for you. I know you love Dubrovnik . . . and famous walls. Now, you have *everything you need*?" Their code so everyone, anywhere around would hear them.

Julia tossed her purse in, "Yes, I have my cell phone and passport in my purse."

He took her hands again, smiling. "Good. Call me lunch, and call me tonight." She kept saying 'yes' to him, and he kept kissing her. Then he said, "Remember, I love you very much." She looked at him, not sure why he had said it in such a way.

"Of course, I love you too, and I'll call and see you soon." As sliding into the car, Tomis still holding her hand, then finally let it go. Ivo had watched it all in the side rearview mirror, and amazed at how emotional Tomis had gotten. He could only remember him acting the same way before, when their father died . . . then he slowly remembered how when Tomis' wife and daughter died. They had to remove Tomis' hands from each closed caskets before the burial.

As Marijana drove south, the rising sun beckoned another beautiful day, and Julia watched as the coast quickly came into view. The lovely red tile-roofed, white stucco houses brought a smile to her face, with remembrances of many Mediterranean-style coast places she'd traveled.

She'd told of her preference of the twisty-turny coast road, which reminded her of famous California Highways, rather than driving inland on the new highway. It didn't really save much time for the lost of views. "So, Ivo, start telling Inka about *the* Zadar, what is *not* in my guide info."

She looked over at Inka, "You translate and I'll take the notes." Julia had done her homework, as usual, and knew Zadar the fastest growing new 'hot spot' for tourists. Located in the central Dalmatia region, while Dubrovnik Airport still handled more tourist visitors, Zadar Airport catching up fast. In fact, the Irish, low-cost carrier, Ryanair announced a new route to Zadar, from several European cities, including Brussels.

Zadar one of the Adriatic's most historically-interesting towns, with a mixture of Roman ruins, from its days as a colony, to the Byzantine-style St. Donat church. The ruins actually went back to the Third century BC. And, with King Tomislav, Zadar came in around the Sixth and Seventh centuries. In the 16th-century, walls were built by the Venetians to fight off the Turks, after they finally subjugated the rebellious city.

A wealth of sight-seeing, like peeling back layers of time and cultures. Ivo commented on its most modern sculpture, the Sea Organ, on the northwestern corner of Zadar's Riva - seaside promenade - a few steps from the ferry station.

Inka mentioned with pride, how being a remarkable piece of urban-architecture. He explained the Sea Organ *captured* the movement of the waves, to transform them into music. The pipes were built into perforated stone stairs, which stretch 70 meters along the coast.

Even without the music, the white marble steps, sloping into the sea, truly extraordinarily beautiful, and a perfect vantage point to appreciate Zadar's splendid sunsets. It even won the European Prize for Urban Public Space, and now Zadar's most beloved monument. Julia complimented Ivo on his detailed description, and her looking forward to seeing it.

Ivo then wanted to talk about Split, their Wednesday visit, as it's Croatia's second largest city. It also had the UNESCO World Heritage Site, the Diocletian's Palace. Both fascinating port cities, and excellent jumping-off points for exploring the wonders of the many islands, just offshore.

Julia then began to share, after Tomis joined her in Dubrovnik for the weekend, they were going to travel back-up to Rijeka by ferry, stopping at several of the islands. She didn't know which ones, so asked Ivo which he liked the best.

They had all talked for over two hours, and Julia felt they were definitely getting closer to understanding each other. With Inka translating, Julia shared some of her travels in Asia and Australia, especially the Great Barrier Reef, with Ivo actually asking her some questions.

Marijana then spoke up, they'd soon be crossing the bridge over the bay, and Zadar less than an hour away. She stopped in busy morning traffic heading into Zadar, needing to make a right-hand turn.

The right-hand drive still strange to Julia, and it felt funny sitting there in the road. She had been showing Inka some of the Zadar brochures, when something out the side window, behind Inka caught her eye. A huge construction-style truck now barreling down at them. She'd just uttered Marijana's name, when it slammed into them.

Julia heard her gasp with pain, as Marijana's door crushed against her. It shovied her towards Ivo, while the airbag exploded on her. Inka had been thrown into the middle of the seat, in front of Julia. Inka then started to bleed from some object, while the metal from the car frame had pushed into her back and side.

The car had been knocked-off its two side-wheels, and settled back against the giant truck bumper, now practically in the dashboard. Julia saw the two men get out of the truck, and one ran around the front of the car, while the other around the rear.

She assumed they were coming to help, and she had moved forward through the front seat split, to see how badly Marijana hurt. She knew Inka more frightened, with probably a whip lash or an injury to her back. But at least Inka still conscious, if not cognizant.

Ivo quite shaken, but uninjured so opening the door, as the man coming around. Marijana, barely conscious, told Julia to push her panic button on her belt next to her gun, on her right-hand side, since she couldn't move. But the door so shoved into Marijana, Julia couldn't get her hand in or touch her, without her groaning in pain.

(In Croatian) Ivo yelled at the other man, who had been the passenger in the truck. "What are you doing? You could have hurt us?"

And, he yelled back at Ivo, "Shut up Fool! I'll hurt you if I want!" This snapped Inka out of her daze, and she realized a set-up and Ivo involved. They were trying to kidnap Julia and Ivo. Julia's door opened, and the driver of the truck tried to reach in and grab her.

Inka then yelled in English, "Julia looks out! He is NOT trying to help, he trying to take you!" She turned in the slot, and saw him trying to come further in to grab her fully. Julia gave him one of her practiced punches, clipped his jaw hard, and another practiced kick to his groin area. He fell back into the door yelling in agony, with blood pouring out of his mouth, as he must have cut his tongue, when she socked him so hard.

The other man hit Ivo in the temple with his gun, and in Croatian yelled something, then called him a fool again. Ivo then called out, "Julia leaves purse and please get out car!" She looked at the two of them like they were crazy. The man fired the gun, and yelled at Ivo again. "Julia, please get out - he shoots Marijana!"

Julia saw the situation, and did not want anyone else hurt. "OK, OK, do not SHOOT!" She started to back out of the car, and leaned toward Inka whispering. "Help Marijana, call Tomis as soon as you can to bring help. Tell them everything you heard." The man fired his gun again, and yelled at Ivo again.

"I'm coming assholes," Julia said, as she backed out of the car. The man she had hit and kicked grabbed her again. This time she hit him again, but with her elbow into his throat. He fell on the ground gasping, as she may have crushed his larynx. The other man came at her. Ivo tried to slow him down, since he couldn't stop him.

Julia looked him right in the eyes, "SHOOT ME ASSHOLE! I'm not worth a cent to you DEAD!" He knew enough English to understand her, and stopped in his tracks. He then went to hit her in the head with the gun, but Julia too fast for him, and had ducked. "Touch me again ASSHOLE, and I WILL KILL YOU. I will go - but DO NOT TOUCH me." In Croatian, he yelled something at Ivo again, and hit him this time in the jaw with the gun butt.

In shocking pain, Ivo cried out, "Julia, please cooperate and go." The man pushed Ivo into her, but she had quickly put her hands in front of her, so her kind of bounced off of her. She then took Ivo's arm and helped him over to the van, which had pulled up next to them. Two men had jumped out of it, and were trying to help the man on the ground, who Julia had almost killed.

Not in very good shape, barely still breathing. The man with the gun giving the orders, and when they looked at Julia, she knew he'd told them not to touch her, she'd cooperate.

She helped Ivo into the van, and climbed in next to him. He began quietly apologizing. "I so sorry. This all my fault. My big gambling debt. They say not hurt you, only want money. They lie. Tell Tomis, I so sorry. I . . ."

The gunman yelling at Ivo again, and it sounded like some cursing, as rather pissed at how wrong it had all gone. Ivo'd also obviously under-estimated Julia, her non-fear of them, and relentless power to not be a victim. But, the gunman now planned, he'd get his revenge.

Ivo looked at her and tears came into his eyes. She put her arm around his shoulder, as she had done to Tomis, just the other night regarding *his* frustration with Ivo. The irony not lost on her, and she leaned over to kiss his cheek. She felt so incredibly sorry for Ivo, his weakness, his addictions, and also having been born *second* to a brother. As well, Ivo knew he'd always be *second* to him in life.

Julia began whispering in his ear. "It is all OK, and we'll be OK." He began to sob quietly, and she tried to cover it up, so the gunman would not yell terrible things at him again. She kept squeezing his shoulder, and telling him it would all be OK.

The two van-men had put the injured man in the far back, and one man who stayed with him saying something in desperation to the gunman. He yelled back with the intonation equivalent to, *he really didn't give a shit*. The other man pleaded, and the driver then also said something to the gunman, so he finally said OK.

Julia guessing they may be dumping him off at a hospital, as she doubted any of them knew how to do a tracheotomy to give him air, so he could breathe. Right, of course, within a few minutes they had pulled into the emergency drive-through. The two men pulled him out, carrying him to the door. Julia carefully turned to watch. What they didn't see, which she did, as the one climbed into the back again, to pull the door closed, the guard stepped-out forward, then pulled out his pen and small notebook to write down the license plate.

They were soon speeding over the bridge Marijana had mentioned, so Julia knew they were heading for the Zadar port. Sure, they'd have some more compadres there. This whole thing had been clumsily-conceived, and carried out worse. It had to be their arrogance, in thinking their Labor politician, and insider-State Police official would protect them.

The port also probably their escape route, by using the shady- owner's ferry, the one who wanted Tomis out of competition. Julia looked down at Ivo leaning against her chest, and figured he may have passed out from the multiple blows, or just in a deep shock. Either way, at least quiet and the gunman had quit screaming at him.

Julia then noticed the man sitting on the floor in the back whispering to himself, and not a *happy-camper*. Larynx-guy must have been a friend, and he figured he'd probably die. This all definitely *not* what he'd signed up for. She wondered what his addiction had been, to have gotten him in such trouble to have to do this.

~ ~ ~ ~ ~ ~ ~ ~ ~

Keeping her head low, Inka had leaned over to see as much as she could out the window, but not making any sudden moves with the gunman still there. When she saw the man on the ground, and realized what Julia had done to him, shocked at her capability to fight back. She tried to get her phone out of her purse, and finally reached it. Still holding it down inside her purse, in case the gunman looked in at her, she had flipped it open to find Tomis on her list of numbers.

Inka heard Marijana groan again, but afraid to move forward, fearing gunman would shoot, if he saw her move. She finally found his cell number and pushed it. A strange voice answered by the second ring, and now in the dilemma. The men had not left yet, they were just lifting the guy from the ground into the van. She began to whisper in English "Help, Julia needs help."

The voice on the other end the security supervisor, as he held Tomis' phone when in a meeting. "Who is this? What?" Inka then realized it had to be one of the security people, so she began repeating it in Croatian. Now, he repeating in Croatian, asking who would be saying this.

Finally, the van pulled away, so Inka ducked her head down to yell into the phone what had happened. He then recognized her, and knew not a decoy call to send them off on a wild-goose chase. Of course, at the moment she should have been looking out the window to get the license plate of the van.

The supervisor immediately got up and knocked on the conference room door. As he walked in, he told Tomis in front of all of the union men present, Julia had just been kidnapped and Ivo injured.

He passed the phone to Tomis as he stood up, and told him, Inka calling from the accident.

He then added Marijana badly injured, as the thugs had crashed a construction truck into their car and destroyed it. Several union people stood up adamantly, saying they'd not support that kind of a criminal act. Inka also clarified to Tomis, she could tell from their accents they were *not* Croatians.

The supervisor then left the room to call the State Police in Zadar, who had actually just pulled up in front of the meeting place in town. They took off for the accident, and had the ambulance meet them there. It came from the hospital, where the larynx-man had been dropped off, and in the process of being given a tracheotomy. Considering the circumstances of his drop-off, the hospital security man had handcuffed him to the bed railing.

The supervisor then took the liberty to call the President, knowing his personal involvement. After telling him Julia had been kidnapped, he said he'd call to have a helicopter released to Tomis. The supervisor then called all of his men into his office immediately.

Tomis slumped back down into his chair trying to grasp it all. The union representatives now arguing among themselves, as to having allowed the Organized Crime to get involved with them in the first place.

When Tomis told them the details of what they'd just overheard, he added Inka said Julia bravely fought back and almost killed one of the men. Several more union men sthen aid they'd give the State Police all of the information they needed to pick-up those others responsible.

Just as the supervisor walked back in, Tomis getting several of them to respond with details. The supervisor said he'd stay to do all of the follow-up on tracking them down. He then told Tomis the helicopter would be waiting for him, and he'd have Luka drive him with several other of his men. The supervisor then said, the kidnappers would probably be calling shortly with the ransom demands, so get his phone connected to their tech guy, to make the trace.

As Tomis then headed for the door, the supervisor called to him, and threw his vest at him. He sternly told him to put it on now, as they may have snipers waiting for him to expose himself. The shocked union people now even apologizing, so would be supporting and standing firmly with Tomis.

~ ~ ~ ~ ~ ~ ~ ~ ~

Nothing original, or unique about the dilapidated, old warehouse which they had pulled the van into. Enough light pouring through the cracks and broken wooden slats, it would be easy for the State Police to find the van inside.

Scattered everywhere, lots of old shipping stuff, ferryboat parts and other nautical looking gear. The one van man carried some old rope, and the other carried the plastic tie-straps from the back of the van. Julia held onto Ivo, now basically conscious, and helped him out of the van.

They followed the two men from the van, who followed Gunman up some rickety steps. She easily figured, definitely a psychopath, so not sure how to play him. They all went into a dirty, glassed-in office, over-looking the huge warehouse below. Gunman pointed to a chair toward the back, against the wall, and simply said "Ivo." Julia lowered him onto the chair, which creaked with his weight. Surely it would've broken if she had dropped him down on it. He pointed to the chair in the corner, a few feet from Ivo, and said "You." She carefully lowered herself onto it, as probably even older, and in worst shape.

At least, she thought to herself, if she needed to break free, she could slam the chair against the wall, and shatter easily. Gunman put his gun on the filthy desk, and sat in the old, torn leather chair behind it. When he leaned back, it slammed into the wall and scared the hell out of him. Julia knew better than to laugh at him. The first van-man, she decided to call *Mutt,* because bigger and heavier, used the rope to tie Ivo to the chair.

The second van-man, she dubbed *Jeff,* simply to coordinate them, as thinner and slightly taller. Also, the one who had talked to himself, on the floor in the back of the van. Julia knew he'd be the vulnerable one, though she may have killed his friend. But she wanted to think, and relatively sure, they saved him at the hospital.

Mutt had tied the rope around Ivo, and Julia noted they were ferry dock slip-knots. She'd seen how quickly they pulled loose, from the year and a half she rode a San Francisco ferry to a job. The only problem, you had to know which way to pull them, but Ivo should know it. Jeff followed with the plastic tie straps, and made sure Ivo's tight.

Mutt stayed far away from the front of Julia, having heard how she'd kicked his friend in the groin, and tried to tie her as quickly as he could.

She had purposely not sat back on the chair, and even leaned forward as far as she could, so it would not be noticeable. Since tying it from the side, she'd pulled against it and he thought it tight. With Jeff, she kept smiling at him, though trying to stay to her side as well. She turned her wrists, as much as she could on the side, so when he pulled the tie strap, he also thought it tight.

Julia looked at him, smiled and said 'thank you' in her fractured Croatian. He stared at her, not knowing what to think of her. She then leaned over and whispered to Ivo. "Tell him his friend is alive. The hospital saves him, he is alive."

Julia realized Ivo might not have even known about the whole hospital scenario, as so out of it himself. Then Ivo spoke to Jeff, and an amazed look came over the man's face. He looked at Julia, and she began to smile, as she nodded her head. "OK, friend OK," she whispered slowly.

Now Gunman yelled at all of them, and obviously told them to shut up. A bench off to the other side of the door, across from the desk. Mutt already sitting on it, so Jeff headed there, but turned again to look at Julia and smile. She returned his smile and kept nodding her head.

The Gunman had been staring at his phone, and it finally rang.

He spoke in a very garbled speech, which did not have the same cadence as the Croatian Julia had heard the past weeks. She had hoped these were not Tomis' countrymen, and now sure they were not.

Julia had no idea what their background, as it had been such a mixture of people living in the old Soviet Yugoslavian group of nations. Gunman had written down one number and laughed loudly, then another. The first she figured the amount, probably quite ridiculous, which why he laughed, and the second probably Tomis' business cell phone. No doubt about it - Gunman at best a sociopath, and worst a psychopath.

Suddenly Julia began to think of Inka and Marijana. Inka could be quite resourceful when she had to be, as she'd tried to instill as much empowerment in her the last few days, they had worked together. She knew Marijana would probably have to have her arm operated on, as she had seen the elbow-bone sticking out.

The crash jolt and airbag, probably gave her a bad whiplash. And having seen it all, one reason why Julia had hit the poor man so hard with her elbow, as the driver. Though just following orders, but a truck of such a size quite deadly, even to a heavy-duty, security- ladened Mercedes.

Julia decided to take some deep breaths, and put the Golden Light around her for protection, with the White Light in front of her for guidance. She began to talk to herself - *"You know this, you've done this thousands of times for numerous reasons, and it has always, always worked."*

Julia closed her eyes and visualized the biggest, deepest Golden Light around her, and a brilliantly White Light in front of her. Now, her intuition jumped in, *"Julia, you are physically strong, mentally brilliant and emotionally powerful. You can play them with sympathy and compassion, , . . if it doesn't work, you will project your strength and will. You know you are NOT and never will be a victim."* She truly did believe, nothing could penetrate God's Golden Light, and she had securely put it around herself.

Julia also knew she'd go down fighting, but it would never have to happen. She also began to send the Golden Light to surround Ivo, to give him strength to do whatever he needed to do to make amends to Tomis. She knew right now, Ivo truly very lost, so also very weak, as filled with guilt. To Julia, it seemed, as if Ivo only wanted to just curl up and die. This the culmination of a very, failed-life. He'd always been a huge disappointment to his father, and to Tomis.

Julia continued to unobtrusively send Ivo the Golden Light, and to watch him, to see if open to getting connected to it at all. She'd expected Gunman to call Tomis any minute, and she wanted to use the time to get

Ivo's attention. Sure enough, Gunman looked at the paper and began to punch the numbers in. A sureness, of not having to use any filter to disguise his voice.

It gave Julia a deep, heavy chill down her spine. Then Gunman losing control of the call, so Tomis, he must have yelled some demand. She leaned over, calling to Ivo several times, he finally looked at her and she said, "He is calling Tomis, pay attention!"

Julia then watched Gunman lumber over to her, and shove the phone at her from the side. Even he wouldn't taking any chance of standing in front of her. "Fuck-off asshole. You will die!" He didn't need any English.

~ ~ ~ ~ ~ ~ ~ ~ ~

Tomis, getting to the helicopter, had to remind himself, as all year he had dealt with these death threat problems, he'd been through worse in the war. Just a quick detailed-memory of losing his wife and daughter could throw him, when the call came in from Gunman. Luka pulled over and called the trace tech to connect his call. Tomis put the call on speaker, so all four of them in his car could hear it.

Gunman said, (In Croatian) "Because Tomis you want Croatia to join EU, so badly, you must pay the ransom in Euros, not Croatian Kuna." Gunman laughing, not even trying to disguise his voice. Tomis cut him off, and demanded to talk to Julia. Gunman laughed again and said, "You don't want to know how much money we want?"

"No," Tomis said, "I will pay. Let me talk to Julia." Tomis kept looking at Luka to see if they had gotten the trace yet, and he kept shaking his head, no.

Gunman had waddled over to Julia and shoved the phone into her face. "Fuck-off asshole. You will die!"

"Julia? JULIA, JULIA DO NOT SAY THAT TO HIM!"

"Tomis, is that you? Oh, Ivo is hurt, but not too bad." "Julia are you OK, have they hurt you at all?"

"No, Tomis I am fine, *totally fine*, but I'm afraid I may have killed one of them. They dropped him off at the hospital close to where we were hit . . . " Gunman grabbed the phone back, and she called him an asshole again. Tomis and his men couldn't help but snicker, as they knew the foul terms.

(In Croatian) "Now, I tell where . . . " Gunman so wanted to be in control.

"No, I want to talk to Ivo NOW. I WANT TO TALK TO IVO NOW!" Gunman stepped over to Ivo and shoved the phone in his face.

"Tomis . . . "

Tomis did not want him to talk. (In Croatian) "Just listen. You must protect Julia, please you must do this for me. They will kill her, you must try to stop it, please. . . . She has become my life, I cannot live without her. I cannot survive *this again*. Only answer me in English, so he does not understand."

"I promise Tomis, I save her. I sorry, all my fault."

"It's OK Ivo, just save Julia." Gunman grabbed the phone away, and said no more talk. He gave him instructions as to where to place the 350,000 Euros by three o'clock and hung up. Tomis calculated it out, over two and half-million kuna, or half a million U.S. dollars. The State Police had already said, they'd have a bag with fake Euros in whatever amount necessary waiting for him, when he got there.

(In Croatian) Luka then said, the tech-trace man says they must have a phone with a blocker. He could only get the cell phone tower location in Zadar. Luka then asked how they were going to find her if they couldn't trace the call. He then asked if she had taken her purse with her passport in it?

(In English) "Oh, my God," Tomis excitedly said. "I forgot about her secret weapon." When his men looked at him strangely, he realized he had spoken in English and repeated himself in Croatian. He quickly called the President, and before he gave him an update, he asked him to call the American Embassy and have them put a trace on Julia's passport. They'd need her number from immigration, so had to get it first.

The President asked if sure she had it on her and Tomis laughed, "Yes, she showed me this morning before she left. She calls it her secret weapon." The President couldn't imagine where she'd hide it, as sure they'd searched her.

"I forgot, she'd given me the key words we had set up, "fine, totally fine," so they didn't find it on her." The President said he'd call him back as soon as the signal had been traced. Tomis told him they were getting into the helicopter now, and it'd be almost an hour until they arrived, but the State Police already had men searching the dock area.

~~~~~~~~

Julia began to wonder how this would all play out, and who would ultimately get the money. Certainly Gunman had not been the brains, as someone else had called to tell him the amount and Tomis' cell number. Could the head-honchos be coming there, to make their ferry escape south to Serbia-Montenegro. Or maybe, a straight shot over to Ancona, Italy with regular ferry passages, so they'd not even be very noticeable.

Curious as to which way they'd all make their escape. On the other hand, if Tomis caught her signal, they'd not found her passport, he could be having it traced right now. They'd have to work through the American Embassy and Immigration to get it coordinated. She then thought of Cara, since she'd put her down as her American contact in the States. Julia hoped they'd not called her yet.

The bottom line, the phone call had been 'proof-of-life,' and technically they no longer needed her or Ivo to get the money, though an exchange. If Tomis, or more likely the State Police did not see her, they probably would do the shoot-to-kill thing. She went back to her own deep breathing, and continuously sending the Golden Light around Ivo, then again around herself.

Julia kept watching Ivo, he had definitely changed, as if he set some goal for himself. Yes, he had promised Tomis about saving her, so now thinking how he could. Julia took her one hand and pointed to her other wrist, getting Ivo's attention. She wanted him to turn his wrist, so she could see the time. They were supposed to get to Zadar by nine-thirty for their schedule ten o'clock appointment. Almost eleven, which about what she'd figured, making the accident around nine.

Gunman then barked at Mutt and Jeff, who quickly reported to him, then their foot steps clunking down the old stairs. He'd most likely sent them to keep a lookout. The Gunman pulled a pack of cards out of his back pocket, and began to shuffle them on the dirty table, without even brushing off a clean spot. He must have figured he no longer needed to watch his prisoners.

He twirled his gun on the table, and smiled as if a job well done, looking at her, then over to Ivo with a nod. He truly must have believed his connections to the Sabor, the State Police, and top heads of the Organized Crime protected him. Julia almost laughed out loud, and quickly pulled her lips in to control it. None of them, would have made it in a high school play, much less a grade B movie about even 'would-be' gangsters.

~~~~~~~~~

In the helicopter, Tomis' phone rang through to the head set, and the supervisor calling in with his report. He had started to laugh. (In Croatian) "That is some lady you've got there. From what Inka said, and the hospital reported, Julia first hits this guy in the jaw - it is cracked, and kicked him in the groin - his left ball is purple and the size of a ball. Then, when she is finally getting out of the car, he is stupid enough to grab her again, and she chops him in the larynx and cracks his windpipe. He would have died, had they not dropped him off at the emergency room." He laughed again.

"The security guard got the license, so we have traced the owner of the van. State Police is searching the old warehouse buildings at the dock. We've already picked-up about a dozen people, from what the union guys told us. The guy with the cracked windpipe can't speak, but in exchange for a reduced sentence, he's writing down all the information on who hired them, and how they were paid. I need to tell you, the State Police will be going in with shoot-to-kill orders, as the guy said they *were* instructed to kill her and Ivo."

Tomis could not laugh at Julia's actions, but also not really surprised.

"Also," he continued, "you may have already realized from what Inka said, Ivo is involved with this regarding a gambling debt. Apparently, from what Inka said, they had promised Ivo, no one would get hurt. Then they laughed, saying they had lied to him, and he had been stupid enough to believe them." He paused with no other comment necessary.

"Oh, just wanted to let you know Marijana is still in surgery for her arm, broken in about eight places, two ribs and some whip- lash. Inka has whip-lash and pulled some muscles in her back. Apparently, the guy with the gun hit Ivo several times, as she said bleeding from the forehead and jaw. You would not believe the size of the truck, and how it totaled the whole side of the car."

Finishing up, he added. "Let me know when you get there, we're moving in on the big guys here. They nailed the Sabor member, and arrested him at his home, where he made the phone calls from Saturday night to set it all up. They have the final results on the ferry owner, and one of the boats is gone, so he's probably down at Zadar. I'm letting the State Police know to arrest him on his boat. And, the last piece, we got the State Police supervisor, who had been on the Sabor payroll, when he tried to remove the bug from his phone. Hope you get as good of a clean-sweep down there, as we did up here."

Tomis trying hard to breathe deep, but his adrenaline racing, as containing his fear not easy.

Dock-side in Zadar, the State Police were again stealthily- moving to the end of the farthest pier, where a very, out-of-place ferry, with the suspect-competitor's name on it, tethered. The two quasi- lookouts, also filled with arrogant-thinking, assuming they were not only above the law, but smarter than them. There were enough various crates or small containers to make it easy for the Police to get the drop on them, before they could even retrieve their weapons.

They pulled them away, threatening silence with their hand clubs. They waited to put the cuffs on until they were far enough from the boat, to attract any attention of others. The remaining half-dozen Police, quietly moved onto the ferry, and down the three different stair cases, while another went up to the pilot house. They were coordinating to hit at the same time, to catch all on board off -guard, with several more Police coming to surround outside the boat.

When they pounced in the main deck cabin, four men were seated and another four standing around as supposed guards. Two immediately drew their weapons and shot instantly, the other two dropped their guns, then raised their hands. The State Police Supervisor and his assistant, went directly over to three of the men they knew to be crime leaders, then jerked them up, off the couch.

As one protested, hit directly with the gun butt, and accused of resisting arrest. The fourth man, the ferryboat owner, quickly begged, he'd been forced to help with it all. Again, heavily hit on the head, and accused of resisting arrest. In all, they had gotten ten men, including the schmucks who worked on the boat.

Practically the same scenario taking place back in Rijecka, with Tomis' supervisor coordinating with the State Police. They had gotten the confession from larynx-man, and also cooperation from the crooked State Police supervisor. The Chief had promised him a protected incarceration, rather than being put in with the general-prison population, who would have killed him within the first twenty- four hours.

They'd known for some time, who all of the Organized Crime were behind most of the snipers and attempts, but now they had the extensive evidence to put them away for good. Carrying-off the attack with over two dozen Police, would not have been easy, except again for the pure, utter-arrogance of the gangsters, thinking they could not be penetrated or caught.

This time, four men shot instantly with drawn weapons, and another half dozen severely injured for resisting arrest. Over a dozen were hand-cuffed and lead-off to the waiting van. Adding insult to injury, each time any one of them spoke, they were again struck. Tomis' supervisor called again, just as they had landed and brought him up to date on their final successes, and where to go. The State Police had not needed Julia's passport for her location, as they had found the old building, and seen the van's license plate through the broken slates.

Tomis headed there with his adrenaline pounding, and sweat pouring out of him. The last puzzle piece would be the rescue, the most difficult and dangerous for Julia and Ivo. By the time their cars had reached the old warehouse building, the State Police made Tomis wait back behind their vehicles, over a block away.

They saw he had his vest on, but still insisted he must wait there. One of the assistant supervisors came to speak to him, and explained they were getting their snipers in place, before they went in. He pointed out Mutt and Jeff, who had been easily caught, as they had no guns and surrendered quietly begging for leniency. They both told about how crazy the guy with the gun, and he planned to kill the prisoners because he could, and also wanted to do so. They added, especially the woman had made him angry. Jeff asked if his friend OK, and they said yes.

The shock of it all had hit Tomis in the helicopter. But, he'd kept telling himself, the State Police knew what they were doing, and would make sure Julia safe. Now, not so sure, and his mind kept racing. This could *not* be happening again to a woman he loved. But no idea of all the happening?

When he heard the shots fired, it took three of the Police to hold him back from rushing into the old warehouse. Tomis screaming to them after the next shots to let him go, and his mind froze. By the time the all clear came, so frazzled, he had no idea how his feet rushed to catch-up to the Police. The siren of the waiting ambulance wailed, racing forward.

~ ~ ~ ~ ~ ~ ~ ~ ~

In the glassed-in warehouse office, Gunman had become engrossed in his card game, oblivious to his surroundings. Ivo took the opportunity to lean over and whisper to Julia. "Man in charge ... do this . . . name ... " He gave her the name of the man, who had made the deal with him, to erase his large gambling debt.

Though leaning as far over as she could, she wanted to make sure she got the name right. "Say again." Ivo repeated the name, but a little too loud this time, and Gunman heard him talking, and yelled at them both. He got up to go over to them, and heard some noise, but not sure if on the roof, or in the old warehouse. He turned and went out the door to call to Mutt and Jeff from the top of the stairs. When he heard no answer, he yelled louder and saw a quick shadow near the high windows.

He quickly came back in, grabbed his gun off the table, shouted wildly something to Ivo and went back out. From the look on his face, Julia knew not good. "What is it Ivo?" Leaning over, Ivo realized the chair really old and rickety, so he began to rock back and forth. She watched him brace his feet on the floor, and on the second try the chair had snapped. He managed to catch himself against the wall to not fall.

"He kill you and me," he said. They heard shots, probably from the Gunman, and he came back in yelling at Ivo again. He stood over Julia, trying to get the ropes off of her, and turned to face Gunman, who immediately shot him.

Though his body had railed from the impact, he turned to purposefully throw himself on her, trying to protect her. The fall snapped Julia's chair. She went down clunking her head first against the wall, and solidly on the floor. The Gunman took one step forward to shoot Ivo in the back, as he pulled the trigger, the sniper shot him several times, felling him in his tracks.

Coming up the stairs behind several of the State Police, Tomis had pulled his vest off, feeling it restricting him from moving fast enough. He saw the dead Gunman first, and the two medics squatted around Ivo and Julia.

(In Croatian) The one checking her neck pulse, nodded Julia alive. But the one checking with Ivo said, he'd not live long. They both began to lift him off of Julia, and Tomis quickly said, "I will take him, he's my brother."

He moved over to the wall, to get out of the medics' way, and slid down holding Ivo to his chest. As he thumped to the floor, Ivo opened his eyes. He then asked, "Did I save her?" And, Tomis told him 'yes,' hoping it would be true. "I sorry Tomis, please forgive me for Celia, too?"

Again, Tomis told him 'yes,' and again true. He pulled Ivo closer to him, until he felt his last few breaths escape, and his whole body released. He kissed him on the forehead, with tears pouring down his face, and glanced over to watch the medics work on Julia.

The one told him, though unconscious, she probably had a concussion from the two knots on her head. The other then added, s very lucky, the way his brother had turned. The bullet shot at his back, had gone a further distance through him, so never came out to hit her. He then added, he had saved her life, even though he already had another bullet in his stomach.

~ ~ ~ ~ ~ ~ ~ ~ ~

Julia still unconscious, and they knew she had a concussion, but were not sure how severe. Tomis sat on the edge of the hospital chair softly stroking her face, careful to not touch the stitches on the corner of her forehead leading into her hairline. Her lovely face had not been scarred, though it would not have made a difference to him. Yet, the little scar on her forehead, would be a reminder of how she'd been hurt because of him. The fact nothing else broken, amazed the orthopedic doctor, who said her back had been badly wrenched.

And, once the swelling had gone down, they'd know if any other damage to the spine. She had responded well to nerve tests, so they knew no damage or pinching had occurred. Each time Tomis looked at her for more than ten seconds, tears would begin to swell in his eyes. He had to shake his head away, and swallow hard to get a grip once again on his emotions.

Again, it truly amazed him how much, he deeply cared for her, in the very condensed time they'd spent together. Hours after the rescue, still in his clothes, coated with Ivo's blood, and dirt from the floor while by Julia's side watching it all. The Emergency Medical Techs had gotten the ropes off, and put her on a flat plastic stretcher, banding down her head, so unmovable. He thanked God the Zadar hospitalso close, and also a good one.

The whole horrific kidnap-situation had kept them rather busy, compared to the usual mundane Tuesday. Starting with larynx-man, and the men who were shot, nearly all had died including Gunman and Ivo. Tomis' mind kept replaying Ivo's last words of trying to save Julia, and his own forgiveness of Ivo regarding his wife Celia. Julia's immoveable body, brought back feeling Ivo's last breaths escape from him. Tomis whispered, "God, please let Ivo be at peace, now."

The Coroner fulfilled Tomis' request to do Ivo's autopsy first, so he might be sent over to the funeral home to prepare his body and casket to be returned to Rijecka for burial. In his breaks from waiting in Julia's room, he had called Ivo's ex-wife and told her what happened. He'd told her he would be flying him down tomorrow, or the next day latest. She only wanted a small private funeral, as she knew few people would attend anyway.

Tomis also called his CFO, for arrangements of Ivo's insurance money and pension-retirement to be sent to his ex-wife and daughter. He clarified also, Ivo had been killed on the job, so the double- indemnity clause in affect. Since the helicopter had to be returned to the State Police post, Tomis asked Luka to request they wait, for Ivo's body to be taken back. He added, he'd travel with them, then drive back alone. Without comment, they both knew security no longer needed.

As he studied her face, he thought he saw her eyes move and immediately called for the nurse. The doctor had said, the first sign of waking up - a good sign regarding the concussion. The nurse ran in and out, then the doctor came in just as Julia's eyes were flickering to open. The doctor had said, she'd be groggy from all of the pain drugs. Speaking English to her, which totally threw her, as to where or who he could be.

Julia then recognized the lovely accent, as Tomis had stood and came into view. "Jelly, do you hear me? Do you know me? It is Tomis." A big smile came across her face, just as the doctor turning her back to him, so he could look closer into each eye. He turned to the nurse, and issued an order for new brain scans, then to Tomis, telling him he had five minutes, and to not touch her head.

Before he could tell her what had happened, she spoke. "Hi, my love. You look terrible. Is Ivo OK?" He sank down in his chair with his head near her chest on the bed and began to cry, not being able to hold back the tears any more. "I'll take that as a 'no.' . . . I think he saved my life, I certainly hope you caught all of the bad guys." He pulled himself back-up, and shook his head, remembering the drugs, but not believing she could crack a joke, after all she had just gone through. He pulled himself back together, and she'd tried to reach her hand to touch him, but both of them were occupied with IV needles or monitoring machines.

"Ah, Julia. I so frighten for you. I so sorry . . . all my fault "

"Don't go there Tomis, I insisted and you know it. Ivo told me all his fault for the gambling debt. Oh, he gave me the name of the man who had made the deal with him it sounds like scissors – say some of their names and I'll recognize it."

"No, no, do not worry about now, we caught most, I think."

"No, I insist. I want to make sure no one gets away with all of this." He knew better than to argue, and started saying some of the key names and after the third one, she responded. "Yes, that's it. Is he involved with the gambling? Did they catch him?"

"Yes, he is gambling *King Pin*, I think you say. And, yes they catch him, but I call supervisor and tell him you confirm from Ivo."

"Tomis, I'm so sorry about Ivo. He really had no idea they'd planned from the start to hurt or kill us. I never asked, did he have a wife or children. ?" The nurse and two techs came in the room and quickly swooped Julia away.

Tomis called after her, "I here . . . I love you." He slouched back into the chair and wept openly. His phone started ringing, and he took it out to see who would be calling now. Since the President, he answered (in Croatian) and gave him an update. He then informed Tomis, the American Ambassador at the Embassy had just held a news conference and all of the newswires now carrying the story around the world.

"It not completely accurate, and gave little credit to the State Police for their excellent job of ridding the country of the Organized Crime. He said Julia supposed to be here consulting on tourism, but had made some statement regarding Croatia joining EU, and some irate groups oppose it, kidnapped her. In the process of resisting, she received a concussion. But he did give credit to Julia, I guess, when he called her '*Karate Kid*,' whatever it mean." He paused, then added, "Let me know when you want me to put out the correct version, and what you want me to say."

Tomis not surprised, Julia had been so right about the Ambassador being "patronizing and arrogant," and she had not gone through him or informed him of her work. But now, more concerned about Cara, as Julia had said, she never missed watching the early morning news reports on her conservative station. She'd said they usually played up the negative about every thing. He knew she got up early with the dogs, so decided he needed to call her before she heard the worst of it.

He told the President, "I want her totally away from them, so I'll let you know tomorrow. Now, I need to call Julia's friend, to let her know before the news." Tomis hung up, and took another deep breath. Not a call he would be comfortable making, but then nothing all day had been easy. He searched through his phone directory and her number not there, then he remembered he had put it in the international phone for Julia to use. He called his office in Rijeka to have them get the number, and wrote it down.

Tomis sat back in the padded chair and took some deep breaths, as he put the numbers into his phone. He heard it ringing and knew Cara always checked the caller ID, so would think it Julia. "Well, what the fuck? I didn't expect to hear from you until this weekend. What's up, you calling at this hour?"

"Cara, good morning. It is Tomis . . . " His voice sighed, with bearing bad news.

"Oh, my God!" Her voice sank, as seriousness took over her demeanor. "No, don't tell me . . . is she dead or kidnapped?" If she hadn't been sitting down, she must have then.

He took another deep breath. "She is not dead, but she kidnapped, but free now . . ." He went on to tell her the whole story, as best he could, though she kept interrupting him, saying she *knew* Julia would piss the gangsters off.

He had to chuckle, then finished by promising if the doctor said it was OK, he would call her back for Julia to talk. Thirty minutes after hanging up, Julia everywhere on the news with a more negative impact, suggesting a mouthy American woman had gotten *herself* in trouble. Still, many of her fans would hold their breath, waiting to hear of her recovery, as she'd almost become a martyr in her support of Croatia.

Exhausted, Tomis closed his eyes until the noise of Julia's bed returning woke him. He'd just rose to talk to her, when the doctor came in, and again told him he had five or ten minutes at most. They were taking her into surgery for several blood clots. It could be two to four hours depending if they found any more once in there, as she'd hit two areas of her head. The doctor turned to Julia, to tell her the shorten version, and not to talk or get agitated, then left.

Tomis stood over Julia and held his finger to his lips, "You are not to talk. Listen. I call Cara, and I call her again." Julia's eyes widened, and he quickly put his finger to her lips again. The President called, … and said your Ambassador had news conference, so I call Cara … before she hear you on news." Julia settled back down. I wait for you and . . . also, I make changes.

He took a deep breath. "I tell you later   Also, Marijana out of surgery, and she good, … but long time to get better. … Inka get whip-lash, I think correct word … and need back brace. She visit you later in wheelchair." He had picked-up her IV hand, and bending over to kiss it when the nurse came back in with more drugs. "I love you Jelly. I wait here for you. … You will be all better, …

Doctor say." He watched her eyes close, as they again whisked her out.

Luka'd been waiting in the hall with a fresh change of clothes for Tomis. He gave him some other instructions, and closed the door on the private room to take a long, hot shower. With hours of nothing to do by Julia's side, his mind and emotions had become occupied with her. And, most of all he thought, *how she'd become so intertwined in his life, in ways he couldn't fathom, or even think about being without her. No doubt a challenge, also in ways he could not have imagined before, any woman could be.*

Yet, she never ceased to amaze him with her brain, or her quirky-ways of looking at life, and appreciating every little gift of life. And, the sex - he thought of again telling her as sensuous-sexy. Not only he'd never known any like it before, but the fun she put into it. Who laughs so much with sex?

Still, her love, not just for him, but her sincere caring for people, he'd never seen up-close in anyone else. Tomis had seen her few vulnerable spots, and as she admitted several times, she could be difficult, and definitely stubborn. Most of all, the challenge would be how *he could change himself,* so she could not refuse to be *with him.* She said she'd given up being a workaholic, but still liked to do work sometimes, then so could he.

When he had changed and refreshed, he called his manager Jossip. He gave him the update on Julia and told him, he - Jossip would be taking over as Interim COO - Chief Operating Officer, with him fully in place by December 1. Jossip to bring his Assistant Manager up to speed on his job as Manager. He said not to hesitate to call him if any questions, though he felt him more than capable of doing the job on his own.

Tomis then called Anton, updated him on Julia, and told him of Jossip's promotion to COO, and to give him his full support. Also, he told Anton, he'd be promoted to General Manager of the trains, and to make sure his Assistant Manager trained to move-up to his position. Again, he repeated to call him if needed, though he knew Anton capable of doing the job.

Tomis then called his security supervisor, and told him the name Julia had confirmed. It would come under the 'dying declaration' testimony of Ivo, so could be used as further evidence to convict the man.

Tomis got up to open the door, and a few minutes later Luka had reappeared. He asked his bloody, dirty clothes be trashed. Luka then informed Tomis, his eighteen-meter sailboat would arrive in Zadar in three days. Tomis smiled, as it should be perfect for Julia.

With the media everywhere and more coming, he wanted to protect her from them. Yes, a hero to many, but she did not need to relive it all again. He'd thought the sailboat the best place for her to recuperate in privacy, while enjoying the water and island views.

Tomis then decided he wanted to go back down to the water, but not to the place where it had all happened. Luka drove him down to the Sea Organ - the urban sculpture at the seaside promenade, near the ferry station. They sat on a bench looking out on the water, as the sculpture captured the wave movements to transform them into eerie music. Both talked only sporadically.

The long security contract would end now, so too, their intertwined relationship into friendship. They'd been through a long, quite difficult year of dealing with the Organized Crime, to keep him alive. Tomis also deciding how to tell Julia about asking Ivo to save her, and how his wife and daughter really died. Julia had told him many times to stop holding onto his guilt, and *move past his past*. So, time for a fresh start on everything, including his past.

Epilogue
Life Blips

Suddenly, once again you saw . . .
life, love and its blips,
dropping off the radar screen,
and staring you in the face.

Is the lonely, empty lighthouse
repeatedly searching for solace,
Or is it bravely standing alone,
to protect us from the pain?

Being a logical person, it seemed strange,
yet having no fear of the unknown,
I had such faith in the illogical idea,
everything would come out all right.

Don't be afraid of death - a voice said,
Be afraid of the un-lived life.
Savor and enjoy each moment of being –
no matter what you are doing.

Every challenging relationship, difficult life situation, unforgivable act, surprising event, betrayal *and* blessing, plays a role in our life purpose. We choose which path we are on with every choice, decision, action and thought. There is no magical formula, or wand to understanding our life purpose, we are *always* on purpose, it is a process of becoming.

No one, and no-thing can force us to follow any path. If we sit around and wait for our purpose to be revealed, we may wonder why we have the same life experiences, again and again, *and* blame the Universe for them. Our journey allows us to step forward into a bright, new, promising future we create, one step, thought, decision and choice at a time.

~ ~ ~ ~ ~ ~ ~ ~ ~

When Tomis got back to Julia's room the door open, but her bed not yet back. Instead, a nurse's aid arranging the half dozen vases of flowers and plants which had been delivered for her. Still, over on the bedside stand, the small bouquet of mixed, wild flowers he'd picked up from the shop when out for a walk, while Julia still unconscious. He realized she had probably not seen them, because she could not move her head any direction. He asked the nurse if she could find out if Julia still in surgery.

Tomis then remembered he needed to call Cara back. He told her of the surgery, and it would be many hours now before Julia would be able to talk, but he'd call again. He then called the President, and brought him up to date about the promotions of his managers. (In Croatian)

The President then asked, "So, are you ready then to be my Consultant to the Tourism Board, and represent us at all of the International Tourism Conferences and Conventions?"

How perfect, Tomis thought, as he'd forgotten of the long ago request. As much as Julia loved to travel, and as much as she'd been doing with Croatia's tourism companies, they'd make the perfect team.

"Only, if you let me pick *my own* Consultant to take with me!" "Of course, . . . how perfect to get the two of you! Why didn't I think of that?"

"You do have to pay for each of us, and all of the expenses. And, no *Motel 6,* as Julia says." The President did not understand, and *colloquial*-Tomis just said, "Never-mind." He laughed, thinking how she'd have loved the joke.

The President got really excited, "Of course, we'd pay! With business the two of you would bring in, it'd be more than worth it. So, she'll stay and do the job when she finishes the training programs?"

"Oh, Mr, President, you are going a little too, fast. She isn't even out of surgery yet. But we will have time, I've sent for my sailboat. I want her to recuperate on it, away from the media. But, you can go ahead and give the correct version of it all to the media." Tomis feeling very positive, and could feel his Golden Light.

"Good idea, and I won't say anything regarding the new jobs, until I hear from you. But, I'm glad about the promotions, and I'm sure your other investors will also be happy for you."

The opportunity Tomis wanted for them both to do together, and how being such a workaholic, he'd totally forgotten about it. Now getting excited to share the news with Julia, though he knew he had to tell her about Ivo and his wife Celia first. He began to wonder, if she'd understand or blame him, yet she'd said to let go of guilt. He looked at his watch, and thought of how she loved to take his hand and check it, like he'd become an extension of her.

It put a smile on his face, thinking of her little habits, he'd learned so quickly. They had changed and influenced each other way beyond either's full comprehension. Over three hours, since she'd been taken to surgery.

Just then a nurse came in to tell him, Julia had been taken to recovery, and would be brought to her room in about thirty minutes. She said the doctor would be in soon, but she heard everything went well. Tomis thanked her, sat down and cried again. So very grateful his prayers had been answered.

Still sitting with his head in his hands, when the doctor came in. He rose to meet him and gave him a big hug, with 'thank yous' over and over again. They did find more clots, than the first scan had shown, as he expected, but sure they got them all. He said they'd do more scans daily for a few days. Tomis then asked how soon until Julia could be released, and explained he wanted to get her away from the media onto his sailboat.

The doctor looked at him, and agreed since the lobby had almost filled-up with them. He'd have to go down shortly and give an update. He then said, if she's still clear after three days, he'd release her, and promised not to tell anyone else. He then commented to Tomis on what a *tough-lady*,, as he'd heard of the damage she had inflicted on the other man.

Julia barely awake more than fifteen minutes at a time, most of Tuesday evening. Tomis dozed off and on himself. His body still ached from the tension, as he felt like he'd been beat up, or hit with the truck himself. Wednesday, the doctor had said, Julia would be out of it the most, so Tomis flew-out early on the helicopter with Ivo's casket and his men - soon to be former security - returning to Rijecka.

The Priest had said the smaller chapel would be best. There were perhaps a dozen friends, neighbors and co-workers in attendance, besides his ex-wife and daughter. Little else to be said or done, as he reconfirmed to Ivo's wife to never hesitate to ask for his help. As Tomis walked out the chapel door, he took a deep breath and looked up to God. "Ivo is yours now God, I think he is finally at peace, and maybe happy in what he did."

Tomis truly hoped now, all the *consequences* left over from their civil war were done, all the hate, revenge, revelry, power- grabbing and death. No one ever really 'won' from a war, and peace always a long-time coming into fruition. He felt his own life so full of new possibilities.

Tomis, back on the road by two o'clock, his brother buried, yet his whole body throbbed from the emotional torrents within him. His maroon Mercedes had practically sat in the garage for over a year, as the secure cars and drivers had taken over his life. He then realized, the first time he'd driven himself, since their trip up to Lake of the Clouds. The thoughts of their glorious adventure brought, not only a smile, but relaxation to his body.

The rest of the drive, he kept playing back those four days they had together exploring the beauty and nature's glory - as Julia called it - of the Upper Peninsula of Michigan. It truly felt, like it had been years prior, not weeks. Shortly before five o'clock, Tomis walked back into Julia's room, and it filled to overflowing now with flowers and plants. "You have your own garden, Jelly."

"Oh, Tomis, you're back. You look exhausted. This could not have been easy for you." Close, but still she had no idea what he'd been through with it all. Yet, not ready to share what he knew he needed to. He played with her shortened hair, giving her a light kiss on the lips, smiling and so happy to be back with her.

~ ~ ~ ~ ~ ~ ~ ~ ~

Getting ready to leave the hospital, Julia had made sure the nurses knew to distribute all her flowers, except the small, wild flower bouquet from Tomis. Those she wanted to take with her to the boat. In her short walks around the hospital, she had visited Marijana and Inka, to see how they were doing. Inka had already started physical therapy. So she wanted some of her flowers to go to them. She checked if any children in the hospital, so they'd get some from her collection, too.

About an hour before sunset on Friday, the nurses escorted Julia in her wheelchair, out the back way and into an ambulance, waiting with Tomis inside. Once they got her inside and laying back down, it scooted away with no siren to attract any attention. At the dock, the Captain waited next to the special ramp for the wheelchair, and assisted Tomis with the medics to get her to the deck for the sunset. "I have new name on boat, do you see?"

Julia took off her sunglasses to peer at the lovely styled-writing

- *'My Jelly'* "Oh, Tomis, I love it!" She giggled at his amazing detail, in the things he did for her, even after breaking-away her protective heart shell. He pushed her chair to the bow with a wide open deck.

Within minutes of settling her in, the Captain slowly guided the boat away from the dock, and Julia waved bye to the medics. Tomis had only kept one female nurse, with good English, to help with her. And, she also offered to help with a little cooking and clean-up.

Though Julia couldn't have any alcohol, he did have some ginger ale waiting for her, she liked so much. With her little bandaged cap, over the shaved area of her head, she sat wrapped-up on the deck with Tomis next to her, holding her hand. They 'oohed and awed' together, as the sun played with the clouds across the water, and finally disappeared leaving the sky a molten-blue.

"See, we finally get to 'ride-off into sunset together.'" Tomis stopped to think of how long ago she had said it, and laughed, as he kissed her. The doctor had said, she needed at least one day in the wheelchair to get her equilibrium to the boat. He also *insisted* no sex until her head had fully healed. Julia just laughed. "We'll see about that!"

The deck lights came on, and Tomis went to help the nurse serve their light dinner. They enjoyed the moon, the music and he insisted then, time for her to go to bed. The nurse pushed the chair into the bedroom, and Tomis scooped Julia up and placed her easily on the bed, with extra pillows to prop up her head. Julia noticed right away, he'd pulled out the sofa bed for himself, and it had been made. "Oh no you don't. I don't care what the doctor says, you will sleep next to me, even if we can't have sex."

When Tomis began to protest, Julia said "Thank you," to the nurse, and asked her to close the door behind her. "Tomis, it is not as if you will jump around on the bed. I've missed you for too long. Even after they put the little bed in my room for you, I know you haven't gotten much sleep. We can at least be close to each other."

Tomis had been given her suitcase from the wrecked car, but also picked-up a couple of nightgowns, which snapped or buttoned in the front, so she didn't have to put it over her head. Julia thought they were sweet, since they definitely were not sexy. Since not to move around too much, he proceeded to help her undress and put one on, but she continually teased him. When he had taken off her bra, she asked him to kiss her breasts. "I cannot do that . . . you know other things happen . . . we are not to do." So serious, she giggled.

"OK, I'll be a good girl tonight, or I know you will threaten to send me back to the hospital. But tomorrow, we will play, at least a little." He'd gotten the nightgown on her, and snapping it up, before he helped her off with her panties.

Tomis kept looking at her face, as he reached his hands under the nightgown up to her waist, and started to pull the panties down. Julia then grabbed the nightgown and pulled it over her face, so he could see her naked body.

"Julia don't do that! This is … difficult for me, … too. Please cooperate …with me." He'd pulled the nightgown back down, and the panties off as quickly as he could.

"Well listen to you," moving her head from side to side, " *'Julia don't'* - you used a contraction! How about that!" Tomis looked at her, shook his head and chuckled.

"I miss your silly jokes … so much. All I do … last four days

… is think of you and things you say and do. You are so much my life . . . I can not say how much . . . " He carefully kissed her on the lips, then reached over and turned-off the bedside lamp.

He then gently laid down on the bed, next to her on his side, and only once kissed into the crevasse of her neck. He then put his hand lightly on her stomach, content to be touching her, if only a little. Julia reached over and put her hand on his, then couldn't say another word, as her eyes had again filled with tears. She knew no one had ever loved her the way he did. As much as sex had been a major part of any of her relationships, this so much more.

Tomis made sure, he woke up before Julia, so she could not tempt him again. He knew he'd not be very strong, yet afraid of the excitement hurting her head. He wanted to get the deck canopy set-up for shade, as he remembered how sensitive she would to the sun. When breakfast almost ready, he went in with the nurse to wake her and bring her out to eat.

"Ana give you shower … or bath later, I want you to enjoy morning sun. Then … after lunch, we walk around boat … and see how you do." Once settled on the deck, Tomis told Ana, he'd call her when ready to bathe. They ate and Tomis talked about the islands they continuously passed, but Julia felt him waiting for the right time to talk to her. Finally, breakfast finished, she took a deep breath and asked.

"Tomis, my love. I know you have some things you want to tell me. Now is good."

Yes, time for more truth, the whole truth, the complete gut- wrenching truth. How much soul-bearing could one man do? As if a modern Job, being tested by having his loved ones hurt? Whether or not Julia ready for it, truly another thing.

He took several deep breaths, having tried to practice this several times. "OK, this is long, please be patient . . . and help me with words. I want you to understand all." He looked at Julia and she nodded, with almost a fear coming over her, but she stopped it, knowing she needed to know, whatever he *needed* to say.

"In warehouse, with kidnap, I speak to Ivo on phone. I know, Police tell me, …they know Gunman plan to kill you and Ivo. So, I ask Ivo to please save you. I tell him, … you become my life, and I can not live without you. I say, I cannot survive this *again*. … Another breath, as he continues.

"I tell him to answer English, so Gunman not understand, and Ivo say he promise to save you." He looks at Julia waiting for her questions. "Julia, I not know … how Ivo plan to save you." He breathed heavy.

"What do you mean by 'again'?" She is confused, but afraid of his answer.

"I finish and explain. When I arrive with medics, they say you alive,… but Ivo die soon. I hold him in my arms, he ask if he save you, and I say 'yes' . . . and he is happy. He then say sorry, and … please forgive him for Celia, . . . my wife   " Julia couldn't help it, she'd taken a quick breath of shock.

Tomis said nothing, but continued. "I say 'yes,' … I forgive him. …I then feel his last breath leave his body. . . . Do you understand … he die happy? . . . You talk about guilt and forgive. … I forgive him long time ago, but *he* … not forgive *him*. Ivo need to save *you* to forgive *him* Do you understand?"

Julia burst into tears, and Tomis rushed across to her. The last thing he wanted would be her to get upset. He was afraid of more vessels in her head popping.

"Julia, … please don't cry. Please, I know this is all very difficult, but it is good thing . . . important we talk about it. … I need to tell you story of my wife, … and why Ivo feel guilt."

Tomis handed Julia a napkin from the table, to wipe her eyes and nose, taking deep breaths to control her emotions. "Is your head OK? Any pain or hurt?" She nodded 'no' and smiled slightly at him, so he sat back in his chair, but held her hand for contact.

"OK, this is long time ago, … when war first start, almost twenty years. My wife and two children live close to Zagreb. Momma and Talia move to Istria - very safe, … close to Rijecka, where Poppa and Ivo live, … to protect business and work." He breathed easier, letting go.

"I drive Rijecka, and work Monday, every day Friday, … come back Zagreb. I want Celia move to Istria, she insist 'no.' Friends and Aunties in old building we live. I home Friday night, Poppa call… can not find Ivo, and … men destroy building, … boat, fires, … come fast help, and I go. Later … men come to our apartment building - like military, but . . . " He looks at her for a word. Julia said, "Marauders . . . or gangs?"

"Yes, bad men . . . kill, . . . rape and destroy . . . most building. I help Poppa stop men at port, . . . put out fire, fix boat. . . . Never see or find Ivo, . . . he *never* come help. . . . Then phone call in morning from Auntie, Celia and Milos in hospital . . . I go back Zagreb . . . fast to hospital. Doctor say Celia . . . rape many times, . . . cut with knife many times . . . and Milos daughter . . . hurt and cut many times." Tomis had to stop and take many deep breaths. It'd been forever, since he'd mentioned any of this to anyone. His pain, still so very deep. Julia held the napkin over her mouth, to control a response to his horrific words.

"When I get close . . . to Celia, she say stop, . . . she is *poison*, . . . not to touch her, . . . not her hand, face . . . nothing. And, say . . . Milos is *poison*, too. Not touch her." Julia had to adjust her hand, as Tomis unknowingly squeezing it. She decided better for her to hold his hand, so he wouldn't think her rejecting him, with what he had just said.

"I talk to her . . . again and again. I love her and . . . tell her we can . . ." He looks at Julia.

"Get over it, or move past it?"

"Yes, you say before, move past it. Still, she say NO. Next day, I want to take her to Istria, . . . but she want to stop at apartment building . . . to get things . . . her and Milos. I do not want . . . her to go in damage building, much destroy . . . but she insist and . . . insist take Milos to help. I go to Auntie . . . in next house, where son Stepan stay.

. . . I come out . . . to go in our old building, . . . and I hear two gun shots

. . . " Julia gasped again and grabbed the napkin to hold over her mouth.

"Celia find Poppa's gun . . . from old war. I give Stepan back to Auntie . . . and run-up stairs to our rooms." Tomis watched Julia, as they both had tears in their eyes. He stops to take a deep breath.

"When I hear gunshots … on Tuesday … at warehouse and run-up stairs, … I think I see … wife and daughter again, . . . not you and Ivo." Tomis moved to his knees, and hugged Julia around her waist. She put her hands on his head, holding him as she could. Several minutes had passed, before either of them got any composure.

"Oh, Tomis. That is so very sad, and so much for you to have carried for so long."

"When Celia shoot … our daughter and self, … she never give me chance to … move past rape. I know … most men can not . . . But I think . . ." His shoulders dropped, heavily.

"No, Tomis." Julia chose her words carefully, but her training kicking in now. Yet, she didn't want it to come off as, perfunctory or rehearsed. With a deep breath, she began. "She believed you never could, no matter what you would have said or done." She took a breath.

"As much as you want to blame yourself, it has to do with the *culture* of your country, and its religion, … and how most everyone felt about those things, … and those people back then. Mixing of the cultures and religions, were never acceptable to them. Under Yugoslavia, they'd been forced to live together by the Soviets, for so many generations."

With another breath, Julia resolutely continued. "But, the *hate* taught from parents to children, … NO One is born with it. And, few can *move past* what has been ingrained, from being repeatedly told to hate them." She paused again.

"It is part of your freedom now, and what it does for people, as they get educated in a more open and accepting, honest way. We talked about this, and teaching people to accept one another, and not punish the *victim*, especially one of rape. It's not just here in Croatia, many, many countries feel the same way. Eventually, the world will learn, we truly all are equal and children of the same God."Julia pulled him up to her, and kissed him passionately. She finally felt his shoulders relax, knowing she had more than understood. "I love you Tomis, and I think you have taken a great leap, to healing, a very, old wound. Not only regarding your wife and daughter, but with Ivo, as well. As you said, he died at peace … and happy. He had the opportunity to somewhat make-amends for his pastguilt." She breathed easier as getting all of it out.

"I, of course, am very grateful to him, as I'm sure you are, also. We are all *moving past our pasts*. It's not easy, but we can do it. We can also honor *them,* by making a difference in other people's lives together, what do you say?" He nodded his true agreement and continued to sit at her feet. He held her legs for some time, with neither of them talking, just watching the islands go by.

Tomis at last spoke. "I want to keep kissing you, and hug you and not let go, but can not now. So, I call Ana to come get you for bath or shower." He stood up, and called out to Ana in Croatian, asking her to come get Julia for her bath. He truly felt so much better about himself.

"Oh, … you are so chicken! We have not had a shower together in a long time!"

He feigned a shock-look on his face, and laughed rather hysterically. "Now I 'chicken'? Not sure what it mean, but not nice I think. Don't worry Jelly. Soon, … your head heal, so we be together." She could bring such positive energy in her silly jokes.

When Ana brought Julia out later to the deck, she had her all dressed, with shoes on her feet instead of the slippers. "You look wonderful and all refresh." Tomis bent down to kiss her, and put the brake locks on the wheelchair. He called up to the Captain, and the boat stopped. Julia turned at the noise.

"It is anchor-drop in water, so we do not move." He reached under her arms, supporting her back, as much as he could. "Any hurt in your back?" Julia slightly moved her head 'no,' and took a deep breath. She knew to be serious about this movement. He slowly lifted her up to him, then slid his arm around her back to keep her supported.

Having only walked the hospital halls a few times, Julia still a little nervous. "Put your arm around me." She did, and actually grabbed him tight. He smiled, "It is OK, I not let you fall."

She looked up at him, taking another breath, and smiled knowing, he never would. Slowly, Tomis walked her around the deck, stopping every few feet, to ask if everything OK. She'd nod, and they'd continue. Ana sat in the back watching, and the Captain smiled down from the pilot house.

As Julia began to relax her grip, Tomis corrected her. "No, hold tight." She resumed, and he then walked her down the side of the boat to the port. He had her sit on a cushioned bench. "How do you feel?" He sat down next to her, still supporting her back.

"My legs are like Jelly, and you didn't even kiss me!" They both laughed, and he leaned over to kiss her. He knew they'd be all right again, with everything.

"Oh, no! I am Jelly! I'll never be able to get up!" They laughed, so he kissed her again.

"We sit, and now I tell you some good news." He then proceeded to tell her how he'd made Jossip the COO, as he'd promised her, and Anton the General Manager, as well. She smiled from ear to ear, so very proud of him.

He then took a deep breath, and she stared, wondering what he planned to spring on her. "And, the President offer me a new part-time job, and I can have a Consultant join me." He looked at her intently. "I say *part-time* job, . . . so no more workaholic!"

Julia got it, and shouted "Yeah!" She leaned over and kissed him on the cheek. "So what is this new part-time job?"

"It is National Tourism Consultant - I go to conference and convention around world and talk about Croatian Tourism. Do you know Consultant who want to join me?"

Julia's face lit-up like a Christmas Tree, about to explode from the lights. "OH MY GOD!?!?! Tomis, this is sooooo exciting! Talk about *the* Perfect job!"

He got his devilish look on his face. "Do I make you *offer ... you cannot refuse*?"

Julia threw her arms around him, as he tried to calm her. "You Bet'cha Baby! Off to My Next Big Adventure! I'll follow you any where, any time!" She kept kissing him and laughing. "We can do trips around Croatia, take photos to show them, oh this is going to be fun!"

"Oh, and no worry, no *Motel 6*." They laughed and kissed. This so much better than the romantic adventure, she'd hoped for. It's all about, *"Never say Never!"*

Importance of the European Union

Tomis had learned from his father regarding the United States, equality and English. He also learned Stalin even worst than Hitler, since he killed his own people, and some believed even more than Hitler did. A key survival point: You can *work* with some one if you have to, and even *put-up with* them, if you must, but you don't have to *join or become* like them. In life, we may take many paths, and even go on mini-journeys off the beaten path or detours. But, when we look back, they have all contributed to our journey of life, and who we have become.

Encapsulated in Croatia's modern history of a people, who were first controlled by the Ustashe regime of Nazi Germany, and under the Stalin Communists, followed by the dictator Tito. Yet, these resilient-Croatians, never let go of their idea of freedom, continually worked *and* fought to get it back, as their choice. Croatia, proudly became the European Union's 28th Member State on 1 July, 2013.

Sixty years before, at the end of the last great war, a group of futurists in Europe said, "How can we keep this from ever happening again? We always end-up conquering one another. For hundreds and hundreds of years, it's all we do - assemble armies and conquer each other." So they put together the seeds, of what became the European Union, beyond the realm of the United Nations, as just for them. They had a goal. They said, "What if we could build something, like the United States did - one currency, a group of countries who could become *States* with no restrictive borders, and we'll call it the European Union?" They did it, and yes, it took 60 years.

Yet, just like the United States, is *not a perfect union*, as some States don't always want to totally cooperate with others, and still sometimes hold onto past, outmoded-beliefs. But, with changes influenced by the media, especially social media, they are slowly letting some go. Though some politicians preach prejudice and discrimination to a few die-hards.

The EU idea has worked for most members. There are issues and problems, which they need to solve, as they arrive. When you put things together *equally*, you *unify* them, it creates a new stability - new energy. When you pull things apart, you create things which are unstable.

Bottom-line, they can work together to *influence* other people, in nations who do not respect the equality and freedom of their people. And, need to rid themselves of their Dictator controlling them, keeping them from a free-open economy. But those people themselves, have to rise-up from the inside, on their own behalf to rid themselves of these greedy-gangsters, stealing their freedom and equality.

Some people believe, there'll come a time when our Earth, will have only five groups with only five currencies. They'll represent major continents, which have come together much like the Europeans did. Currently, there's another group doing it in South America. They have a vision. "What if we could put all the countries together without borders, with one currency, all within just two generations? We'd have a much stronger economic influence on Earth."

And again, they must first rid themselves of those criminals and politicians who only want to control them and the economy for their own greedy behalf. Africa will do it eventually also, within 50 years. Unfortunately, the same negative forces exist, of an organized crime, power hungry others, with greed to take more than given. There are also successes, who have gone before them, to help them to persevere, be resilient and never give up their belief.

The Europeans knew the result of the unification meant, Countries which *depend* on each other for trade, won't go to war with each other. Which can only be done with removing the power-hungry, who want to control people, and their money. All it takes is two generations to create this kind of equality and peace. When parents tell their children to hate another culture, or group of people, they perpetuate *old negative energy.* Look at the Middle East, where religion is used as the excuse to kill. The hatred, anxiety, death, the torture and humility of eons continuing.

The unsolvable problems can be solved by the young people of Earth, when they see the positive others have done, too. They are starting to understand the folly of hate-separatism, and in various countries they are rising-up. The world will see the change, what a consciousness-shift brings, because they see the potential of what good can be done, by truly letting go of the past.

~ ~ ~ ~ ~ ~ ~ ~ ~

Julia knew why she must stay - not just to travel and have a good time with Tomis, but to tell any and all bullies, people won't crumble to old barbaric ways, eliminate the criminals, any way needed. Yes, scary and exciting at the same time to do it. The importance of international travel, meant seeing other places and people. Then, to realize, as well in showing them we are *not* so different, but quite alike in who we are. For anyone, travel to different countries helps to eliminate negative, old ways of thinking, which have kept most people separated, not believing in equality. It also helps to get rid of prejudice, and old leaders who want to keep people separate.

In the coming New World, people know and accept we are all One, so we deserve to be treated as such equally. This is not just for Croatia, or all those participants of their civil war. This is for all countries, who do not allow their people freedom, independence or equality. This means for all of their males *and females*, of any religious belief. We are ALL ONE, and we can live in peace with each other, with love, not hatred toward one another. It is the way of the New World, which the young people will make happen, as they demand their freedom to follow those beliefs of equality of all.

Acknowledgements

Greater appreciation to my two readers, Pat Brown and Patricia Dahlke for corrections and suggestions. And, Dorothea Olson's knowledge and suggestions of the Upper Peninsula tourist area.

Author's Biography

Originally from Chicago, Alice Parker has degrees in psychology, marketing, and English ESL-bilingual–bicultural studies in graduate school. A Dale Carnegie Trainer for 3 years, leading classes, she's traveled to 36 countries and 40 states – lived in 6, and wrote for an international business-travel magazine, and others.

A corporate business trainer in Japan for 7 years, then 8 years in San Francisco as HR Mgmt. to 1000 employees. As a Life Coach, she used her published Self-Help book, *Move Past Your Past - A Process for Freeing Your Life,* to do numerous workshops. She's passionate about her poems and empowering published memoir *Choices, Changes & Friends - 1970s After Divorce.* Four friends got their divorces together in the crazy 1970s, with satirical humor they dealt with it all and grew into independent women.

In the Dallas area since 2013, member of Poetry Society of Texas, winning 1st in State several times, and past President of the local Mockingbird Chapter, 3 years. Alice is also a proud member of the weekly, international poetry group, Corroboree.

For over 10 years she has taught memoir writing classes, and did editing to help her students publish. Her most recently published book is on Australia, *A Trip To Oz - A Memoir of Self-discovery thru Australian Adventures.* And, her other 2 finished biographical books regarding the American Occupation of Japan is: *Occupied Hearts - Love the Long Way Around and Japan as the Occupier & Occupied.* Both are based on true stories.

www.ingramcontent.com/pod-product-compliance
Lightning Source LLC
Chambersburg PA
CBHW070902120626
46546CB00001B/100